4.50
N

THE DEVELOPMENT AND ORGANIZATION OF EDUCATION IN CALIFORNIA

THE DEVELOPMENT

AND ORGANIZATION

OF EDUCATION IN CALIFORNIA

Charles J. Falk

SAN DIEGO STATE COLLEGE

HARCOURT, BRACE & WORLD, INC.

New York / Chicago / San Francisco / Atlanta

Acknowledgments

The author thanks the following publishers and copyright holders for their permission to use the material reprinted in this book.

CHANDLER PUBLISHING COMPANY for excerpts from Theodore Bass and Arnold Wolpert, *Teaching in California.* Copyright 1963.

THOMAS Y. CROWELL COMPANY for excerpts from James C. Stone, *California's Commitment to Public Education.* Copyright 1961. For material from Henry Magnuson, "Enrollment in California Public Schools, October 31, 1960," *California Schools,* Vol. 32, No. 2 (February 1961), pp. 49 ff.; and from Carl Frisen, *Enrollment in Public Schools for California, 1947–75* (mimeographed; Sacramento: California State Dept. of Finance, 1960).

THE FAMILY OF WILLIAM WARREN FERRIER for excerpts from William Warren Ferrier, *Ninety Years of Education in California, 1846–1936* (Berkeley, Calif.: Sather Gate Book Shop, 1937). Copyright 1937 by William Warren Ferrier.

HOLT, RINEHART AND WINSTON, INC. for excerpts from Stuart G. Noble, *A History of American Education.* Copyright 1938, 1954, © 1966 by Stuart G. Noble. Holt, Rinehart and Winston, Inc., publishers.

HOUGHTON MIFFLIN COMPANY for excerpts from William L. Langer, ed., *An Encyclopedia of World History.* Copyright 1948. For excerpts from Arthur B. Moehlman, *School Administration.* Copyright 1952.

THE DEVELOPMENT
AND ORGANIZATION OF EDUCATION IN CALIFORNIA, *Charles J. Falk*

Library of Congress Catalog Card Number: 68–29032

Printed in the United States of America

To my own native Californians:
Helen, Margaret Ann, Linda,
Kimmie, Kent, Marc, and Danny

PREFACE

Although there is a wealth of books and other material available on the history of California and some on the professional aspects of teaching in the state, there has been no concise and current textbook on the history of education in California available for students taking courses in the social foundations of education or in public school administration.

Two of the sources to which I have often referred as a college teacher provided the incentive I needed to undertake this volume. They are the privately published *Ninety Years of Education in California, 1846–1936*, by the late William Warren Ferrier, and the Stanford University Press publication *Education in California* by the late Roy W. Cloud. These books and the original sources to which they refer are essential to serious research in the history of California education.

Roy Cloud and his brother Archibald, a San Francisco educator, were an essential part of California's educational history in the first half of this century. They moved in the company of California's best-known educators— such people as Susan M. Dorsey and Mark Keppel of

Los Angeles, State Superintendent and U.S. Commissioner Will C. Wood, City Superintendent Willard Givens of Oakland and San Diego, Superintendents John Sexson of Pasadena and Walter R. Hepner and Will C. Crawford of San Diego, and a host of others who left their mark on California's educational system. I am grateful for my personal acquaintance and association with many of these men and women who have shaped California's school system since 1930. I am also in considerable debt to the generation of Will Angier, business manager of the San Diego City Schools, Judge Jacob Weinberger and Mrs. Mildred Hale, who served on local and state boards in the 1920s and 1930s, and Dr. Edward L. Hardy, who played no small role in making a state college system out of normal schools. In a sense, the Clouds belonged to both generations. The fact that the Cloud family has provided teachers for the public schools in the San Francisco Bay area since Civil War days no doubt accounts in part for the zeal with which Roy Cloud documented the state's educational history while he was the chief executive of the California Teachers' Association.

The teachers of California have a special obligation to understand California's education system and how it has developed. Many teachers, especially those not trained in California, are painfully ignorant of the system in which they work. Aside from its use as a textbook, this book can serve as a handbook for orientation and reference for teachers already in practice.

The history of education, though often identified as a course in itself, can serve more practical ends when it is understood as a backdrop for many courses—for example, school law and finance, the organization of systems and schools, and curriculum development. So far as history itself is concerned, however, this book is relevant not only to education but also to the history of California as a state, a subject that is often taught as if the education system had no part in that history. The usual textbook on the state's history and government offers at best a few paragraphs on the development and organization of schools. This blind spot in history courses must be eliminated, for the history of California's system of education is related in important ways to historical development in other realms such as politics.

In writing this book I have sought the help of my colleagues and experts in several fields. The original materials for the book were used experimentally for four years by a group of professors of education at San Diego State College. Their success has justified the revision and expansion of classroom aids into a single volume. Those who used the materials and suggested expansion of the legal, financial, and curricular aspects of the book have my sincere thanks.

A special word of thanks is due to Professor Lionel V. Ridout of the history department of San Diego State College and to Dr. Charles Lienart of the school of education for their willingness to read and criticize early drafts of the historical and administrative sections of the book. I am deeply indebted also to the family of Professor Ferrier for permission to make generous use of the materials in his book. In effect, this book has many authors and collaborators.

C. J. F.

CONTENTS

THE DEVELOPMENT AND ORGANIZATION OF EDUCATION IN CALIFORNIA

HISTORICAL NOTES

ON CALIFORNIA SCHOOLS BEFORE 1850

By education in California we generally mean the present school system of the thirty-first state. Most of these pages are therefore concerned with the development and present status of this extensive system of public schools, colleges, and universities. Some references will be made to the private schools and colleges. And, lest we seem to neglect completely the educational patterns that preceded our Yankee system, brief reference will be made now and in Appendix One to the Indian, Spanish, and Mexican educational efforts in California.

Organized educational efforts in California go back much further than many people realize, and we are ill-equipped to evaluate these earlier efforts in terms of the circumstances under which they were made. People are wont to say, for instance, that the Mexican government did little for California education after it achieved independence in 1821 and that Spanish colonists did almost nothing to develop a system of schools and colleges in California. In fairness to both of these governments, however, it must be recognized that California was the Ultima Thule of Spain's empire in the Americas and of the

Mexican Republic. Though Spain had claimed California for 227 years, California was colonized only in and after 1769. Spain had a scant 50 years to develop schools in California, and Mexico had only 25 to create a school system. Until Spain began her colonization of California, Indian education was all the education there was.

The California Indian

Before 1769, the sole occupants of California were some 130,-000 Indians with a neolithic culture very much like what their ancestors had brought across the Bering Strait at least 9,000 years earlier.[1] However, recent studies of Indian origins set their arrival in California much before this, as evidenced by these observations from a recent Bureau of Indian Affairs pamphlet:

> California's kindly climate was a lure that attracted more wandering Indian bands to settlement than did most other regions of America north of Mexico. Before the coming of the white man, this area and the pueblo region of the Southwest were the two most densely populated of all the land areas which today comprise the United States.
>
> The Indians brought with them fire and tool-making skills. From Alaska to South America, their stone artifacts are found in caves and under the earth. They probably came first in the Pleistocene epoch, near the close of the last glacial period, 15,000 to 20,000 years ago, although some scholars contend the migrations began as early as 45,000 years ago. They were hunters and fishermen, and their migration was trickling and episodic over many thousands of years. But when they reached California they settled down to a more stable way of life.[2]

[1] Harold E. Driver, *Indians of North America* (Chicago: Univ. of Chicago Press, 1964). Note especially Driver's summary statement (p. 4): "If the date of 11,000 years ago for man's first appearance in the Valley of Mexico is correct, the crossing of the Bering Strait by the ancestors of these people must have taken place several thousand years earlier."

[2] Bureau of Indian Affairs, U.S. Dept. of the Interior, *Indians of California* (Washington, D.C.: Superintendent of Documents, U.S. Government Printing Office, 1966).

It is reasonable to assume, however, that the California Indians were not the most technologically advanced of their race and that some ancestors of the Incas, Mayas, Toltecs, and Aztecs moved through California to more invigorating milieus where they developed advanced civilizations. The Indians who stayed behind to roam the foothills, valleys, and deserts of undeveloped California have not been praised by historians for their vision and ambitions or for their ability to improve the neolithic culture that their ancestors brought from Asia. But they did survive, and survival is not only for the fittest but for those who can teach the techniques of survival to each succeeding generation.

It cannot be argued that the California Indians had an organized system of education as did their Aztec brothers. The Yuma tribes—which included the California Diegüeños, Maricopas, and Mojaves—though often living in settled communities, did not develop the simplest forms of agriculture. They were hunters and fishermen who lived on fish, game, small animals, and vegetation, including roots dug from the soil. In a society so primitive, education was a simple and informal affair. After their infancy, young Indians had to be taught how to stay alive in the wilderness, how to get their food, and how to live in reasonable harmony with their fellow tribesmen. This Indian culture was strongly matriarchal, and the squaw was the principal teacher of the tribal tongue, the legends, and the simple crafts such as basketry. The young braves, after their initiation into male society, learned the arts of weapon-making, hunting, fishing, dancing, and war-making.

That the California Indian had even the crudest educational practices is strange to those who consider the aborigines somewhat less than human. Henry K. Norton, who devotes the initial chapter of his *Story of California*[3] to a thorough vilification of California Indians, sums up his thesis in this manner: "It is strange and so far inexplicable that there should be found here, surrounded by peoples in much higher position in the human scale, a race so little above the brutes." It is true that the California Indian did not leave the archeologist permanent structures, elaborate artifacts, or extensive evidence of his culture as the Aztecs, Incas, and Pueblo Indians did. But he was *homo sapiens,* speaking a variety of languages and dialects, living by sets of tribal and family rules, and, above all, teaching each succeed-

[3] Henry K. Norton, *The Story of California* (Chicago: McClurg, 1923).

ing generation to survive in the rugged and debilitating conditions of undeveloped California.

That there remain a scant 20,000 California Indians today can be taken as proof that the Indian learned and taught survival better before the white man came than he did thereafter. Yet the stereotype of these aborigines, created after the Spanish occupation of California, lays the blame of their decimation at the Indians' own door. This stereotype was perpetuated by Hubert Howe Bancroft, Charles Edward Chapman, Father Zephyrin Engelhardt, and other historians of the early mission days. The sources suggest that the California Indian was lazy and listless, filthy and prone to disease, noisy, superstitious, and an inveterate gambler.

It should be noted that this picture of the Indian has some of the white man's vices and diseases in its background. The Indian was not as immune to vices and diseases as he was adverse to acculturation into civilized life. It was precisely the restrictions of civilized life and the resultant epidemics of smallpox, measles, tuberculosis, and other diseases that caused to a considerable degree the decline of the Indian. Even with allowances for those who adjusted successfully to the white man's ways, the Indian ways of life and education seemed better for Indians. For, as Herbert Spencer implies, no knowledge can be of much worth if you do not survive.

It can be argued that survival alone in a neolithic culture is not a great prize or that most Indians were not capable of lifting themselves up by newly acquired Spanish bootstraps. It can also be said that where there was a substantial amount of acculturation, as in the case of the mestizos, the survival rate was higher.

Our purpose is not to lay the blame for the decimation of the Indian population at the door of the Spanish conquerors. The American Indian in general, and the California Indian in particular, has been alternately blamed and pitied, but he has seldom been given credit for what he did well. He chose the best environment he could find and learned to live with it. For many millennia each generation of California Indians passed along to its offspring the techniques of survival in a wilderness. In essence, this is the substance of Indian education.

California Under Spanish Rule

We know much more about the educational system that Spain brought to California than we do about the primitive Indian patterns of education. As we have already noted, the chief problem of Spanish educational endeavors in California is that they came so late and continued for scarcely 50 years. Spain laid claim to California in 1542; 280 years later, in 1822, Spain was no longer active as an educational force in California. Its years of effectiveness lasted from 1769 to 1818 or 1819 (the last years of the revolution). Indeed, California was the scene of Spain's frantic and ultimately futile effort to occupy, colonize, and develop this Ultima Thule of her vast but shaky empire. The immediate occasion for the occupation of California was Spain's suspicion that Russia had designs on northern California. In 1768, the viceroy of New Spain in Mexico City was ordered to frustrate Russian hopes in California; in 1769, the occupation of California began, 227 years after the first of a series of explorers staked out Spanish claims there.

One might reasonably suppose that, after 250 years of experience in conquering, civilizing, Christianizing, and educating the native populations of South America, Central America, and Mexico, the Spanish king and viceroys would have been able to do a superior job of civilizing and making effective citizens of the 130,000 Indians scattered throughout California. That Spain could not or would not do this reflects upon her imperial policy, which was unable to withstand the revolutionary movements of the late eighteenth century.

The vast Spanish empire in the Americas began to fall to pieces during the American Revolutionary War. After scattered uprisings in the early 1700s, serious revolts were organized from 1780 to 1782 by Tupac Amaru, a Peruvian descendant of the Incas, by Berbeo and José Antonio Galán in New Granada (northwestern South America) in 1781, and by Francisco de Miranda in Venezuela. Independence from Spain was declared in Paraguay (August 14, 1811), in Chile (February 12, 1818), in Peru (July 22, 1821), in Mexico (February 24, 1821), and in Bolivia (August 6, 1825). With the seed of discontent so generously and widely sown, a lush harvest of revolutions ripened quickly.

The failing empire undoubtedly was well organized on paper. Under the Spanish king there had been from 1503 a *Casa de Contratación* to control colonial commerce and maritime enterprise and from 1524 a *Consejo de Indias* with supreme authority over the judicial, administrative, and ecclesiastical affairs of the "Indies," but these legal entities in Spain were very remote from the lands they controlled.

Conquistadors and colonists (*encomenderos*) were given early control of specified colonial towns. The Indians of these towns paid tribute, labor, and services to their *encomendero,* who was obligated, in return, to give the Indians protection, indoctrination in Christianity, and civilizing instruction. The top colonial administration of New Spain was fixed first in an *audiencia* (court) in 1527, but this proved ineffective, and Antonio de Mendoza was named viceroy in 1529. He took office in 1535. But the king, the *Casa,* the *Consejo,* and the viceroy were unable to control the abuses of the *encomenderos,* who bled the natives white by extracting high tributes and using forced labor in the mines, on the haciendas (plantations), and in public works.

Hence, the New Laws of 1542 were enacted in Spain to control the abuses of the local *padrones.* Under the New Laws, fixed quotas of tribute, labor, and service were set, the viceroyalty, or *reino,* of New Spain was given a capital, Mexico City, and a second viceroyalty of Peru was established in Lima. Not only was enslavement of the Indians prohibited but they were made wards of the crown. Because of this, more than 200 years later the California *padres* claimed to be mere custodians of mission properties, administering them for Indian owners who presumably were still wards of the crown.

The Spanish kings, however, were so far away from their Indian wards, their crown lands, and the sources of their major income that they were forced to expand systems of control in the Americas. Therefore, additional viceroyalties were established in New Granada (northwestern South America) in 1717 and in La Plata in 1776; captaincy-generals were established in Venezuela (1773), Cuba (1777), and Chile (1778). *Audiencias* likewise were ordered for Buenos Aires (1783), Caracas (1786), and Cuzco (1789).[4] For still more local control, municipalities had their councils of *regidores* (appointed by the king) and their *alcaldes* (a combination of mayor, sheriff, and justice of the peace). After 1714, all this vast machinery of colonial government was controlled by a minister and a secretariat of the Indies, created by the Spanish Bourbon dynasty.

[4] William L. Langer, ed., *An Encyclopedia of World History* (Boston: Houghton Mifflin, 1948), pp. 497–500.

But, for all this administrative control, the kings of Spain were never able to develop the human resources of the empire effectively. The colonies were valued chiefly for their economic resources such as gold, raw materials, and trade, all of which Spain needed badly. In the colonies themselves, the officials and upper classes thrived in considerable wealth at the top of a caste system strangely out of tune with the democratic ideals of the eighteenth- and ninteenth-century world. What had grown most and benefited least was the population of the empire.

Langer accepts the estimate that the Spanish population in the Americas reached 160,000 by 1574, and he gives these figures for the entire population at the end of the colonial period: 3,276,000 whites—Spanish blue bloods, creoles (natives of Spanish blood), immigrants from Spain and from other European countries (the Scotch, Irish and so on—for example, Bernardo O'Higgins, who laid the foundations of the Chilean state); 5,328,000 mestizos—natives with mixed white and Indian blood; 7,530,000 Indians; and 776,000 Negroes, half of whom lived in Cuba and Puerto Rico. In New Spain (Mexico and California) alone there were 1,230,000 whites, 1,860,000 mestizos, and 3,700,000 Indians.[5]

Spanish colonial officials and important churchmen composed the top social groups, while creoles and socially superior Spanish immigrants came next. High-ranking mestizos and Indian nobles outranked the mulattoes, zambos (Negro-Indian mixtures), and Indians (the largest group of all). Negro slaves were the real outcasts. The population was obviously weighted on the poor and low-caste side and, in early California, on the side of the Indians, who were rarely found ready for full citizenship.

The inability of the Spanish authorities to make the most of the vast human resources on the American continents was certainly a major cause of the sudden collapse of the empire. To say that this was the sole cause is to oversimplify; however, most of the other causes were related to this basic failure. From the 1400s, Spain's chief domestic concern was the unification of the Iberian peninsula, and Spain was frequently at war with neighbors and competitors in the business of empire-building. As a result, the treasury was wanting funds to build ships and keep armies in the field. The best sources of gold and trade were the American colonies. Finally, staunch Chris-

[5] *Ibid.*, p. 496.

tian faith and devotion to the Catholic cause created problems for Spain, for the church, and for the empire.

There are perhaps few people today who will deny that the church-state union that characterized Spain's empire was at least an occasion for many imperial problems, to say nothing of the continuing problems of Latin American nations. When the foundation stone of church-state union was laid in the 1400s, no ecclesiastical or government authority could foresee its ultimate impact on the Spanish empire, on Californian or Mexican history, or on present-day Latin America. That the ecclesiastical power wielded by the Spanish government in New Spain and New Granada had salutary effects no one can deny, but few today will doubt that it was a mixed blessing.

The Spanish empire was born because Ferdinand and Isabella wrested Granada from Moorish control. The missionary overtones of Spanish conquests were echoes of the Christian battle cry against Islam and the Spanish Inquisition after 1480 (against infidels and heretics, including Moslems and Jews). Their "most Catholic Majesties," [6] Ferdinand (of Aragon) and Isabella (of Castile), married in 1479, were in effect fighting the last, local Crusade against Moslem power in Spain. As an expression of his appreciation, Pope Martin V agreed to a concordat with the Spanish throne in 1482 that restricted the power of Rome over the Spanish Church. The union of church and state in Spain gave the monarch a free hand in ecclesiastical matters in Spain and in its future colonies. He became the grand master of powerful religious orders of the knighthood and gained the right to promulgate even papal decrees in his possessions. In 1492, the fall of Granada was followed by the expulsion of Jews from Castile and the subsequent expulsion of the Moors in 1502.

This turn of events played into the hands of Spanish explorers, conquistadors, and viceroys. To claim land for the Spanish throne and for the church was one and the same thing, for the crown had almost complete control of ecclesiastical affairs in Spain and the Spanish Indies. The decrees of Pope Alexander VI (the *Inter Caetera* of May 4, 1493, and the *Eximiae Devotionis* of November 16, 1501) gave the Spanish crown these privileges: (1) dominion over the Indies, (2) the sole right to convert the natives, and (3) "the titles and the first fruits of the Church in the Indies."

In his *Universalis Ecclesiae*, Pope Julius II (1503–13) granted Spain

[6] A title conferred on the royalty of Spain by Pope Alexander VI, the Spanish Rodrigo de Borja (or Borgia).

"the real patronage of the Indies" (that is, the right to create dioceses, to name bishops and assign ecclesiastical benefices, and, in effect, to handle church affairs). So the earliest dioceses and archdioceses in the empire were created by royal decree, and the missionary activities of the religious orders and societies (Dominicans, Franciscans, Carmelites, and Jesuits) were assigned and transferred by the Spanish viceroys.

This control over the religious orders had considerable effect on the ultimate establishment of missions in *Las Californias* (lower and upper California); however, the earliest missionaries seem to have volunteered to accompany the conquistadors. The first Franciscans arrived in New Spain about 1524. Eleven years later, one of the original "twelve apostles," Padre Martin de la Coruña, was with Cortés when he sailed into Santa Cruz Bay near the present city of La Paz, Lower California, on May 2, 1535. The attempt of Coruña and his confreres to establish a mission failed within a year. In 1596, when Sebastian Vizcaino set out to found a colony in Lower California, he had four Franciscan priests and a lay brother aboard.[7] This second attempt also failed within a year. Then in 1683 the Jesuit fathers Eusebius Kuehn (the well-known Padre Kino) and Pedro Matías Goñi joined Fray José Guijosa of the Order of St. John of God in an attempt to establish a mission north of La Paz. Two and a half years later, in 1685, these Spaniards and their missionaries withdrew from the Californias.

For fear that some foreign power would claim Lower California, however, Viceroy Montezuma assigned to the Jesuits the task of establishing missions there and enlisting soldiers to protect the missions. The Jesuit superiors, Fathers Kino and Salvatierra, had the viceroy's orders on February 5, 1697, and Father Salvatierra was almost immediately appointed the superior of these missions. During the next 60 years, 56 Jesuits served as missionaries in the Mission of Our Lady of Loreto and in the eight other missions that the Jesuits opened in Lower California. Sixteen of the 56 Jesuits died at their posts, two as martyrs. Nevertheless, Charles III ordered the expulsion of the Jesuits in 1767. Viceroy De Croix actually issued the royal decree in July, 1767, and the Jesuits were brought to Mexico by ship in February, 1768.

De Croix then assigned the Franciscan Friars of the Apostolic

[7] See Father Zephyrin Engelhardt's article on "California Missions" in the *Catholic Encyclopedia*, Vol. 3 (New York: Appleton, 1908), pp. 177–78.

Missionary College of San Fernando to the Lower California Missions. Fray Junípero Serra was one of the first 15 Franciscan volunteers to go to Loreto. The Franciscans planned to establish five missions and did establish Mission San Fernando at Velicatá in 1768. A few years later, on April 8, 1770, the Dominicans secured a royal order to found missions in Lower California. By this time Fray Junípero and his fellow Franciscans were establishing themselves in San Diego and Monterey.

The foregoing events are proof that the king of Spain and the viceroys took the grants of popes Alexander VI and Julius II seriously. The grants were no great boon to the missionary orders and societies that came and went as they were told to do by the kings and viceroys. It is really a marvel that the hard-working and long-suffering missionaries remained the royalists and highly patriotic Spaniards that they were. However, there was some exhilaration and much satisfaction in claiming new lands for the crown and the cross simultaneously.

The ecclesiastical grants to the kings of Spain were given before the British, Dutch, and French became involved in colonial pursuits, and when England first claimed American territory she was a Protestant antagonist of Spain. Long before Francis Drake menaced the Peruvian coast and before he claimed California territory for Elizabeth in 1579, Spanish American governments had been operating with a political and ecclesiastical arm. For that matter, the ecclesiastical arm was more powerful than the political; the Spanish empire functioned better through its missionaries and bishops than it did through its viceroys, captaincy-generals, intendants, and governors. After all, those Indians and mestizos who never became full-fledged citizens did become sons and daughters of the church. Even when, in the days of revolution, they proved themselves anticlerical, they seldom admitted to being anti-Catholic. If the political and educational forces in the empire had been as effective in making citizens (that is, not mere wards or dependents) of the Indians as the missionaries were in making them Christians, the Spanish empire might have developed peacefully into an effective modern state. Instead, when California was first colonized, the empire was already falling apart.

The last brief chapter of Spain's colonial efforts in North America took place in California a few years before our Declaration of Independence. Apart from the colonists' intentions to frustrate the ambitions of Russia and England in California and the intentions of the *padres* to convert the Indians, the colonization of California was no enthusiastic enterprise. Spanish colonists in California at no time numbered more than a few thousand in sparsely populated towns. In 1813, the Mexican Revolution had begun, and by 1822 the imperial role of New Spain in California was ended. So the effective years of school work for the Spanish barely stretched from 1770 to 1815.

During this brief span of years, most of the 21 California missions were established. Undoubtedly they represented the most outstanding Spanish educational efforts in California. The story begins with the founding of the first mission in San Diego on July 16, 1769, and of a second, Misión San Carlos at Carmel, on June 3, 1770. Carmel was to become the headquarters of the first mission *presidente,* Fray Junípero Serra, who started from an earlier plan to create three missions in California. Before he died in 1784, however, Father Serra had founded directly or had supervised the founding of the first nine California missions. The second nine were founded under the presidency of Fray Fermín Francis de Lasuen, the successor of Serra, who was a man scarcely less purposeful and courageous than Fray Junípero himself.

After Lasuen died on June 26, 1803, the last two missions proper (Santa Inéz in 1804 and San Rafael in 1817) and the *asistencia* of San Francisco de Solano in 1823 finished the long chain of the California mission system. From 1769 to 1845, 146 Franciscan *padres,* most of them Spanish by birth, served the California missions. According to Father Zephyrin Engelhardt: "Sixty-seven died at their posts, two as martyrs, and the remainder retired to their mother-house (El Colegio de San Fernando in Mexico) on account of illness or at the expiration of ten years of service." [8]

It is only natural that these loyal Spanish churchmen should have created *el camino real* (the royal highway) to make the missions accessible to one another. In the fulfillment of their chief purpose, the *padres* claim to have baptized 90,000 Indians, blessed the marriages of 28,000, and buried 70,000. Engelhardt says, "the largest number of neophytes harbored, fed, clothed and educated at all the missions at any one time was nearly thirty thousand." [9]

The education of the Indians, organized around the religious and vocational goals, provided some training in building skills, farming, animal husbandry, cooking, sewing, Spanish, and Christian doctrine. "Secular education, so called," according to Engelhardt, was not neg-

[8] *Ibid.*
[9] *Ibid.,* p. 182.

lected, for the *padres* devoted "their spare time to teaching reading, writing and a little arithmetic to those boys who evinced any inclination for these branches." [10]

For the children of the Spanish colonists, education was often a less formal matter. There was a concentration of these children around Monterey, but otherwise they were scattered in small towns on the ranches or near the missions. As with the British colonists in the East a century and a half earlier, the Spanish colonists were beating down a wilderness, and there was precious little time for formal schooling. The rudiments of the Spanish tongue were learned from the parish priest or from a miscellany of untrained teachers. In this latter group are such examples as José Manuel Toca, a ship boy who served as a teacher in Santa Barbara, and Manuel Vargas, a retired army sergeant who taught and laid on the rod at San Jose, Santa Barbara, and San Diego from 1794 to 1800. Besides, the *padres* of the missions assisted bright boys, particularly if they seemed destined for the priesthood. The most education-oriented of the settlers sent their children to better schools and colleges in Mexico. Other than this, Roy W. Cloud in *Education in California* summarized the situation in this way:

> Diego de Borica, the seventh Spanish governor of Alta California, fought apathy in his endeavors to bring some light of education to the young Spaniards, but with little success. The schools mainly were taught by soldiers, some of whom had no education themselves beyond the ability to read and write. Inadequate teachers, together with a scarcity of books and consequent lack of any obvious need for either writing or reading, made many parents hostile or indifferent to Borica's program. [11]

It is fair to assume that no formal schools, outside the mission schools, could have been functioning in California before 1775 and that few schools under New Spain carried on normally after 1815 or 1820, although the Mexican Revolution in its early stage had little effect on California. In the early years, the chief concern of the colonists was to establish themselves safely in a vast wilderness; and in the last years of Spanish California the governors and *padres* alike

[10] *Ibid.*

[11] Roy W. Cloud, *Education in California* (Stanford, Calif.: Stanford Univ. Press, 1952), p. 19.

were sifting conflicting reports on the Revolution and getting little financial aid or support from either Spain or Mexico City.

From 1808 to 1814 Spain was a battleground in the Napoleonic Wars or was in the control of Napoleon. In 1812, Spanish liberals assembled in the *cortes* of Cadiz adopted a constitution for Spain, modeled on that of France. It was later rejected by Ferdinand VII when he was liberated by Napoleon; but by that time the long-neglected Spanish empire in the Americas was irretrievably in revolt.

It was 1818 before the Spanish constitution of 1812 was submitted to the people of California, whose governor, Pablo Vicente de Solá, laughed it off as a fantasy of Mexican dreamers. In February, 1821, though, the Mexican "dreamer" Iturbide proclaimed the independence of Mexico from Spain and declared himself Emperor Agustín I. Word of these events came to California in December, 1821. In 1825, Californians had official word that there was indeed a Republic of Mexico under the new and lasting constitution of 1824, which was modeled after the Constitution of the United States. Obviously, none of this protracted turmoil and government change benefited education in California. The people could only hope that the new Mexican government would become effective soon.

Mexican California

Mexican Californians had less than half the time that Spain did to develop schools. Mexican rule in California actually began in 1824 and ended, in effect, in 1846. The capital at Monterey and the scattered towns were, in terms of the transportation facilities, a continent away from the federal capital in Mexico City. If little was done, it was because there was little to work with during those 24 years of Mexican school development.

With the benefit of hindsight and through comparison with the schools of California nearly a century and a half later, many Californians tend to minimize Mexican efforts and early achievements in the promotion of education on the West Coast. Actually however, Mexican governors and *alcaldes* did much to promote reasonably good education, as the following examples show.

The eighth Mexican governor of California, José Figueroa, an Aztec

Indian, gave the first big push to education by calling for better schools in Monterey, Santa Barbara, and Los Angeles and for new ones in Sonoma, Santa Clara, San Jose, San Gabriel, San Luis Rey, and San Diego. He spoke like a Thomas Jefferson on education, holding that education of the individual was necessary for an enlightened society and true progress. Figueroa got tax support for a normal school at San Gabriel and directed each town to send its most promising young men, white and Indian, to the normal school for teacher training.

In the 1830s the thirteenth governor, Juan Bautista Alvarado, though plagued by lack of funds, promoted good. schools, imported teachers from Mexico, and welcomed Yankee educators from the eastern United States. Alvarado instituted classes in typesetting and printing in Monterey.

The last Mexican governor,[12] Pío Pico, advocated compulsory education by requiring parents to send their children to school and to pay school taxes where schools existed. He wanted schools opened wherever a sufficient number of pupils justified them, and he proposed that teachers' salaries be paid from the public treasury (state fund). The *alcaldes* in the pueblos, however, who were responsible for putting the governors' orders into effect, were not always so enthusiastic about schools.

Americans like Richard Henry Dana found education in Mexican California poor, but the cause of the deficiency is attributable to a notable lethargy in the people and to the problems of education and government that the Republic of Mexico inherited from Spain. Also, no small measure of the blame can be ascribed to the fact that much of the sparse Mexican population of California was beyond the influence of the governors in Monterey.

The population of Mexican California, apart from Indians and some Yankees, probably never exceeded 10,000, but there were fluctuations, especially in the Mexican War years. Though few battles of the Mexican War were fought on California soil, 1846 to 1848 were years of uncertainty. With few exceptions, the schools, so painfully developed, were closed. An almost complete educational hiatus separated Californian education that had been from the school system that was yet to be.

The present system of public education began in 1849 as a brief outline of a broad plan written on several pieces of paper. This brave

[12] See Appendix Two for the exact succession of Mexican governors of California.

and terse constitutional provision (Article IX of the first constitution of California) has tempted enthusiastic Californians to think that in 1850 all sorts of schools were neatly placed in every part of California. This definitely does not agree with the facts of the situation. The state school system during much of the 1850s existed chiefly on paper and in the hopes of enthusiastic pioneers. An educational vacuum had settled on California in and even before 1846, and the 1849 command "Let there be light" did not have the immediate effect of the first creation story.

San Francisco alone among California cities offered some public education before the first constitution was adopted. This city of 25,000 inhabitants was unique. Elsewhere the first problems were to get gold out of the hills and lawless conditions out of the towns and cities. It would take 10 to 12 years to get the educational show well on the road, and then Civil War conditions would play into the hands of the economy-minded California townsmen and miners who were against generous spending for education. Even in 1850, most of the children of the 92,527 California citizens were not bothered with the dread of school restrictions and school tasks. Most of them were out of school altogether.

THE LEGAL FOUNDATIONS

OF CALIFORNIA'S SCHOOL SYSTEM

In theory, Mexican civil law was to have prevailed in California until the United States Congress arranged a territorial government, but the Congress repeatedly failed to act. The *de facto* government was military (under General Stephen Watts Kearney, Colonel Richard B. Mason, and General Bennett Riley), and there was very little of that. Consequently, the people took matters into their own hands by setting up school boards like that appointed on February 2, 1848, in San Francisco and by organizing a constitutional convention in Monterey.

General Riley on his own initiative had called the delegates together, but the general's authority was disputed. The delegates had no mandate from the Congress to establish even a territorial government; but, on their own initiative, they proceeded to write a state constitution for California. So it was that California never had territorial status. One day it was foreign territory; the next it was the thirty-first state of the Union. In the field of education, we passed from a land almost devoid of all schools to a state with a full-blown school system, on paper at least.

The First Constitution
and Its Educational Provisions (1849)

The foundations of this state's school system were laid by the constitutional convention that met from September 1 to October 13, 1849, in Colton Hall at Monterey. The 48 delegates that finally affixed their names to California's first constitution were men of widely different training, backgrounds, and interests. Five were European by birth: John Augustus Sutter (Switzerland), Pedro Sansvaine (France), Miguel de Pedroena (Spain), Hugo Reid (Scotland), and the Irishman, W. E. Shannon. Another seven were Mexican Californians by birth: M. G. Vallejo, Manuel Domínguez, Antonio M. Pico, Jacinto Rodríguez, José Antonio Carrillo, P. N. de la Guerra, and J. M. Covarrubias.

The remaining 36 Yankee delegates came from 13 of the 30 states then in the Union in these numbers: New York, 12; Maryland, 5; three each from Kentucky, Massachusetts, Ohio, and Virginia; and one each from Connecticut, Florida, Maine, New Jersey, Pennsylvania, Tennessee, and Rhode Island.

The educational and occupational background of the delegates in Monterey provided additional breadth of interests and experience. Fourteen were lawyers, ten were farmers or ranchers, and six were merchants. Among the remaining 18, there were a surveyor, a U.S. engineer, two traders, an army man, a navy man, a lieutenant with the volunteers (*vigilantes*), two printers, a banker, a physician, and men who gave these less familiar listings of occupation: "Military" (M. G. Vallejo of Sonoma), "Negotiant" (Pedro Sansvaine, the Frenchman who had lived in California since 1837), "Elegant Leisure" (B. F. Moore of San Joaquin, born in Florida), and *Labrador* (José A. Carrillo of San Francisco, who obviously was not a farm laborer).

It is significant that the best state school systems in 1850 were found in New York, New England, and Ohio. It is also interesting to note that, while the constitution of California leaned heavily on the U.S. Constitution and the constitutions of seven states (Iowa, Louisiana, New York, Michigan, Mississippi, Tennessee, and Wisconsin), 66 of the 137 sections in the first constitution appear to have been taken from Iowa's constitution and 19 from that of New York.

It seems that the delegates from Kentucky were very much impressed by the brevity of the new constitution of Iowa, which had been admitted to statehood in 1846. Luckily, Iowa started its statehood with a good school system, having profited from the school systems of Illinois, Indiana, and Ohio and having had territorial schools since 1838. After 1820, New York was reputed to have had the best schools in the nation. Therefore, the influences of Iowa and New York on the educational provisions in California's first constitution (Article IX on the state school system) were very valuable.

The school systems in New England, New York, and Iowa were characterized by the control of state boards of education and superintendents over local school districts. Local school boards in towns, townships, and cities, though they were immediately responsible for the operation of district schools, were being subjected to increasing controls written into state constitutions and statutory law.

Many states were able to provide financial assistance to local districts largely through the sale of public lands, which, together with school taxes, created state school funds. The chief concern of most states was for a system of "common" (elementary) schools, though, because most secondary education was provided by private academies and most higher education was offered in private colleges. So, when Californians were writing their first constitution and their first school laws, they had these national precedents to follow.

The discussion of the future of education in California was begun in Monterey on September 25, 1849. All 48 members of the constitutional convention, sitting as a committee of the whole, had the opportunity to discuss the educational provisions of the constitution. There was common agreement on the general pattern of the state school system, but there was some heated debate on the extent of the educational offerings and on the financial support of the system. That there should be a statewide system of common schools operated by the local townships under the supervision of an elected state superintendent of public instruction was the first point of agreement of most of the convention. There was no controversy on the founding and funding of a state university by the legislature "as soon as possible." The university was seen as having such branches as the public convenience might demand and as promoting literature, arts, and sciences as might be authorized by future federal land grants.

Robert Semple of Sonoma, the president of the convention, presided over the sessions on education and offered some of the best suggestions. On the afternoon of October 4, these constitution⸰⸰ ᵣ for public education in California were adopted:

Section 1 An elected state superintendent of public instruction was to head the schools of California.

Comment The position and the title came from the New York constitution. All delegates in Monterey agreed without question to this position, the duties of which were left to the legislature to define. The legislature of 1851 defined the duties as largely fiscal and administrative. Judge John G. Marvin of Tuolumne County, editor of the *Sonoma Herald*, was the first superintendent of public instruction, elected October 7, 1850.

Section 2 A state school fund was to be created by the legislature from money derived from the sale or rental of public lands.[1]

Comment This section was the occasion of considerable discussion, since gold mines were still to be found in these lands and also because the state might have needed these revenues for other purposes. A farmer from Sacramento, delegate M. M. McCarver, closed the issue by favoring the placement of "every farthing of this income in the hands of the State for the purpose of educating our children."[2] The debate on the resources to be used for the original state school fund is reported in more detail later. (See Chapter 3, pages 109–12.)

Section 3 School funds were to be provided for at least three months of school in each school year.

Comment An amendment to increase this to six months was lost. Eventually the term was increased to six months and more, up to the present, when 175 school days have become the minimum school year. The penchant of Californians to keep obsolete laws, however, is dem-

---

[1] Most of this public land was to be provided by federal land grants. These land grants, begun by the Northwest Ordinance of 1785 and 1787, were continued and became increasingly more generous during and after 1850, when the Congress established the Oregon Plan of common-school land grants. California was the first state to receive the benefits of the Oregon Plan, which reserved the sixteenth and thirty-sixth section of land in each township for school purposes. See Arthur B. Moehlman, *School Administration* (Boston: Houghton Mifflin, 1951), pp. 459–60.

[2] Roy W. Cloud, *Education in California* (Stanford, Calif.: Stanford Univ. Press, 1952), p. 21.

onstrated by the fact that in 1967 the constitutional minimum for the school year remains at six months.

Section 4 The constitution sanctioned the use of penal fines for school and libraries to be apportioned on the basis of the number of inhabitants in each district.

Comment There was a motion to change "inhabitants" to "children," but it was lost when Delegate Charles T. Botts, a Virginian who had been a resident of Monterey for 16 months, indicated that grown men often needed and wanted education as much as children. This was the first word spoken for adult education in California (and this in 1849!).

Section 5 The constitution charged the legislature with the task of founding a state university with funds from the rent or sale of other lands.

Comment This section anticipated federal land grants for the development of land-grant colleges to promote agricultural and mechanical arts education. (See the Morrill Acts of 1869 and 1890.[3])

These five sections of Article IX were discussed and debated intermittently from September 25 through October 4, 1849, when the delegates voted 26 to 10 for the Article. On October 13, the convention finished its final draft of California's first constitution, which outlined the state government in twelve articles as follows:

    I. The Bill of Rights of California
    II. Suffrage (citizenship and the electorate)
    III. Distribution of Powers (legislative, executive, and judicial)
    IV. The Legislative Department
    V. The Executive Department
    VI. The Judicial Department
    VII. The State Militia
    VIII. State Debts
    IX. Education (the school system of California)
    X. Amendments and Revisions of the Constitution
    XI. Miscellaneous Provisions—e.g., San Jose listed as the permanent seat of government, disfranchisement for dueling, oaths of office, the

[3] *Ibid.*, pp. 463–64.

system of county and town government, the fiscal year to start July 1, the validity of civil marriages, the right of married women to own separate property, the provision that all laws were to be published in both English and Spanish

XII. State Boundaries

Although California was not admitted to the Union until September 9, 1850, her first governor, Peter H. Burnett, and the legislature were elected on November 13, 1849, a very stormy day. But the rains did not prevent 12,872 voters from accepting the constitution, with only 811 against it.

It was up to the legislature to implement the provisions of the constitution; but the constitution provided no guidelines on state and school finance, and it failed to put restrictions on the power of the legislature in matters of finance. It soon became clear that the legislature was to have a free hand in the creation, encouragement, and financing of the school system. The constitution was not specific on the types of common schools it wanted (elementary or secondary), on the rights and responsibilities of local school organization and administration (in counties and school districts), or on the relationship between public and private education.

The first constitution was put together in some haste by a body of wise men with varied backgrounds. It had its weaknesses as well as its strengths. On the surface, it was a sufficiently clear and concise document, devoid of administrative and legislative detail, but it was sketchy in parts and almost completely silent on the subject of finance for the state government in general and for public schools in particular. The legislature was, therefore, left entirely free on matters of taxation and the sale of public lands. That the early lawmakers did not always use this financial freedom wisely was to become apparent to Californians some 20 years later, but that the constitution was sketchy in other matters was soon apparent to the legislature itself.

As early as 1859 and 1860, the legislature proposed a second constitutional convention, but the people voted down this proposal, and in 1873 they refused another such proposal. Finally, in 1877, the voters agreed to a revision of the state constitution and adopted the second constitution on July 4, 1879, some 30 years after the first one. In those 30 years, each succeeding legislature did as much or as little for the California school system as it saw fit, which meant that there were good years and bad years for California's schools during that period.

Basic School Legislation
in the Formative Period (1851–1879)

The first statutes on the public school system of California were enacted in the spring of 1851, at a time when the lawmakers were preoccupied with the massive task of getting the ship of state afloat. Still, busy as it was, the legislature had a constitutional mandate to establish a state school fund—that is, to authorize the sale or rental of public lands and to create the political machinery whereby the benefits of the fund could be apportioned to local school districts. Since the lawmakers would need guidance and encouragement in creating the architectural design of the state school system, they assumed that the constitutionally elected state superintendent would offer the best recommendations for school legislation.

It became the chief project of early state superintendents of public instruction to importune the lawmakers with organizational, financial, and educational plans and to convert the constitution's educational ideals into actual effective schools in the widely scattered communities of California. Under pressure from the state superintendents or on their own initiative, the legislatures during the architectural period (1851–79) enacted many basic school laws.

THE LEGISLATIVE DESIGN FOR PUBLIC SCHOOLS

The fundamental design of the state system was drawn between 1851 and 1862 under the first three state superintendents of schools in California. Judge John G. Marvin of Tuolumne County, an attorney and former army quartermaster, served from January 1, 1851, until he was succeeded by Colonel Paul Kinsey Hubbs, a former U.S. consul to France, on January 1, 1854. Both of these men were concerned with school finance, taxation, school administration, and the selection of teachers. Colonel Hubbs was succeeded in 1856 by Andrew Jackson Moulder, the first professional schoolman to be elected and once reelected to the state superintendency. Superintendent Moulder's professional interest gave him concern for the training and licensing of teachers and for the function of boards of education, as well as for school finance and administration organization.

The legislature followed the interests and counsel of these three men until January 1, 1863—the date, incidentally, of the Emancipation Proclamation of Abraham Lincoln—the eve of the Civil War. During these 12 years (1851–63), the basic design of the school system was gradually developed in the following way.

The first school law in California was passed by the legislature on May 1, 1851, and signed by Governor McDougall. It provided for the sale of public school lands, the reapportionment of school funds, the formation of local school committees, and the definition of the duties and functions of the state superintendent of public instruction.

Sale of Public School Lands. The federal land grants made vast acreage available for school purposes, but until California's surveyor general specified the location of these acres the land could not be sold. Thereafter, it was up to the legislature to sell or rent the land and to create the first state school fund. It was decided that the interest only on the sales receipts was to be allotted to the counties for the support of the common schools. The county apportionments were then to be made on a census of children between the ages of seven and eighteen.

Reapportionment of School Funds. The county government (the county assessor) was to reapportion school funds to local school districts on the basis of attendance. The 1852 law made the county assessors of all counties superintendents of schools, *ex officio.*

Formation of Local School Committees. Local school committees (or boards) of three annually elected members were authorized to supervise school affairs, examine and hire teachers, build schools, and report annually to the state superintendent.

The first local boards of education were set up, as could be expected, in cities like San Francisco, whose common council created California's first school district under state law on September 25, 1851. Even in more rural areas, school boards were elected in towns and settled communities. That the local districts did not suddenly flourish is clear from Superintendent Marvin's report of April 11, 1853. At this date there were only 20 public elementary schools organized by law in all of California. Seven of these were in San Francisco County, three each in Napa and Solano counties, two in El Dorado, and one each in Santa Clara, Sonoma, Monterey, Contra Costa, and Yuba counties. The state census in 1852 listed 17,821 children between four and eighteen years of age, and state aid for such children as were in school amounted to $22,172.84.

The 1851 legislators, perhaps foreseeing the difficulty of getting public schools established and wishing to take advantage of existing private schools, authorized the distribution of state school funds to private, religious, and sectarian schools on the basis of attendance. This section of the 1851 law caused a great uproar in the assembly and occasioned heated public debates until 1855, when the opposing factions finally agreed that only the public schools should receive public support. Thereafter, state laws and constitutional provisions have repeatedly forbidden the use of public funds for religious, sectarian, or denominational purposes.

Definition of Duties and Functions. The duties and functions of the state superintendent of public instruction were defined by the 1851 legislators. They ordered that the schools under his control include primary, intermediate, and "grammar" grades. The type of studies for these levels was also specified. The "grammar grades" offered advanced, quasi-high school courses.

Thus, the first legislators planned a system of local school districts in California counties, under state control and with some basic state aid. But the sale of public land did not produce much money for the state fund. Therefore, Marvin, the first state superintendent, went before the 1852 legislature with pleas for more money (in fact, for $50,000), for a state school tax, and for established county superintendencies to distribute school funds locally. Surprisingly, he got much of what he asked for and, in addition, a greater definition of public school organization.

The school law of 1852 included these provisions:

1. State, county, and city school taxes were approved by the legislature in these amounts

   a. The state tax levy was five cents on each $100 of assessed property value.

   b. Counties were authorized to levy a school tax of not more than three cents.

   c. Incorporated cities were authorized to levy a three-cent tax.

It was further stipulated that all of the state school funds were to be used for teachers' salaries and that half of the money raised by county taxes was to be used for these salaries. This implied that the cost of buildings and equipment would need to be borne by the local school boards. The state school fund was to be apportioned to the counties for local school districts on the basis of a child census (of children five to eighteen years of age), but no school could receive public money unless it was free of denominational and sectarian bias, interest, or control. Constables were to be the census marshals for the districts.

2. Public school organization and administration were set up

    a. A state board was to have three *ex officio* members—the governor, the surveyor general, and the state superintendent of schools.

    b. The county assessor in each county was still to serve as the *ex officio* superintendent of schools, and the county superintendent's duties, largely fiscal, were defined.

    c. The three members of each local district board were to be elected for a term of one year. Their duties were defined as managerial and operational. The boards created and ran the schools, hired the teachers, and kept school records.

3. The state superintendent, county superintendents (assessors), and local trustees were to carry out their duties as described in this law.

4. The school year of at least three months was to end on October 31 of each year. (This is the origin of the October report, which is still required in each district. Originally it was a final report in each school year, ending in October.)

5. All teachers were to be examined before they were hired.

6. The state superintendent was authorized to call an annual meeting of all teachers in Sacramento. (This is the origin of teachers' institutes in California. Out of these state meetings grew the organizations that ultimately led to the founding of the California Teachers' Association.)

7. The use of denominational and sectarian books in the common schools was forbidden.

In 1855, the legislators established the county superintendency as a separate elective office with defined duties, provided for the election or appointment of city boards of education and city superintendents, and permitted city councils to levy a 25-cent school tax. It also set the rules for the formation of new school districts.

The legislatures were prodded by the state superintendents, who prepared biennial reports on the status of education in California. The first state superintendents were not trained educators, as we noted, but the third state superintendent, Andrew Jackson Moulder, had been a teacher in Virginia. He fought strongly for increased public support and for better schools but had difficulties with the legislature, largely because of inadequate state funds. Nevertheless, he managed to get the following measures passed:

1. County school taxes, which had already increased to 10 cents, were raised again to 25 cents per $100 assessed valuation (1860).

2. County boards of examiners were composed entirely of teachers and were permitted to issue county teaching certificates (1860).

3. The state board of education was authorized to adopt a state series of textbooks and to compel their use (1861).

4. Provisions were made for the establishment of the first state normal school.[4]

Superintendent Moulder retired to private life and a brokerage business on January 1, 1863, and was later appointed to the Board of Regents of the new University of California. Moulder was succeeded by John Swett, a San Francisco school principal. The latter's superintendency (1863–67) marks the greatest gains made for California schools before the second constitution.

JOHN SWETT AND THE CIVIL WAR DAYS

If Horace Mann deserves to be called "the father of American public education," John Swett earned no less a title than that of "father of the California public school system." No pioneer educator did more for this system than Swett, the son of a New England schoolmaster who reached the state superintendency by the way of the principalship of little Rincon School at First and Folsom Streets in San Francisco. He took office on the day the emancipation of slaves was declared, the worst possible time to become state superintendent in California, for the slavery issue was hotly debated in California and the sensitive legislature was prepared for a possible wartime economy. Like his predecessor, John Swett was a devoted schoolman, profes-

---

[4] This normal school was opened in San Francisco on Monday, July 21, 1862, on the ground floor of the high school on Powell Street. Six candidates were admitted for a tuition of five dollars per month. The California State Normal School was moved to San Jose several years later; it is now San Jose State College.

sionally trained, and a zealous fighter for the cause of public education. Among his many achievements for the improvement of public education, only a few can be listed here. They include:

1. Defeat of the wartime economy move, which might have ruined education in California (1863–65).

2. Conversion of the earlier state board of education to the present type of appointed board—that is, a board that adopts rules and regulations for the conduct of schools in the whole state, adopts uniform textbooks for the whole state, establishes a course of study for district schools, and issues teachers' certificates and diplomas. The state board had nine members in Swett's day. Today it has 10 members, all appointed by the governor.

3. Secured finances for county teachers' institutes.

4. Provided for furnishing school supplies (ink, chalk, pens, and paper) at district expense.

5. Established an eight-member state board of normal school trustees. (For the evolution of this board, see Chapter 2, pages 64–66.)

6. Established a system of school libraries with partial state support.

7. Provided for the granting of life diplomas to teachers with 10 years of experience or recognized normal-school diplomas from other states.

8. Required district trustees to keep schools open five months a year.

9. Raised the rates of state and county school taxes.

Swett failed to get himself reelected in 1867 largely because of the overconfidence of the teachers that he would be reelected and specifically because he, a Unitarian, was branded an infidel. He lost the election by 1,600 votes and returned to teaching as a high school science teacher.

Despite all opposition to him and despite the unsettled conditions of the Civil War years, John Swett proved himself one of the chief architects of the public school system of California. For more information on his life and contributions, see Chapter 5, pages 173–75.

Swett's three immediate successors to the superintendency built on his foundation of free state-supported education and so closed the architectural period. We shall now examine their contributions.

THE CLOSE OF THE ARCHITECTURAL ERA

Superintendent Oscar P. Fitzgerald, a Methodist minister, was chosen to run against John Swett when orthodoxy became a campaign issue in 1867. Not only was Fitzgerald considered orthodox, but he had served as a professor in the church-affiliated College of the Pacific[5] at Stockton, California. It was to be expected, too, that he would have considerable interest in creating the University of California out of a college in Oakland that had been originally developed by a group of Protestant ministers.

Swett had been opposed to an abortive attempt to create a state university and had pushed the development of the California State Normal School. This school, which Fitzgerald moved in 1870 from its original San Francisco location to San Jose, became one of the superintendent's pet projects. Although he fulfilled his regular duties as superintendent satisfactorily, Fitzgerald will be best remembered for his part in the state legislation of March 21, 1868, which created the University of California.

To Fitzgerald's successor, the Prussian-born Henry Nicholas Bolander (1871–75), goes the credit for getting a straight seven dollars per pupil in annual state aid and for getting state school apportionment classified as a fixed charge. In 1875, state aid amounted to $1,-215,207.04.

Ezra S. Carr (1875–79) was elected to the superintendency on the Republican ticket in 1875, when he was professor of agriculture at Berkeley. His tenure in office was marred by law suits and injunctions over state textbooks. It ended the period under the old constitution.

To sum up the achievements and deficiencies of the first period of our public school system in California, we need first to remember that the system did not really get under way until 1854 or 1855, that the Civil War years of 1861–65 were detrimental to educational progress, and that during the 15 years following the legislatures were chiefly concerned with the creation and stabilization of a state government in California and with subsidies that would induce telegraph and express

[5] Now the University of the Pacific.

companies, railroads, and business interests to take part in the development of a great state. The constitution had put few restraints on legislative powers, so the lawmakers became generous patrons to growing corporations and somewhat reluctant builders of the school system.

Yet, despite these problems, the bases of the school system were established by 1879. The state superintendency and the state board of education had created a highly centralized system of elementary schools and facilities for teacher training and certification. A normal school and a state university were operating, and state funds for public education were regular items in the state budget.

At the county level, the fiscal and educational responsibilities of the county superintendents and county boards of education had become both clear and fairly effective.

City school systems with at least some high school facilities had developed in San Francisco, Los Angeles, San Jose, Santa Cruz, Stockton, Alameda, Oakland, Vallejo, and Santa Rosa. School districts had reached the corporation status, with rights and responsibilities to tax and to do their share in the support of public education.

Some basic principles on public education were established. The first was that free public education in the common schools should be made available to all the children of California and that facilities for secondary schools and in higher education should be encouraged. The second principle, that state aid and public support should be limited to the public schools, was not so readily adopted. Private and parochial schools, which often preceded public schools in California cities, expected and did get public support for a brief period (1851–52). The 1851 state school law included these provisions:

> If a school be formed by the enterprise of a religious society, in which all the educational branches of the district schools shall be taught, and which, from its private and public examination, the Committee will find it to be well conducted, such school shall be allowed a compensation from the Public School Fund in proportion to the number of its pupils, in the same manner as provided for district schools by this act.

> Schools established under charitable auspices, orphan asylums, schools for blind, almshouse schools, etc., such as shall be subject to the general supervision of laws on education; but under the immediate management of their respective trustees, managers, or

directors; and said schools shall participate in the apportionment of the school moneys in the same manner as other common schools.[6]

It is clear that the 1851 legislature hoped to use the elementary schools, academies, and welfare institutions of various churches and private individuals at a time when almost no other schools were available. But the legislature, bent on promoting public education, stipulated in 1852 that no books of a denominational or sectarian character could be used in the common schools. The contradictions between the 1851 and 1852 laws created a major controversy in the formation of California school districts, particularly in San Francisco, as we shall see in Chapter 2.

A third principle established in the architectural period was the recognition of a united teaching force as a potential in the development of public education in California. This force, first welded together in the early state teachers' institutes after 1854, eventually became the California Teachers' Association. (For its effects on California's schools, see Chapter 5.)

On the negative side, little was done in the early days for rural schools or compulsory education. Moreover, in a highly centralized state school system, county and district school authorities had little control over teachers' licenses, choice of textbooks, and financial affairs. When a second constitution for California was proposed, school people hoped to correct some of the earlier deficiencies.

The Second Constitution (1879) as Written and Amended

The 1849 constitution of California was a brief document that enabled state government in California to get under way. The first constitution had been deficient, as we have said, in outlining the authority of the legislature in particular and almost mute on matters of state and educational finance. The legislature itself was soon aware of these deficiences and repeatedly proposed a second constitution. The people turned down these proposals until the depression of 1873, which gave citizens strong reasons for serious thinking.

By 1878, an accumulation of popular discontent with the first con-

[6] Cloud, p. 249.

stitution developed. Gradually, powerful political organizations had exerted control over the legislature, and just as gradually the agricultural South had developed sectional disputes with the mining and trading North. Private monopolies acquired cheap land, secured water rights, and developed railroad interests. Chinese "coolies," imported in large numbers for railway construction, were considered a threat to white workers.

In education, state and county superintendents and teachers became impatient with inadequate state support of the schools and with the slow progress of the school system. As a result, the California Teachers' Association, newly organized in 1875, began under its president (State Superintendent Ezra Carr) to consider school reforms that might be written into a new constitution. In fact, at the CTA's annual meeting of 1878 at Sacramento, the members made proposals to be submitted to the constitutional convention, which was about to meet.

This constitutional convention was brought about in part by the new Workingmen's party. When the people at large realized the need for a new constitution, the elected delegates were called to a first meeting in the state capital on September 28, 1878. The elected delegates had the following affiliations:[7]

Workingmen's party	50
Republicans	11
Democrats	10
Independents	1
Convention	3
Nonpartisan delegates	77 (a slight majority)
Total	152

[7] These figures of Cloud (p. 67) do not agree with the California State Assembly Handbook, *The Constitution of the United States and of the State of California* (1967), which offers these data on the delegates:

> . . . There were 85 nonpartisan delegates, 50 "Kearneyites or Workingmen's Party delegates" and 17 elected on the regular party tickets, nine of whom were Republicans and eight Democrats. The large number of foreign-born delegates caused considerable comment at the time. There were 35 foreign-born delegates in the convention, most of whom were Irish and 19 of whom were from San Francisco. (Bancroft, XXIV, 373, 407.)

The delegates, assembled in Sacramento, argued and wrangled for five months (Sept. 28, 1878–March 1, 1879). They felt that a mandate of the people required them to clear up these abuses:

1. Corrupt politics (bribery, perjury, and excessive lobbying)

2. Unequal representation of the North and South in the legislature

3. Abuses by railroads and corporations in securing public land, subsidies, and special privileges

4. Unequal tax assessments

5. The threats of Chinese coolie labor

Special committees of the delegates worked on separate articles for the new constitution. The education committee, headed by Judge Joseph W. Winans, had a revised draft of Article IX ready on December 13, 1878, but there was great difference of opinion about the contents of this article. Despite the recommendations of the CTA, the teachers feared that the centralized state system then prevalent would disintegrate into a motley pattern of county and local organizations without the unifying benefits of the state school organization. Finally, Article IX, as adopted by the whole convention on March 1, 1879, had these major provisions:

1. The terms of the state and county superintendents of schools were extended to four years.

2. Money derived from the sale and rental of public lands allocated to education was to be kept entirely for that purpose. The interest derived therefrom was to be used solely for public schools. No public money or public school was to be used for any sectarian purpose.

3. Every school district was required to keep its free public schools open for six months each year.

4. Public schools were to include high schools, normal schools, evening schools, and technical schools, but state public school funds were to be applied exclusively to the support of the primary, grammar, and state normal schools.

5. Adoption of textbooks was assigned to local boards of education and county superintendents, as was the granting of teachers' certificates.

6. A fund of public money for the state university was to be maintained at all times, a college of agriculture and mechanic arts was founded, and no person was to be denied admission to any state-supported college on account of sex.[8]

In addition to this framework, other articles of the new constitution affected education in the following five areas:

1. No taxable area (district or county) was allowed to spend beyond its actual income, although it was granted the right to bond itself for improvements, always provided the interest on such bonds could be comfortably met out of current taxes.

2. A state poll tax of two dollars was levied on every male citizen over 21 years of age, the money to be paid into the state school fund.

3. The legislature was denied the right to pass local or special laws dealing with the management of common schools.

4. No public funds were to be used for any sectarian purpose.

5. Property used exclusively for public schools was to be exempt from taxation.[9]

All of these school matters, along with the rest of the constitution, were approved by the convention on March 3, 1879, and adopted by a small majority of California voters (77,952 for, 67,134 against) on May 7, 1879.

The entire constitution turned out to be a lengthy, discursive, moralizing document of over 65,000 words, wide open to future amendments. The State Assembly Handbook has these pertinent observations on the amendments: "The large amount of legislation contained in the Constitution has necessitated frequent change. From 1880 to 1940 inclusive, there were amendments proposed to 733 sections of the Constitution, of which 343 were adopted and 390 rejected." [10]

[8] Cloud, pp. 70–71.
[9] *Ibid.*
[10] California State Assembly Handbook, p. 102.

In California, constitutional amendments have been used and abused to bypass the legislature and to fix permanently in the constitution matters that have no place in the basic law of the land. They include racetrack regulations, minimum salaries for teachers, and formulas for the apportionment of state aid for public schools. As the economy and the value of the dollar change in good times and bad, minimum salaries and specific dollar formulas frozen in the constitution can be detrimental to the very people the amendments are intended to help. For instance, at a given moment there could be a constitutional minimum for a teacher's salary of $2,400, a legislative minimum of $4,500, and a school district minimum of $5,000 to $6,000. If there were a financial disaster, the constitutional minimum could become the maximum teacher's salary. This did occur in the depression of the 1930s, when the constitutional minimum was $1,300.

These and other deficiencies of the constitution have been well known for years. Periodically there is talk of or agitation for another revision or a complete recasting of the basic law of California. In 1933 and "at every session of the Legislature from 1935 to 1947, there were proposals for a Constitutional convention and for revision of the Constitution . . . but none of them passed." [11] Finally, in 1947, a joint committee consisting of 10 members from each house was appointed to study the constitution and prepare a draft of a revised constitution. The State Assembly Handbook summarizes the effect of this effort:

> Very little was accomplished because the advisory committee recommended that the committee restrict itself to the elimination of obsolete provisions in the Constitution rather than a revision in substance and that recommendation was accepted by the committee. A series of seven Constitutional amendments were submitted by the Legislature to the voters for the purpose of eliminating purely obsolete material from the Constitution. After submission it was discovered that one of these proposals might contain defects in drafting. At the special election November 8, 1959, the voters adopted six of these proposals thereby eliminating the more obviously obsolete proposals of the Constitution. These amendments on the whole eliminated approximately 14,500 words from the Constitution.[12]

[11] *Ibid.*, pp. 102–03.
[12] *Ibid.*, p. 103.

To summarize this discursive, much-amended document is a thankless task, but we shall endeavor to give the scope of the constitution's present content, particularly as it relates to public education.

California Constitution (1879–)

Preamble   "We, the people of the state of California, grateful to Almighty God for our freedom, in order to secure and perpetuate its blessings, do establish this Constitution." (from the 1849 Constitution)

Article I   Declaration of Rights

A bill of rights, including the rights of private property and the state's eminent-domain rights (whereby property can be condemned for schools and other public purposes).

Article II   The Right of Suffrage

The qualification of voters and the loss of the right to vote by criminals and the insane.

There can be no property test for voters and no poll tax.

Literacy in the English language has been mitigated (November 7, 1950).

Party conventions and direct-primary elections.

Secret ballots are used, and voting machines may be used.

Article III   The Separation of Powers

The powers of state government are legislative, executive, and judicial.

Persons charged with the exercise of one power may not exercise either of the others except as permitted by this constitution.

Article IV   Legislative Powers

The Senate and the assembly and qualifications for membership therein.

The 1879 constitution trimmed back the powers that earlier legislatures had exercised under the old constitution. It prohibited special or local laws and the use of state funds for sectarian purposes. It included powers of initiative, referendum, and recall.[13]

Article V   The Executive Branch

The qualifications, terms of office, and the powers and duties of the governor, the lieutenant governor, attorney general, secretary of state, and superintendent of public education—all of whom are elected executives.

Vacancies and succession to the governorship.

Article VI   The Judicial Department

Provisions for the state supreme court, appellate, superior, and lesser courts, for judges, trial, the right to be represented by an attorney, and so on.

Article VII   The Pardoning Power

The pardoning power of the governor, partly from the 1849 constitution, but with additions.

Article VIII   The State Militia

From the 1849 constitution.

Article IX   Education

[Because of its importance, this article is detailed at the end of the outline.]

Article X   State Institutions and Public Buildings

The establishment and supervision of penal institutions, the separate treatment of female felons, and the control of convict labor.

---

[13] It should be noted here that amendments to the California Constitution do not appear at the end of the original constitution, as in the U.S. Constitution. Instead, the original articles have new materials written into them or old materials deleted by repeal. As a result, we find these amusing notations in Section 19 of Article IV (as summarized in the State Assembly Handbook, p. 126):

> **Section 19.** (b) The Legislature may provide for the regulation of horse races and horse race meetings and wagering on the results. (New section adopted November 8, 1966, as amended November 7, 1916 [initiative measure], repealed November 8, 1966.)

Article XI　Counties, Cities, and Towns

> Boundaries and county seats.
>
> Charters and officers of counties and municipalities.
>
> County employees, roads, and local utilities.
>
> Local taxes and debt limitations.

Article XII　Corporations

> The formation of corporations, corporate franchises, and the control of corporations.
>
> The railroad and public utilities commissions.

Article XIII　Revenue and Taxation

> *Ad valorem* property taxes and exemptions therefrom.
>
> Tax assessment and the state and county boards of equalization.
>
> Bank and corporate taxes.
>
> Tax exemption of municipal bonds (1902), church property (1910), college property (1914), and orphan asylums—all private, nonprofit organizations.

Article XIV　Water and Water Rights

> A major problem in early days, as well as now.

Article XV　Harbor Frontage (Tidelands)

> Riparian rights.

Article XVI　State Indebtedness

> This article has been amended several times, including state bonds to be loaned to school districts for school buildings.

Article XVII　Land and Homestead Exemption

Article XVIII　Amending and Revising the Constitution

> Proposal by the legislature, by the people through the initiative, or by the constitutional convention; ratification by the electorate.[14]

[14] See note 13, page 36.

Article XIX   *Chinese Coolie Labor Restriction*
Repealed November 4, 1952, as obsolete.

Article XX   *Miscellaneous Subjects*
An assortment of provisions relating to the seat of state government, marriage, suits against the state, conditions of labor.

Article XXI   *Boundaries of the State*
As they now stand.

Article XXII   *Schedule*
Process for putting this constitution to vote and into effect.
When laws are in force, conflicting legislation, prior validations, and ratifications.

Article XXIII   *Recall of Public Officers*

Article XXIV   *State Civil Service*

Article XXV   *Aged and Blind Act*
Repealed by Article XXVII.

Article XXVI   *Motor Vehicle Tax and Revenue*

Article XXVII   *Repeal of Article XXV*

Article XXVIII   *Open-Space Conservation*

NOTE   Articles XXIX through XXXIII have been repealed.

Article XXXIV   *The Public Housing Project Law*

Because of their importance, the constitutional provisions for schools in Article IX will now be outlined in detail:

Section 1   A general diffusion of knowledge and intelligence being essential to the preservation of the rights and liberties of the people, the legislature shall encourage by all suitable means the promotion of intellectual, scientific, moral, and agricultural improvement.

Section 2   A superintendent of public instruction shall be elected by the qualified electors of the state at each gubernatorial election.

He shall enter upon the duties of his office on the first Monday after the first day of the January succeeding his election.

Section 3   The election of county superintendents of schools for four-year terms.

Section 3.1   The qualifications and salary of county superintendents.

Section 3.3   The qualifications and term of office of county boards of education.

NOTE   Section 4 has been repealed.

Section 5   The legislature shall provide for a system of common schools by which a free school shall be kept open and supported in each district at least six months in every year, after the first year in which a school has been established.

Section 6   Each person, other than a substitute employee, employed by a school district as a teacher or in any other position requiring certification qualifications shall be paid a salary that shall be at the rate of an annual salary of not less than $2,400 for a person serving full time, as defined by law.

The public school system shall include all kindergarten schools, elementary schools, secondary schools, technical schools, and state colleges, established in accordance with law and, in addition, the school districts and the other agencies authorized to maintain them. No school or college or any other part of the public school system shall be, directly or indirectly, transferred from the public school system or placed under the jurisdiction of any authority other than one included within the public school system.

The legislature shall add to the state school fund such other means from the revenues of the state as shall provide in said fund for apportionment in each fiscal year, an amount not less than $180 per pupil in average daily attendance in the kindergarten schools, elementary schools, secondary schools, and technical schools in the public school system during the next preceding fiscal year.

From the state fund, the legislature is then required to provide $120 in basic aid per pupil across the board and never less than $2,400 to any district no matter how small.[15]

The legislature must furthermore provide for the levying of school

[15] The complexities of current state apportionments are discussed in detail in Chapter 3, pages 119–25.

district taxes within legislative maximums for each school district and control the issuances and payments of school bonds within the limitation of Section 18 of Article XI of the constitution.

Section 7   The legislature is required to provide for the appointment or election of a state board of education and a board of education for each county. The state board is required to adopt a uniform series of textbooks, which are to be printed and distributed at state expense for the free use of all elementary pupils (grades 1 through 8). The county superintendents and boards are charged with examining teachers and granting teachers' certificates for their respective jurisdiction.

Section 8   No public money shall ever be appropriated for the support of sectarian, denominational, or private schools, and no sectarian or denominational doctrine shall be taught in any common schools of the state.

Section 9   The University of California becomes a public trust to be administered by a corporation known as The Regents of the University of California. The composition, rights, and duties of the Board of Regents are defined.

Section 10   State protection of the grants, properties, corporate powers, and privileges of Stanford University is established.

Section 11   The California School of Mechanical Arts, endowed by James Lick, is to be exempt from taxation (adopted November 6, 1900).

Section 12   The California Academy of Sciences is to be exempt from taxation but must make annual reports to the governor on its finances.

Section 13   Cogswell Polytechnic College is likewise tax exempt and must also make annual reports to the governor on its finances.

Section 14   The legislature shall have power, by general law, to provide for the incorporation and organization of school districts, high school districts, and junior college districts, of every kind and class, and may classify such districts.

Section 15   The Henry E. Huntington Library and Art Gallery is exempt from taxation, but the trustees must report annually on their financial status.

To summarize briefly, Article IX regulates the organization and conduct of public schools, but some sections in Articles XII (Corporations), XIII (Revenue and Taxation), and XX (Miscellaneous Subjects) also apply to schools and education. For example, school districts may not hold shares of capital stock in corporations except mutual water companies that supply them with water (Article XII). Support of public education and the state university is a fixed charge and so has the first call in the revenue from state taxes (Article XIII). School district bonds are exempt from state taxation (Article XIII). The eight-hour day for laborers, workmen, and mechanics must be respected by school districts (Article XX). The subversive group and subversive persons section of the constitution (Article XX) applies to school districts (since a constitutional amendment was passed on November 4, 1952).

Besides these constitutional provisions for public education, statutes on the organization and conduct of schools have been enacted in almost every session of the legislature since 1851. Quite obviously, in the face of this mass of accumulated legislation, we must resort to the study of legislative trends, particularly in the first 80 years of California's history.

The thirty years between 1850 and 1880 were required to establish a system of public education in California. After this architectural period, 50 years were needed to expand and modernize the system. Only in 1930, at the end of this intermediate period, which closed with the Great Depression, did the school system settle down in its present form.

Progress in School Legislation (1880–1930)

Before the adoption of the new constitution in 1879, California had had a centralized state school system, but the new constitution sanctioned some decentralization by strengthening the hands of county boards of education and county superintendents, particularly in matters of courses of study and textbooks. To offset these dangers the state superintendent, Fred M. Campbell, initiated biennial meetings of county superintendents in January, 1880. He strove to maintain some unity in educational practices through his leadership and secured some general agreement on textbooks that the state planned to print and sell at cost to pupils.

In 1880, most California public schools were elementary schools whose buildings were provided by local districts but whose operational costs were borne in part by state aid. The teachers for these schools, when trained in California, were graduates of the state normal school in San Jose. Public high schools, available for the most part in urban areas only, had begun to operate alongside private academies. A single state university was offering higher education courses in Berkeley and San Francisco.

But progress was in the air; it was encouraged by the new constitution. Bonds for school buildings were legalized by 1881 legislation. From the summer of 1880, summer courses in teacher training were available. The first course was a Chautauqua-type meeting at Pacific Grove in Monterey County. These summer courses and county teachers' institutes sometimes took the place of regular training in normal school. In 1886, Colonel Francis W. Parker, brought to California by an encampment of the Grand Army of the Republic, began a series of talks to teachers on schools and the problems of teaching. Parker decried the large classes and formal methods that prevailed in the common schools. He had little to say about secondary education because there was so little of it in California.

THE DEVELOPMENT OF PUBLIC SECONDARY EDUCATION

Free, state-supported high school education was a long time coming to California. Its development, largely after 1886, was brought about by a series of laws passed, repealed, or amended by legal opinions and court cases and the 1902 constitutional amendment to Article IX, which reads:

> *Section 6* The public school system shall include primary and grammar schools, and such high schools, evening schools, normal schools, and technical schools as may be established by the legislature, or by municipal or district authority. The entire revenue derived from the state school fund and from the general state school tax shall be applied exclusively to the support of primary and grammar schools; but the legislature may authorize and cause to be levied a special state school tax for the support of high schools and technical schools, or either of such schools included in the public school system, and all revenue derived from such special

tax shall be applied exclusively to the support of the schools for which such special tax shall be levied.[16]

This amendment was implemented by the following 1903 legislation:

> **Section 1**   There is to be levied annually during 1904 and 1905 an *ad valorem* tax of 1½ cents upon every 100 dollars of value of taxable property of the state. The amount of tax for the years after 1905 is to be fixed by the Legislature.

> **Section 9**   High schools organized under present law for the establishment of high schools and receiving money under this act shall, within one year after first beginning to receive such state aid, provide at least one course of study as will prepare pupils for admission to one of the colleges of the University of California, and for that purpose said high school shall be subject to inspection by a duly accredited representative of said university. High schools eligible to receive state aid as herein provided shall admit as students only such pupils as have completed the full course of instruction prescribed for the primary or grammar schools of the county or city and county wherein the high school is located, or an equivalent course, or such pupils may show by thorough examination that their qualifications are equivalent to the requirements for graduation from said primary and grammar schools.[17]

However, lest it be erroneously concluded that no secondary education opportunities were available in the early years, a summary of early secondary education is in order. Between 1852 and 1858, the San Francisco Board of Education was in the throes of getting a public, though not free, high school established. Superintendent Thomas J. Nevins had suggested a high school and was instructed by his board to present a course of study including high school courses. He came up with "The Rules and Regulations of the San Francisco High School and Ladies' Seminary," with separate courses for boys and girls, which were approved by the city council on January 7, 1853. Union Grammar School opened on August 25, 1856, with a four-year course, mostly for college entrance. Thirty-five boys and 45 girls were enrolled, and 11 of them (four girls and seven boys) graduated in 1861. By that date, the school was known as San Francisco High School, which on

---

[16] Cloud, appendix 46, pp. 264–65.
[17] *Ibid.,* appendix 47, p. 265.

September 19, 1860, moved into its own building on Powell Street between Clay and Sacramento Streets.

The Sacramento Board of Education opened Sacramento High School on August 25, 1856, and by 1859 it was offering courses in business practice and vocational studies in addition to college preparatory courses.

By and large, however, most grammar school courses and college preparatory work from 1850 to 1890 were offered by private schools, usually church-affiliated, which were generally called academies, seminaries (for girls), or institutes. Ferrier devotes a 44-page chapter to lists and descriptions of them.[18] He concludes his study with this summary:

> The 1890's mark the beginning of the waning of the academies and seminaries. Many went out of existence, and not many came in to take their places. They were no longer needed as they had been for many years. The high schools met the need increasingly and made the academies and seminaries to a considerable extent impossible of maintenance. In 1890 there were only 30 high schools in the state. In June 1893 there were 76; in 1895 there were 98, and in 1900 there were 120. For the year ending June 30, 1890, the enrollment in the high schools was 3,541. In 1900, it was 12,179.[19]

According to Napier, there were already 19 public high schools in California by 1879.[20] Although this was five years after the U.S. Supreme Court decision on the Kalamazoo case, these California schools did not offer completely free high school education. After the Kalamazoo case, it was clearly not unconstitutional under the U.S. Constitution to use common-school funds for the support of high school education, but the constitutional authority to offer free secondary education was not so clear under the state constitution of 1879.

The 1879 constitution included high school among the public schools of California, but it said that public school funds were to be applied exclusively to support the primary and grammar schools of the state.

The great lack of high schools caused the state to approve "grammar school courses" as a link between the public schools and the uni-

[18] William Warren Ferrier, *Ninety Years of Education in California—1846–1936* (Berkeley, Calif.: Sather Gate Book Shop, 1937), pp. 119–62.

[19] *Ibid.*, p. 160.

[20] John J. Napier, Jr., *The Origin and Development of the Public High School in California.*

versity; but in 1886 a popular movement was under way to establish more high schools in cities, towns, and counties. The principal reason for this interest in secondary education was the expanded service of the new University of California and private colleges. In those days the chief purpose of high schools was preparation for college. The entrance requirement at the university and the colleges was graduation from high school or, at the very least, "grammar-grade" education.

The 1887 legislature approved a "grammar school course" for entrance into the university and for a secondary teaching license. On the basis of this legislation, city school districts looked for state support for their high schools, which they had been operating at local district expense. However, on May 16, 1887, California's Attorney General A. G. Campbell ruled that this was not in accord with the state constitution. He did say, though, that grammar school courses were to be construed as elementary.

In 1891, the California legislature passed three bills on high school education:

1. The Caminetti Act, permitting elementary schools to maintain postgraduate courses designed to prepare pupils for admission to the University of California.

2. The County High School Act, providing for the formation of county high school districts and for the establishment of one or more county high schools within several counties.

3. An act permitting any city or incorporated town of 1,500 or more inhabitants to establish and maintain a high school after it had the consent of a majority of the voters for it. Union high school districts were also created by the consolidation of several school districts.

A superior court decision of 1892 (*People ex. rel. Brown v. Union High School District of Solano County*) threw the 1891 law in great confusion, which led the 1893 legislature to repeal the high school law. Sections of the 1891 law were reenacted in 1893 in what was really an 1893 secondary school law. The 1893 enactments avoided the constitutionally questionable sections of the 1891 law, which was declared unconstitutional in the 1893 state supreme court decision on the case of *McCabe v. Carpenter*.[21] It is interesting to note that the

[21] See Cloud, pp. 90–91, especially where Cloud notices that the revision of 1893 prevented an interruption in the establishment of high school districts.

constitutional problem was rooted in a legal technicality. Since the fixing of the high school tax rate was left entirely to the discretion of the county superintendents of schools, the supreme court found that legislative powers were granted to executive officers, which is contrary to the constitution's Article IV on the separation of powers. Since the 1893 enactments did not have these flaws, the laws on the formation of high school districts were constitutionally upheld by the supreme court of California.

The whole problem of state support for secondary education was not finally settled, however, until 1902, when the constitution was amended especially to include the granting of state aid to high schools. This constitutional amendment cleared the road of all hazards: it provided state support for high schools, both urban and rural.

The amendment, adopted by a large majority of the voters, seems to have given the electorate, the legislature, and professional educators an incentive to extend secondary education beyond the twelfth grade. At any rate, shortly after the legislative session opened on January 5, 1907, boards of education of all city and high school districts were authorized to develop what amounted to a junior college course for high school graduates and to charge tuition for it. The new "junior college course" began and remained an integral part of secondary education until the close of the depression era in the 1930s. The thirteenth and fourteenth year offered in California high schools, given after graduation from grade 12, was generally called postgraduate work.

Alexis F. Lange of the University of California, who did much for the improvement of junior high schools and junior colleges after 1912, announced to the 1915 CTA annual meeting that:

1. Junior colleges were progressing and adjusting to meet the requirements of the university.

2. Junior colleges could and should constitute a capstone of secondary education—that is, terminal work for "the great mass of high school graduates, who can not, will not and should not become university students."

3. The function and structure of the junior college makes it "an integral part of the secondary school"; though, as the father of the California junior college movement, Lange saw it also as a two-year

terminal college. Lange stressed three levels of secondary education: junior high school, senior high school, and junior college. For this top level, his so-called capstone, he wanted a vocational department, not entirely separated from liberal arts, and a department of civic education.[22]

Merton E. Hill, a successor of Lange, moved from a high school principalship to the presidency of Ontario's Chaffee Junior College in the early 1920s and became a professor of education at Berkeley on July 1, 1931, while he was president of the California Junior College Association. It was largely through Hill's efforts that junior colleges were reorganized and developed in California after the depression. This was after the old thirteenth and fourteenth years of postgraduate work in high school were abandoned.

Fresno seems to have begun this postgraduate work in 1910, but by 1914 San Diego High School's principal, Arthur Gould, had organized junior college classes. From that time on through the depression, junior colleges remained an integral part of secondary education, though some junior colleges like Chaffee operated separately from the high schools. San Diego, however, offers one example of the program's development. In the middle 1930s, grades 13 and 14 were moved from San Diego High School to San Diego State College, where junior college classes, financed by the city schools, were conducted separately from regular freshman and sophomore classes. Then, in 1937, adult junior college courses were begun in the department of adult education of the city schools, and in 1938 a vocational junior college was opened. In a few years, the terminal, vocational, and academic courses were again brought together in a new junior college organization.

By 1940, therefore, California's junior colleges served both terminal secondary education functions and the new needs for lower-division college work. During recent years, although terminal opportunities have not been eliminated altogether, the California junior college has become a lower-division educational institution. Indeed, in September, 1967, the state board of education requested State Superintendent Max Rafferty to nominate members for a new state board proposed to guide the destinies of these intermediate (lower-division) institutions. It becomes clear, therefore, that California junior colleges are no longer merely secondary schools.

[22] It is worthy of notice that Lange was chosen as the first head of the school of education at Berkeley with the title of director when that school was organized in 1913.

A summary of 10 effective years of 1908–18 of legislative enactments and constitutional amendments should suffice to prove the enthusiasm of Californians for their public schools:

1908   Children were forbidden to work during school hours and at night. High school district boards were to have five members. An eight-year elementary course of study was approved. Supervision by physicians of students' health and development was approved.

1910   State school taxes were discontinued in favor of county school taxes (constitutional amendment).

1911   Free textbooks, printed by the state, were provided for grades 1 through 8.[23]

On January 3, 1911, Governor Hiram W. Johnson, elected on the Progressive Republican ticket, began two terms of office that are known for their progressive viewpoint and for progress in education, among other things. The laws of the following years bear out this contention.

1912   The first Teacher Tenure Law, a continuing-contract law, was enacted.

1913   The state board of education's authority over all schools except the university was defined and the board was authorized to grant secondary credentials and life certificates and to select state textbooks for state printing.[24] Other legislative enactments of 1913 approved the appointment of state commissioners for elementary, secondary, and vocational schools in the state department of education and the establishment in the state department of the California Teachers' Retirement System. The initial retirement benefit of $500 per year after 30 years of service has been vastly improved, as we shall see later in this chapter and in Chapter 5. Finally, the 1913 constitutional amendment on direct primaries took the election of school board members and state and county superintendents out of partisan politics.

[23] The state continues to print and distribute free basic textbooks for all elementary school classes entirely at state expense. Supplementary textbooks, if districts desire them, must be bought at district expense, but they may not be substituted for the basic state textbook.

[24] The state board has used a curriculum commission of teachers and school administrators to study and recommend textbooks for state adoption.

1914   The California state poll tax was repealed.

1915   Intermediate (junior high) schools were organized. School districts were permitted to levy tax for kindergartens. Vacation schools (summer schools) were authorized. School boards were permitted to hire "home teachers." Tobacco and alcohol were excluded from school premises. Three-quarters of elementary school time was required to be devoted to the fundamentals (the 3 R's).

1916   Physical education was required in all schools, with a specific requirement of one hour of physical education in all secondary schools (grades 7 through 14).[25] A special credential was approved for teachers of physical education and industrial arts.[26] High schools in California were required to provide free textbooks for all pupils at local district expense.

1918   Vocational, agricultural, and home economics courses, as provided for by the Smith-Hughes Act, were approved for California schools.

On January 9, 1919, Will C. Wood became state superintendent of public instruction. Wood had been a country-school teacher, a principal, and a member of the Solano County Board of Education, as well as superintendent of the Alameda City Schools. In 1914 he became California's first commissioner of secondary education. Having reached the state superintendency after "the world was saved for democracy," Wood stated his aims of January 20, 1919, as follows: "A school system aiming to prepare for Democracy must itself be democratic. And Democracy means counseling together, cooperating, working out policies that will represent consensus or at any rate majority opinion." [27]

In 1919, California education needed an infusion of democratic ideals, but it also had an urgent need for more teachers. Class sizes had jumped from 35 to 40 pupils to 75 or 80. Poorly paid teachers had been attracted to jobs in wartime industry; rural schools were closing down for lack of staff. The crisis was national in scope, so the NEA and PTA endeavored to call attention to the emergency by establish-

---

[25] Physical fitness as a war-preparation issue caused physical-education associations to initiate this law, which, despite repeated opposition, is still in effect today.

[26] These and other special credentials—for example, in art, music, agriculture, and homemaking—that required less stringent educational preparation than general credentials continued to the early 1960s.

[27] Cloud, p. 140.

ing American Education Week, first observed during the week of November 11, 1920.

The Masonic Lodges of California rallied to publicize a statewide publicity campaign through an annual California Public Schools Week, starting on September 27, 1920. The first job of this original school week was to gain support for a proposed new constitutional amendment initiated by the CTA to increase state school funds and to promote federal aid for education.

MODERNIZATION OF THE SCHOOL SYSTEM IN THE 1920s

The first California Public Schools Week was effective in gaining public interest in school finance and in the general improvement of the state system. The chief effect was the proposal of another constitutional amendment.

The California constitutional amendment, then known as Proposition 16, was adopted on November 2, 1920, by a vote of 506,008 to 268,781. This new law, effective December 9, 1920, contained these provisions:

1. The state school system was to include kindergartens, which had previously been supported at local district expense.

2. "Teachers' colleges" were to replace the old two-year normal school and give a degree in pedagogy. The colleges were three-year institutions until 1924.

3. State school funds were for the first time to be apportioned at $30 per unit of average daily attendance for the preceding school year. This method of apportionment had long been advocated by Ellwood Patterson Cubberley, dean of Stanford University's school of education and former superintendent of the San Diego city schools. (See Chapter 3, page 117.)

4. City and county taxes for schools were required to match the $30 per ADA for elementary schools and to produce at least $60 per ADA for high schools.

5. The legislature was required to provide for local district school taxes. After these legislative provisions were made, local districts could support their schools by state aid (ADA apportionments), county aid (property taxes), and local-district taxes (also on real property).

6. All state aid and 60 percent of the county aid was to be used for teachers' salaries, which needed improvement.

The era of the 1920s was a period of reorganization of California schools, school finance, teacher training and licensing, teachers' salaries and retirement, and the state department of education. It was also a time of conflict for the state superintendent of public instruction.

The economy-minded governor, Friend William Richardson, complained: "Extravagance in educational matters has run riot during the past few years." But before the Richardson regime of 1923–27, and even during it, much good legislation was forced across the governor's desk, as the following items show:

1921 School boards were required to file a budget, but the boards of supervisors were to have no control over this budget. A director of research and foreign languages was added to the state department of education.

1923 Teachers of special subjects were to be paid more than primary teachers. School boards were given increased power to improve school buildings and grounds. City boards of education were required to keep public records of all financial transactions and of all courses of study. Facilities for the education of the deaf and blind were increased. Boards of supervisors were authorized to consolidate school districts when their schools were within three miles of each other. A "supervisor and school administrator" credential was enacted into law to supplement the existing general elementary, general secondary, and special teaching credentials.

1924 State teacher training was extended from three to four years —24 units of education required and the B.A. could be granted. Radio was introduced into the school program.

1925–26 These were years marked by a war between the progressive state superintendent Wood and the economy-minded governor Richardson.

1927 Governor C. C. Young reversed the Richardson policy. State Superintendent William John Cooper, with the aid of the CTA under the strong leadership of Mark Keppel, reorganized and enlarged the state department of education and secured these school reforms: Legislation authorizing school cafeterias was passed. A six-year elementary course of study became standard practice in the 6-3-3 school organization, though the 8-4 plan was not entirely abandoned by the legislature. State schools for the correction of speech defects were approved. School districts were authorized to provide supplementary textbooks at their own expense, though they were still required to use the basic textbooks provided by the state. The state board of education was authorized to establish a California Curriculum Commission composed of teachers and school administrators. The commission still continues to make curricular and textbook recommendations to the state board, and so guides its approval of authorized textbooks and its adoption of state textbooks.

In 1928 the enormous task of codifying all educational legislation from 1851 to 1928 was begun by the state department of education with the approval of the legislature. Mark Keppel, the renowned Los Angeles County superintendent of schools who was most influential in getting the code started, died while the codification was still in progress. The school code, which was California's first, was published in 1929.

The Codification
of School Law (1929–1959)

State laws regulating the management of schools began with the first constitution in 1849, with statutes passed by state legislatures, and with court decisions on school matters. New legislation changed, replaced, and improved older laws. A new constitution, wide open to amendments, was adopted in 1879. During the next 50 years a vast accumulation of new constitutional provisions, volumes of statutory law, and numerous court cases made school law a complex maze of regulations, the sum of which could be found only in law libraries, the constitution, and acts of the legislature or court records.

This impossibly confused mass of scattered laws made the work of boards of education, superintendents, principals, and teachers a confused and risky business. As early as 1915, the CTA, under the leadership of Keppel, strongly urged the codification and indexing of all laws pertaining to public education.

For 12 years, however, nothing tangible happened in the development of a school code, for they were years of strife between the governor and the state superintendent. But in 1927 State Superintendent Cooper assigned Sam H. Cohn to assist Keppel's legislative commission, which eventually got a senate bill passed to codify school law. The job was begun in 1928, but Keppel died in June of that year. In 1929, a new law provided for a school code separate from the political, civil, penal, and other codes of California.

This 1929 School Code was out of date the year following its publication, since new legislation about schools is enacted in each legislature. The situation was particularly unfortunate for the first school code, however, because it was enacted the very year of the stock market crash. The ensuing depression forced revised legislation, particularly as it affected school finances and all other types of state and county finance.

In 1930, the forty-ninth legislature saw 3,000 new bills introduced in its two houses. Among these bills were 138 assembly bills and 90 senate bills directly affecting education, of which 53 assembly and 61 senate bills were passed. This was a mere harbinger. Year by year, loose-leaf supplements to the school code were issued by the state department of education. Thirteen years later, on April 7, 1943, the legislature called for a new education code that would consolidate and revise "the law relating to schools, libraries, and institutions of learning, arts, and sciences and repeal certain acts or parts of acts."

Thus, the School Code of 1929 became the Education Code of 1944, and this Education Code had the following organization and section numbers:

General Provisions (1–100)

Division 1. State and County School Organization (101–500)
    Chapter 1. State Organization
        Article 1. State Board of Education
        Article 2. Superintendent of Public Instruction
        Article 3. State Department of Education
        Article 4. Surplus Property

    Chapter 2. County Organization (501–1,000)
Division 2. Local School Administrative Organization (1,001–5,000) This division was expanded to 159 pages defining the types of school district, the creation and consolidation of school districts, and the duties of governing boards and superintendents.
Division 3. Financial support of the school system (5,001–8,000)
Division 4. System of public instruction (types of education and

instruction at all levels of the school system) (8,001–10,000)

Division 5. Courses of study (10,001–11,000)
Division 6. Textbooks (11,001–12,000)
Division 7. School employees (12,001–16,000)
Division 8. Pupils (16,001–18,000)
Division 9. Equipment and environment (18,001–20,000)
Division 10. Educational institutions (the University, state colleges, California academies, schools for cerebral-palsied children, transportation districts, and scholarships) (20,001–22,000)
Division 11. Libraries (22,001–24,000)
Division 12. Miscellaneous legal items (24,001–50,000)

The 1929 school code had been a major achievement. For the first time in California history, all laws directly pertaining to the public schools were organized in a logical framework and made available to legislators and school people alike. But the defects of the code and the problem of keeping it up to date were noticed almost from the day of its publication.

The first defect was that the code's coverage of law was incomplete. The constitution, general laws, and other Californian codes (for example, the civil code and the election code) carried laws that affected schools and their management. This defect was remedied only in 1944, when a new education code included educational provisions from the constitution and other codes in its appendixes. The appendixes include legal excerpts applicable to schools in 14 other documents: (1) the Constitution, (2) Agricultural Code, (3) Business and Professional Code, (4) Civil Code, (5) Code of Civil Procedure, (6) Election Code, (7) Government Code, (8) Health and Safety Code, (9) Insurance Code, (10) Labor Code, (11) Military and Veterans Code, (12) Vehicle Code, (13) Welfare and Institutions Code, and (14) General Laws.

The 1929 school code and the 1944 education code had other defects:

1. New legislation, new constitutional amendments, and court decisions made it difficult to keep the codes up to date without supplements printed every few years.

2. The original organization of materials and their codification proved inadequate.

3. The indexing of the code itself and of the appendixes was so unsatisfactory that it was difficult to trace laws in the code.

Therefore, in the 1950s educators were calling for another new code with a new organization, new codification, and indexes. Elimination of obsolete material seemed desirable because the presence of laws no longer in effect was, to say the least, confusing to educators and legislators. To clear up these problems, the 1957 legislature created a joint legislative committee to revise the Education Code. (See Chapter 2419 of the Statutes of 1957.) "The act to recodify the Education Code by repealing and reenacting said code . . . [was] approved by [the] Governor February 3, 1951." [28] But Section 1 of the act reads:

> The Legislature intends by this act to rearrange the provisions of the Education Code in more logical sequence, making only such other changes as are necessitated by changing the sequence of existing provisions. The Legislature intends to accomplish this objective without making any substantive change in the law.[29]

This third and latest effort to bring all state laws on public education together in one massive document resulted in two volumes totaling 2,368 6-by-9-inch pages, including tables of content, an appendix of pertinent materials from the constitution, 16 other California codes, general laws, and the indexes. The codification and indexing of this extensive legal publication represent improvements over the earlier codes. Therefore, it is now easier to find specific laws on public education. Although no teacher or school administrator can be expected to have a comprehensive knowledge of the whole code, it does seem desirable that public school employees have an overview of the state law as it is organized in the code. Therefore, an outline of the contents of this education code is provided in Appendix III.

Legislative Trends Since 1933

When the 1929 school code was published, the California system of public schools already bore a close resemblance to today's system. Educational opportunities were available from kindergartens

---

[28] State of California, *Education Code,* Vol. 1 (Sacramento: Dept. of General Services, Documents Section, 1965), p. 31.

[29] *Ibid.*

through junior colleges and adult classes. Teachers could be certificated for elementary or secondary teaching. They could gain tenure and a small retirement benefit ($500 a year after 30 years). A single administration credential was required of principals and superintendents.

The system was financed by state aid (apportioned on an ADA basis), county taxes, and some district taxes. School buildings were usually financed by local school bonds, and, in the lush days of the late twenties, tax money was available in fairly adequate sums. These conditions reflected the boom market in the general economy, which was bedevilled by unrestrained speculation until the stock market crash in October, 1929.

In California, the depression struck late, but its effects lasted until 1938. Major financial, personnel, and program changes affected the pattern of public education particularly as the schools adjusted to the depressed economy.

The first catastrophic effect of the depression on California schools was triggered by the inability of California counties to carry their major load of school costs. Welfare cases due to general unemployment sapped the counties of their resources. Therefore, if schools were to be kept open, a general revision of their financial support was obviously a prime requirement. A detailed account of the shift of financial support of education from the counties to the state, the federal government, and local districts will be given in Chapter 30. It will become apparent that the provision of more adequate and better equalization support for public education has been a principal concern of the legislature since 1933.

The problem has been intensified by repeated population explosions in California since the depression and World War II. The U.S. Bureau of the Census gives these figures for the years in consideration:

Year	Population
1930	5,677,251
1940	6,907,387
1950	10,586,223
1960	15,717,204

The school enrollment in California, which was just over a million in 1940 and about one and a half million in 1950, was divided by grades in 1960 as follows:[30]

Grade	Enrollment
K	307,207
1–8	2,212,239
9–12	785,600
13–14	145,000
Total	3,450,046

In 1966, the total school enrollment in all regular grades and special classes was 5,290,719, an increase of 174,939 (3.4 percent) over the total for the fall of 1965.[31]

This fantastic growth in population and school enrollment has forced the state government and local school districts to provide more school facilities, books and supplies, and teachers for the public schools. It has long been customary for large districts such as the Los Angeles City Schools to estimate how many new classrooms and new school buildings they must provide each month to keep abreast of enrollment growth. New buildings must be paid for by future generations, so local districts are often required to hold school-bond elections, sometimes bonding themselves up to the legal limit.

When district resources have failed to produce needed money for school buildings, the state has come to their assistance. In 1949, for example, a state school-bond issue was approved for $220 million to be lent to specified school districts (for example, those close to military bases) for their building programs. (See Chapter 3.)

Finally, as enrollment increases and buildings are provided, there is the need for more textbooks and supplies and a very special need for large numbers of well-trained teachers. To provide them, school districts and the state legislature have had to provide good salaries and working conditions. Besides providing more adequate teacher-training facilities in California, the state has had to make teaching in California attractive to its own sons and daughters and appealing enough to attract teachers from other states. This was not much of a problem

[30] James C. Stone, *California's Commitment to Public Education* (New York: Crowell, 1961), ch. 1.

[31] California State Dept. of Education, *Enrollment in California's Public Schools —Fall 1966* (Sacramento, 1967).

during the early years of the depression, when jobs, including teaching positions, were scarce. Since 1935, however, as the need for additional teachers in California has increased and then ballooned, the state has been forced to make teaching more attractive. The following statutes and constitutional amendments sketch some of the measures taken to improve teachers' salaries and other fringe benefits:

1935 Retirement benefits were increased from $500 to $600 per year for those with 30 years of service. The cost to each teacher was set at $12 per year.

1937 A minimum salary for California teachers was set at $1,320 per year, though most districts were paying more. Local retirement systems were legalized. The voters of San Francisco, Oakland, Los Angeles, and San Diego established such local retirement systems.

1939 Sabbatical leave for teachers was legalized for school districts wishing to grant such leaves. Sick leave for teachers injured while not on duty was legalized.

1943 A minimum salary of $1,500 per year for full-time teachers was passed by the legislature. A minimum of five days sick leave with full pay and the right to accumulate up to 25 days in any five-year period were made a matter of state law.

1944 The teacher's retirement system was improved and put on an actuarial basis; $30 million in state funds was added to the school system.

1946 A constitutional amendment set the minimum salary for full-time teachers at $2,400, which the legislature could and did increase to $3,400, then to $4,300 and to $4,500. (The constitutional minimum still remains at $2,400. In 1960, the average teacher's salary in California was $6,622.)

1947 Ten days of sick leave with pay were made possible for all teachers. They were permitted to accumulate up to 40 days.[32] Local retirement systems were given the opportunity to transfer their funds to the present adequate system of teacher retirement. (Under the present state system, a teacher retiring at 65 with 30 years of service may collect two-thirds of his average salary in his best three consecutive years.)

Still other inducements are provided by upgrading teacher training in the state, as evidenced by these items of state legislation:

[32] There is no legal limit to the number of days of sick leave that a teacher may accumulate nor any specific time period for this accumulation.

1. State teachers' colleges (the normal schools) were formally legalized in 1935 as general state colleges with broader curricula and a variety of departments.

2. In 1946, senate bill No. 37 appropriated $154 million for construction at the several state colleges. Other appropriation bills have since provided still more money for buildings at the state colleges.

3. The California state colleges have been authorized to award the master's degree, at first jointly with the University of California but now independently. In the 1960s, the graduate programs of these colleges were extended to the doctorate, which in 1967 was still awarded jointly with a California university.

4. The complex system of teacher certification that developed from 1920 to the 1950s has been revised and simplified by a system of seven standard credentials. The nature of the teaching, supervisory, and administrative credentials and the training requirements are discussed in some detail in Chapter 5. It should be noticed here, however, that the state has agreements with other states to recognize credentials or college work toward certificates or credentials.

That young Californians have been attracted to teaching and that teachers from other states have been attracted to California by the improved salaries and other benefits are best illustrated by the fact that the number of regular certificated teachers in California practically doubled between October 31, 1948, and October 31, 1959, increasing from 73,484 to 145,921.[33] In 1967, the total teaching staff in the state school system (from kindergarten through junior college) reached 166,806, but the state system has 197,750 certificated employees.

For over 30 years the people of California and their government have been expected to find billions of dollars and thousands of teachers for public education. They have been called upon to cooperate with many federal projects as well as to obtain assistance from the national government. Special legislation was required for the emergency educational programs such as the NYA and the CCC, for defense education programs such as the training of workers for defense industries and of military personnel and their dependents, and for the education of veterans. More recently, civil-defense education, disposition of federal surplus properties, compensatory education, NDEA, and the proper

[33] Stone, p. 20.

disposition of federal aid to education have required state laws and expanded educational services.

After a brief respite from the curricular and organizational changes caused by World War II, the schools of California made adjustments in science, mathematics, and foreign language courses in the post-Sputnik era. As a result, new legislation and a continual revision of public school programs have piled change upon change. The latest changes of all, since 1957, have increased state control over local school systems and have provided much detailed curriculum by legislation, as we shall see later when we discuss the Fisher Act.

A full discussion of recent curricular reorganization by legislation appears in Chapter 4, and legislation of the reorganization of school districts will be treated in Chapter 2.

THE ORGANIZATION OF CALIFORNIA'S

SYSTEM OF PUBLIC EDUCATION

By September 9, 1850, when California was admitted to the Union, the state legislature was forced to provide a pattern of administrative organization for the public school system. California's first constitution had named only one administrator, the state superintendent of public instruction. The legal basis for state, county, and district boards of education, for county educational authorities, and for state and local taxes had yet to be established in the legislature.

The legislature was instructed to "direct, by all suitable means, the promotion of intellectual, scientific, moral, and agricultural improvement." It was directed, furthermore, to use the proceeds from the sale of public lands and rentals for the use thereof as well as "the estates of deceased persons who may have died without leaving a will or heir" for the sole support of common schools throughout the state. It was presumed that the state legislatures would define the types of common schools (primary, intermediate, and grammar grades or "college prep") and establish a system of state and local school boards and local or county superintendents.

That the constitution left the details of public school organization to the legislature was right but unfortunate, since the early legislatures had much pressing business to attend to besides setting up a school system. The first legislators were primarily interested in getting the state and local governments organized and in establishing an improved and stable economy. Business and commercial interests had to be encouraged. Communication and transportation within the state and with the rest of the nation needed development. Legislators, then as now, were concerned with their local constituencies and communities —urban, rural, or mining communities—and with the different interests of northern and southern California.

The constitution and the legislatures of 1851 and 1852 managed to get a public school system on paper, but most schools in operation before 1854 were private schools in urban areas. The 1851 legislators even made provisions for the distribution of state school funds to private, religious, and sectarian schools on the basis of attendance. This legislation did not seem unreasonable in the light of early California history, for local public school districts could not be expected to spring up quickly, especially in rural areas. Native Californians were used to the lack of public educational facilities, and Yankee pioneers had come to California for other reasons than to be educated. Besides, there had been a long tradition of private schools in California. In the Mexican days, venturesome teachers like William Hartnell and Olive Isbell Mann had set up private schools in Santa Clara and Monterey. In 1848, there was a wave of missionary activity in California, spurred by the American Home Missionary Society, the Episcopal and Catholic churches, the Mormons, the Baptists, and other denominations.

Already in 1848 many active or retired missionaries and military chaplains were promoting the cause of public or private education, and some were actually setting up schools. In Monterey, for instance, Walter Colton, a Congregational minister and former navy chaplain, encouraged his colleague, the Reverend S. H. Willey, to build and operate a school. He built the school so well that the California constitutional convention used the building for its meetings. It eventually became Monterey's historical Colton Hall.

In 1847 William Marston opened a school at Broadway and Pacific in Yerba Buena (San Francisco), where Samuel Brannan, a Mormon elder, preached. Presbyterian missionaries—Sylvester Woodbridge and Reverend J. N. Douglass—Baptists like O. C. Wheeler, Episcopalian priests—Fathers F. S. Mines and J. L. Ver Mehr—and Catholic Fathers Langlois, Nobili, and Ascolti built schools in San Jose, Monterey, and San Francisco.

Protestant and Mormon missionaries from New England and the Middle West seem to have been working toward a public school system like they had had at home. Episcopalians sensed the need for high school and college work in their establishment of Trinity High School and San Francisco College in 1857. Bishop Alemany undoubtedly sowed the seeds of a parochial system in his schools at Mission Dolores, on Vallejo Street, and in Happy Valley; but the Sisters of Charity tried to establish a free school and infirmary under the auspices of the Roman Catholic Orphan Asylum and Free School Society of San Francisco. It was natural that some of these private or sectarian schools would be thought of as the foundation of California's school system.

The ultimate effect of the private and denominational schools was threefold. First, they created interest in education. Second, they were at the origin of the first city districts. Finally, the conflicting denominational and antiecclesiastical viewpoints caused the legislators of California to create a well-defined separation of church and state in educational matters.

In and after 1852, there was so much controversy over state aid for private schools that the legislatures first forbade denominational and sectarian instruction in state-supported schools and finally, in 1855, prohibited public support for private schools. This prohibition was written into the second constitution in 1879. The legislatures after 1852 turned their attention to the creation of public school districts, county-school organization, and state boards of education.

The long and gradual development of the organizational machinery of public education in California cannot and need not be detailed here, but the development and present status of boards of education, superintendencies, departments of education, and local districts are important for the understanding of California's system of education.

Boards of Education—State and Local

Like other states, California has had, and does now have, a variety of state boards dealing with matters of education. Ten states have more than 10 such boards, and one state has only two boards; the rest vary from three to 10. Currently in California there are three major boards at the state level. In addition, there are county boards of education and a board of education for each school district. This apparent duplication of boards has been a source of confusion to people coming from other states, where local control of education resides either in the county or in the local districts (town, township, or school district) but never in both.

In the pages that follow, we shall try to clear up this more apparent than real overlapping of local California school authorities. Here we should note that the legislation of 1851 and 1852 offers clues to the view of the early lawmakers on state, county, and local district prerogatives. The state fiscal officer (the superintendent of public instruction), as the legislature saw it, was to gather attendance records and dispense state funds in cooperation with county superintendents (also fiscal officers) for the benefit of district boards, which actually operated the schools. This, in effect, made the county-school office an arm of the state government.

Following the old American tradition, towns, townships, and cities founded their schools through locally elected boards of education. To weld this motley mass of school boards and school practices into a uniform state system became the responsibility of the elected state superintendent, assisted by elected county superintendents. In California, the *ex officio* or appointed state and county boards were apparently afterthoughts. The members of these boards first served as advisers to the elected superintendents of the state and county schools. The types, membership, and functions of the state and county boards have been changed repeatedly by succeeding legislatures, in ways that we shall describe.

CALIFORNIA STATE BOARDS OF EDUCATION

The functions and organization of California's three state boards of education are listed below with some flashbacks into their historical development. Proposals for a fourth state board for the junior college system, discussed from time to time, have just materialized. Historically, the three basic boards—the state board of education, the board of regents of the University of California, and the board of trustees of the California state colleges—were established in this order:

State Board of Education. This board long had responsibility for all public education policies in the state, except the university. In 1960, the legislature relieved it of its responsibility for state colleges and for rehabilitation education in 1966. Its current organization and duties are: (1) *membership,* ten members appointed by the governor[1] and generally selected from different parts of the state; (2) *term of office,* four years with staggered terms of office; (3) *officers,* president elected by the board (but the state superintendent is the *ex officio* executive secretary of the board); (4) *meetings,* at least six a year; (5) *recompense,* traveling expenses only; (6) *duties,* see Education Code, Division 2, Chapter 1, Article 2, especially these sections:

> **Section 151** The board shall determine all questions of policy within its powers.
>
> **Section 152** The board shall adopt rules and regulations not inconsistent with the laws of this State (a) for its own government, (b) for the government of its appointees and employees, (c) for the government of the day and evening elementary schools, the day and evening secondary schools, and the technical and vocational schools of the State, and (d) for the government of such other schools, excepting the University of California and the California State Colleges, as may receive in whole or in part financial support from the State.
>
> The rules and regulations adopted shall be published for distribution as soon as practicable after adoption.

The board's jurisdiction once covered all public education in California, except control of the University of California—that is, it regulated all elementary and secondary schools, junior colleges, teacher training in the normal schools, and state colleges until the creation of the board of trustees of the California state colleges in 1960.

FLASHBACK The original California state board of education was created by the 1852 legislature. This was an *ex officio* board of three members—namely, the governor, the surveyor general, and the state superintendent of public instruction. That board was changed into a nine-member board of education created during the superintendency of John Swett. The 1866 legislature established a new state board of trustees for the normal school. This board, which continued to 1912, was responsible for teacher education. The original board had the governor as chairman, the state superintendent, John Swett, as secretary,

---

[1] The governor's appointees on all education boards, with the exception of the university's board of regents, must be ratified by two-thirds of the senate.

the president of the normal school as *ex officio* member, and six county superintendents or teachers as appointed members.

As time passed and the number of normal schools increased, the principals of all normal schools and a professor of education at the university were added to the normal-school board.

Although the normal-school board was abandoned in 1912, when the state board of education was reorganized and again given responsibility for teacher education, each normal school and later each state college was left with an advisory board.

In 1912, the Shanahan Amendment to the constitution implemented by statutory laws created a seven-man state board of lay members to be appointed by the governor for four-year terms of office. The new board was essentially the type of state board California has today, except that there are now 10 lay members appointed by the governor.

The Board of Regents of the University of California. Unlike the state board of education, the board of regents is a constitutionally established board. (See the Constitution, Article IX, Section 9, as amended on November 5, 1918.) The organization and duties of the board are: (1) *membership,* eight *ex officio* members (the governor, lieutenant governor, speaker of the assembly, superintendent of public instruction, president of the state board of agriculture, president of the Mechanics Institute in San Francisco, president of the California Alumni Association, and the acting president of the university) and 16 members appointed by the governor (no senate approval is needed); (2) *term of office,* 16 years for the appointed members, with *ex officio* members serving as long as they hold their elected or appointed office; (3) *officers,* board's president and vice president elected by board but its executive officer is the president of the university; (4) *meetings,* regular meetings every three months and special meetings to be called by the president of the board on the request of four members; (5) *recompense,* travel expenses only; (6) *duties,* to manage affairs of the University of California and all its campuses. (Rights and duties are spelled out in the constitution and explained in part in Chapter 6.)

FLASHBACK   The board of regents was created by the state legislature in March, 1868. Its organization, status, and powers were written into the 1879 constitution and strengthened by the constitutional amendment of November 5, 1918. The board has an extraordinary amount of independence of legislative control.

Board of Trustees of the California State Colleges. This latest state board was created by the legislature in 1960, when the control of the state college system was withdrawn from the state board of education. Its organization and duties are: (1) *membership,* 21 members, 5 of whom are *ex officio* (the governor, lieutenant governor, speaker of the assembly, superintendent of public instruction, and the chancellor of the California state colleges); (2) *term of office,* 16 appointed members serving for eight years on staggered terms as appointed by the governor; (3) *officers,* president and vice president chosen by the board and the chancellor appointed as executive officer; (4) *meetings,* monthly; (5) *recompense,* travel expenses only; (6) *duties,* to manage the affairs of California's 19 state colleges. The board hires the chancellor of the California state colleges and his chief assistants. It selects the presidents and principal administrators of each campus and, of course, approves the state college budgets and personnel policies.

FLASHBACK   A board of normal-school trustees was created in 1866, when there was only one normal school in San Francisco (the school that was later moved to San Jose). This original board now has counterparts in the advisory board of each state college. Jurisdictional control of these teachers' colleges (when they were still normal schools) was passed in 1912 to the state board of education and to the state department of education's Division of State Colleges and Teacher Education. Until 1960, therefore, the chief executive officer of all state colleges was the state superintendent of public instruction. An associate superintendent served as chief of the Division of State Colleges.

The local advisory boards of each of the 19 state colleges are not true boards in the legal sense of the term, though they are remnants of an early California practice to have a separate board for each normal school. Another "advisory body," created by the state legislature in 1960, is the Coordinating Council for Higher Education. Although it has sometimes been considered a state board, if not a superior board, of education, its chief function is to advise the governing bodies of public higher education and "appropriate state officials" (the governor, legislators, and state superintendent) on the annual budgets, capital outlays, functions, and plans of the University of California, the state colleges, and the junior colleges. It was organized to coordinate the functions of complex and sometimes competitive state systems of higher education.

Finally, since 1960 at least, there have been repeated suggestions that a state board of junior colleges be created and that, therefore, the junior college system be separated from the rest of the public school system—that is, from the control of the state board of education. Until recently, such a new board seemed a mere hope; but in September, 1967, the state board of education instructed Superintendent Rafferty to nominate members for a junior college board. These board members were named in April, 1968.

COUNTY BOARDS OF EDUCATION

The original county superintendent of schools was so much of a fiscal officer at the outset, in 1852, that the county assessors were appointed as school superintendents *ex officio*. Only after 1855 were the county superintendents elected as independent school officers. They had no advice or assistance from a county board until 1860, when county superintendents were authorized to appoint teachers to a county board of examination with powers to grant teachers' certificates valid for one year. This was a permissive law of which all counties did not take advantage.

The second constitution in 1879 (Article IX, Section 7) provided that in counties then without county boards of education, the district boards of education or the board of supervisors or the county superintendent was required to select textbooks for the county schools and to make rules for evaluating and certifying county teachers. In 1880, after the adoption of the new constitution, the legislature required every county to have a board of education composed of four educators (appointed by the board of supervisors) and the county superintendent of schools as the *ex officio* secretary. These new county boards were required to adopt textbooks, make rules and regulations for conduct of the schools within the county, and elect a president from their own membership. The county boards were strengthened by State Superintendent Campbell (and by subsequent legislation), who recommended that they provide county schools with a course of study or curriculum.

From 1881, the nature and functions of county boards of education in California were established. With only slight changes and added responsibilities, these appointed professional boards continued until November 5, 1946, when a constitutional amendment permitted the creation of elected lay boards of education in counties wishing an appointed county superintendent of schools.

Before 1946, most counties had elected their superintendents and appointed their boards, but San Francisco and Los Angeles counties were exceptional cases. San Francisco has long had a combined city-county organization with an elected school board and an appointed city-county superintendent. In Los Angeles County, the superintendent of schools and his staff have civil service status. In 1947, other counties had options in school organization. The counties that chose to take advantage of the 1946 amendment have elected lay school boards operating on permissive laws:

1. County boards of education, after necessary county-charter revision, can be five- or seven-member boards of elected laymen for four-year terms of office (the same general pattern as school district boards of trustees). Any registered voter is eligible to run for the board except the county superintendent, his staff, and school district employees. The unexpired terms of board vacancies are filled by the remaining board members.

2. The first meeting of each board after July 1 is an organizational meeting wherein the board chooses its president. The board must meet at least once a month with the county superintendent as its *ex officio* secretary and as the board's executive officer. Board members receive a token stipend of $10 per meeting plus travel expenses, all of which comes from the county general fund, not from ADA money or the school fund.

3. The board's power, duties, and responsibilities include the following. The board *shall*

    a. Adopt rules and regulations for their own government.

    b. Review and make recommendations on the county superintendent's budget before it is submitted to the county board of supervisors and on the county school's service fund before it goes to the state superintendent of public instruction.

    c. Prescribe the course of study for each elementary school grade each year. (This course of study does not apply to large city-school districts.)

    d. Employ the county superintendent and his staff (where he is no longer elected).

The board *may*

    a. Adopt an official seal and have necessary printing done.

    b. Adopt rules and regulations governing the administration of the office of the county superintendent.

    c. Accept duties transferred to them by the county board of supervisors—for example, make travel allowances and accept educational-recreational duties.

We should note that the county board of education, like all school boards but unlike the state legislature, may take only actions that the state law requires or permits. It may not, for instance, set the superintendent's salary, which is established by state law for each type of county, and it may not certify teachers except as the state law specifically permits. A county certificate is now issued to teachers by the registration of the state credential in the county office. In a word, the county board, like the district boards, must prove its authority to take any given action. The state legislature, on the contrary, may pass any school law or other law that it wishes, except as prohibited by the state or national constitution. Most of the state legislation on the county-school organization is found in the Education Code, Division 3, Chapter 1 (County Boards of Education—Sections 601–708) and Chapter 2 (County Superintendent of Schools—Sections 751–876). See also Sections 879–81 (County Board of Supervisors) and the California Constitution, Article IX, Section 3.

In view of the code's tendency to interlock the functions of the county boards, the superintendent, and his department of education, it may seem artificial to treat these legal entities separately. Our purpose, however, is to separate the policy-making functions of the boards from the superintendent's administrative duties. The departments of education, generally so designated in county charters, are in reality an extension of the functions of the superintendent, as these are either administrative duties or services to the county schools.

It should be noted, however, that the county-school authority does not actually operate schools except in special cases. The county superintendent in San Diego, for example, actually operates only four schools—the Hillcrest Receiving Home School, Juvenile Hall, Sierra Vista High School, and Rancho del Campo High School—all for delinquent or abandoned children.

The chief exception to this rule is San Francisco, where the combined city-county government provides for a single, city-county board of education for all public schools. With this and a few other minor exceptions, the county-school authority is the local arm of the state government. It enforces state school laws, supervises attendance and financial accounting of local districts, and prepares, as the state requires, courses of study for the county. Beyond this, the county office offers educational leadership and curricular and supervisory services and special assistance, as in the case of audiovisual aid, that local school districts cannot provide adequately for themselves. The actual operation of schools, however, is conducted under the board of trustees of each district.

LOCAL BOARDS OF SCHOOL TRUSTEES

The American tradition of public education began in the New England town, where three of the town's selectmen served as the school committee or board of education. When the Northwest Ordinances of 1785–87 authorized land grants for common schools in the Middle West, the township and its three-man board again became the local school authority. In 1849 and 1850, early Californians were aware of this tradition. They looked for land grants as the basis of a state school fund, the benefits of which would be allotted to the townships or districts. The legislators even ordered that district schools be established on the petition of 50 householders, as had been the case in New England. The formation of district boards was also authorized by the legislators in 1852.

At that early date, local superintendents of schools were not contemplated except in the larger cities like San Francisco. So the district board was all the administration that was available to the small local communities. The board bought the land, built schools, hired teachers, and kept all the records of finances and enrollment. The minutes of the boards of the 1850s and 1860s, like those in San Diego, recorded the purchase of a stove, fuel, and other basic equipment such as desks and blackboards.

District boards were required by state law to keep their schools open three months a year and to report in October of each year to the state superintendent on the enrollment, classes, and conditions of the school. The state school law of 1863 extended the term of board tenure to three years, one member of each three-man board to be elected every year. Up to this time, the custom of electing five-member city boards was confined to the larger, incorporated cities.

The 1879 constitution kept the district-board situation about as it was, except that it required local boards to limit their expenditures to their income. It did, however, open the door to school bonds for buildings and improvements, provided that the interest on the bonds could be met out of the district's current income. The constitution likewise included high schools, normal schools, and evening and technical schools under the name "public schools," but it permitted the use of state funds for primary and grammar schools only. Therefore, if a city or district wished to offer high school, adult, or technical education, it was required to do so out of local funds only.

In more recent years, when high school and junior college districts were authorized, the size, powers, and responsibilities of district boards were adjusted to the type of district they served. Today, the election, terms of office, duties, and responsibilities of all types of local boards of trustees for elementary, secondary, city, unified, and junior college districts are detailed in the Education Code (Part I, Division 4—Local Educational Agencies—Sections 915–1463.1).

To distinguish the functions of the district board from those of the county board of education, it is necessary to see the district board as the agency that actually operates the public schools of California under the state law, under the rules of the state board of education, and usually under the regulations of the county board of education. Despite the common assumption of the people in school districts that their board of trustees can do whatever the board wishes for the local educational program, the local board may take only such actions as the state law authorizes. Section 1001 of the state Education Code reads:

> The governing board of any school district *may* execute any powers delegated by the law to it or to the school district of which it is the governing board, and shall discharge any duty imposed by the law upon it or upon the district of which it is the governing board.

As may be expected, some of the required and permissive actions of the governing boards apply to certain specified districts only—to city districts, unified districts, or junior college districts—while other legislation applies to all school districts. Without attempting to repeat the whole law and all of its distinctions here, we shall list the major powers and duties of local governing boards of trustees:

1. To formulate local district policy—budgetary, personnel, educational, disciplinary—under the law.

2. To employ the superintendent and his staff as well as all other certificated or classified employees—that is, instructional or service

employees—of the district. The board alone may hire personnel, usually on the recommendation of its executive officer, the superintendent.

3. To buy land, build and maintain schools, authorize bond elections, and offer services authorized by law.

4. To hold board meetings and keep records thereof and to see that all required district records (financial, attendance, and so on) are kept and reported annually in October to the county and state.

5. To obligate the district by contracts for personnel, services, equipment, and supplies, and for such textbooks as are not supplied by the state.

Under the state law, the governing board is now the policy-making body of a school district in its financial, operational, personnel, and curricular services. The professional relationship between the governing board and its chief executive, the superintendent, is generally equated to that of a corporation's board of directors and its employed managerial services. Despite much adverse precedent in the past, the governing-board members either individually or as a unit do not and should not involve themselves with managerial or administrative detail. When they do, confusion in staff relations and strife in public relations often follow.

Finally, since the governing board of trustees is the board of a school district and since districts differ, it is necessary to examine the development and types of local districts in California.

The School District in California

The local school district as an operational unit is a basic assumption of California's first constitution, but the nature and functions of the local school districts in California were first defined by the statutes of 1851 through 1855. In reams of legislation enacted for more than a century thereafter, the state legislature has defined the types, nature, organization, and reorganization of local school districts to meet expanding needs and changing conditions.

It is not necessary, or even important, that these legislative changes be followed step by step down the years. It may be of value, however, to examine the conditions under which the first school districts of California were established, to list the types of existing districts, and to consider the proposals of the state for the reorganization of local school districts.

EARLY SCHOOL DISTRICTS IN CALIFORNIA

In a spurt of enthusiasm for public education, John G. Marvin, the first state school superintendent, enticed John C. Pelton, a pioneer San Francisco teacher, to help him prepare suggestions for the legislature of 1851. Among the suggestions that became law on May 1, 1851, was the provision for an annually elected, three-member school committee in each school district to supervise school organization, hire teachers, build schoolhouses, and use public funds therefor. This law gave the green light to the establishment of local school districts; it also provided state funds for private schools. The private school controversy was most intense in San Francisco, because San Francisco holds the honor of being School District No. 1, derived after long experimentation with private schools. Indeed, the city was so anxious to provide schools for its children that it created its own school board two years and eight months before California's admission to the Union.

San Franciscans, at that time, were most impatient to get a system of public schools underway, even before California had a constitution. In February, 1848, therefore, on the motion of Samuel Brannan, the San Francisco Town Council appointed a committee of three men to call an election of a board of five commissioners with authority to hire a teacher. This first school board was composed of C. L. Ross, W. H. Davis, R. Fourgeaud, J. Townsend, and J. Serrine. They opened the first public school in the schoolhouse on the Plaza, but it was not a free school.

Thomas Douglas, an ordained Congregational minister from Hawaii and the teacher of this school, offered the 3 R's and geography at five dollars per quarter and grammar grades at six dollars. Besides, he made this additional offer:

> In any or all of the foregoing, together with mental and moral science, ancient and modern history, chemistry and natural philosophy, it was $8. In any or all of the foregoing, together with geometry, trigonometry, algebra, astronomy, surveying, and navigation, it was $10. With any of the foregoing, together with Latin

and Greek, the fee was $12 per quarter. If any persons were unable to pay the tuition fee, admittance was to be free.[2]

Douglas apparently did a good job, but his competitor for the teaching job instigated an election, which on May 13, 1848, declared the earlier election of the commissioners illegal. The school was closed and, there was not another one opened until 1849.

In April, 1849, however, the *alcalde* (mayor) and *ayuntamiento* (town council) of San Francisco granted the use of the Plaza schoolhouse to Albert Williams of the First Presbyterian Church. Williams operated a school in that building from April 27, 1849, to September of that year. In August, 1849, however, John W. Geary, the new *alcalde* of San Francisco, made a strong plea for a public primary school. There was no action on this plan until April 8, 1850, when the San Francisco Town Council declared a school run by Mr. and Mrs. John C. Pelton "a public school free to every child."

This school had been operated in the basement of the Baptist chapel on Washington Street near Stockton. The husband-wife team was hired for $500 a month to be paid out of the public treasury. The additional teachers required were paid out of the Peltons' salary, which eventually reduced the Peltons' income to $162 a month. But the school grew to the extent that Pelton mortgaged and then lost his own home. Even after the school had closed in September, 1851, there was a legal question whether public funds were rightly used for this "private" school.

Through these attempts to use private schools for public purposes, San Franciscans learned lessons. They remained determined, however; in fact, they were about to organize what can justly be called the California Public School District No. 1. In 1851, the legislature had passed the first California school law, instituted the state school fund, and authorized the establishment of local school districts. It had even authorized the distribution of state school funds among private, religious, and sectarian schools on the basis of attendance, as already mentioned.

This latter, hotly debated issue was not finally settled until 1855, although San Francisco's new school district found a temporary solution. On September 25, 1851, the city council of newly incorporated

---

[2] William Warren Ferrier, *Ninety Years of Education in California—1846–1936* (Berkeley, Calif.: Sather Gate Book Shop, 1937), p. 24.

San Francisco passed Free School Ordinance No. 189 [3] with these among other provisions for free common schools:

1. There were to be five school districts in San Francisco with a schoolhouse in each district. These five schools in different parts of the city were in operation by February 9, 1852: *Happy Valley* (November 17, 1851), corner of Bush and Stockton Streets; primary and grammar; principal, James Denman; teachers, Miss Anna I. Sanford, Mrs. E. Wright, Mrs. J. A. Hazelton, Miss Kennedy; *North Beach* (November 19, 1851), Filbert and Powell Streets at Washington Square; principal, Joel Tracy; assistant, Mrs. E. W. Baldwin; *Central School* (December 22, 1851), Dupont Street near Jackson; primary and grammar; principal, F. E. Jones; assistant, Mrs. E. W. Baldwin; *Rincon Point* (January 8, 1852), corner of First and Folsom Streets; primary and grammar; teacher, Silas Weston; *Spring Valley* (February 9, 1852), Union Street near Franklin; mixed school; teacher, Asa W. Cole.[4]

The annals of San Francisco record another common school and the first grammar school: *Mission Dolores* (May 10, 1852), near the Old Mission, mixed school; teacher, Alfred Rix; *Clark's Point* (later the Union Grammar School), corner of Broadway and Montgomery Street; primary and grammar; teacher, Ahira Holmes.[5]

2. All district schools were to be free and open to children and youth from 4 to 18 years of age.

3. All district schools were to be free of sectarian or denominational influence or interference.

4. All money collected or saved from taxes for these schools was to be kept in the Free Common School Fund of San Francisco, which was to be used for school purposes only.

5. A board of education was to be formed with an alderman, an assistant alderman, two citizens (to be elected), and an appointed superintendent of schools, who was to be the clerk of the board.

6. The board of four members was to appoint a superintendent,

[3] The full text of Ordinance No. 189 is quoted in Roy Cloud, *Education in California* (Stanford, Calif.: Stanford Univ. Press, 1952), appendix 8, pp. 249–51.
[4] *Ibid.*, appendix 9, p. 251.
[5] *Ibid.*

select school sites, build schools, employ teachers, and visit and examine the schools twice each year.

Therefore, San Francisco's Ordinance No. 189 created California's first legally organized school district and San Francisco's first legitimate school board, elected by the common council on October 8, 1851. Mayor C. J. Brenham assumed the presidency of this board of education, which appointed Colonel Thomas J. Nevins to the city superintendency by a unanimous vote.

Other urban communities in California went through similar experiences in getting local districts organized and local boards established. The details of the early establishments in Los Angeles (1851–56), San Jose (1852–56), Stockton (1852–53), Santa Cruz (1853), and San Mateo (1856–65) can be gathered from Roy Cloud's book and from accounts by William Ferrier.[6]

Most of the early public schools were established in the cities; even in the more rural school districts, they began in towns and villages. Such was the case in Contra Costa County (Martinez and Antioch), in Yuba County (Marysville), and in San Diego County. The almost hopeless problem of establishing school districts in vast rural areas is best typified by San Diego County, which originally included the present Imperial and San Bernardino counties and some of Inyo County—an area of over 37,400 square miles. The county assessor was the *ex officio* superintendent of schools during 1852 and from 1854 to 1865. School District No. 1 in Old Town (old San Diego) provided the sole school and sole teacher in San Diego County. The school rarely enrolled more than 50 pupils.

By 1860, there were still fewer than 400 public schools in the whole state. These were common or elementary schools, though some offered upper or grammar-grade work. They were generally operated by local boards of three elected members, though some city districts, like San Francisco, had five-man boards. In the rare cases when high schools were attempted, as in San Francisco (the Union Grammar School after 1856 and San Francisco High School after 1858) and in Sacramento (1857–59), the school boards were urged to charge higher school fees. As a result, most high school and college preparatory courses were offered in private academies. The high school district

[6] Ferrier, chs. 4 and 5.

with its separate board was still 20 or 30 years away. The principle of free secondary education for the whole county had yet to be established by the Kalamazoo Case of 1872–74.

MODERN SCHOOL DISTRICTS AND THEIR ORGANIZATION

Not until 1893 did state legislatures of California begin to establish the current types of local school districts and to regulate the nature and function of the local boards of school trustees. This whole complex system of school districts and boards is condensed in the state Education Code, which lists the types of districts and the nature and function of their boards and executive officers and details how school districts may be organized, consolidated, or even discontinued (see Education Code, Part I, Divisions 4 and 5, Sections 906.5 through 3389).

While the details of the organization and functions of any given district or board must be read out of the law, it will be profitable here to (1) discuss the legal terms used, (2) list the types of districts in California, and (3) outline the functions and responsibilities of local boards of school trustees.

The simple term *school district* always refers to a political subdivision in charge of the elementary school or schools (grades 1 through 8) in its jurisdiction. *Union district* describes a consolidation of originally separate elementary districts so that they can be managed by a single board and administration—elementary or secondary. *Unification* and *unified* signify that all levels of education (elementary, secondary, and junior college) are brought together under one board and administration. *Joint union* implies that a consolidation involves districts in more than one county. The nature of California's geography and population is such that it became the practice to form school districts without regard to county lines, so that part of the district might be in one county and part in another. Joined districts from two adjacent counties are obviously also union districts—that is, a joint-union school district or a joint-union high school district.

City-school districts most frequently means districts that have jurisdiction over all schools (elementary, secondary, and junior colleges) in an incorporated area. This, in effect, makes an urban unified district the same as a city-school district—for example, the San Diego city schools are the San Diego Unified School District. However, it is now possible to make a city-school district of a former elementary school district, if the district has more than 1,000 pupils in average daily attendance and an assessed valuation of $20 million or more. (See Education Code 1204.) If the voters of such a city choose to make "city schools" of their elementary districts, they may have five board members instead of the usual three. The Chula Vista city schools in San Diego County are an example of this local option. For its senior high school program, Chula Vista uses the services of the Sweetwater Union High School District within the boundaries of which Chula Vista lies.

California School Districts are of the following types:

1. *School District* (the basic unit) jurisdiction over the elementary school or schools (grades 1 through 8); board: three members organized as president, clerk, and member; administration: none in a one-room district, principal in a single-school district, or district superintendent over several schools and principals.

2. *Union School District* jurisdiction over all elementary schools in the consolidated unit; board: generally five members, at least one from each component district—president, vice president, clerk, and members; administration: district superintendent.

3. *Joint Union School District* like union school district except that the consolidated unit crosses county lines and is operated under two county superintendents and a district superintendent.

4. *Union High School District* jurisdiction over one or more high schools that serve several consolidated elementary districts; board: five members as in union school district; administration: district superintendent.

5. *Joint Union High School District* like union high school district except that the component school districts are in two counties and are under two county superintendents and a district superintendent.

6. *City-School District* originally in charge of all schools in its incorporated area; now as described on page 78; board: five members or, in unified city districts, up to seven; administration: city superintendent of schools.

7. *Unified School District* jurisdiction over schools of all levels (K through grade 12 or 14) within a city (for example, Los Angeles or San Diego) or within a unified rural area (for example, Mountain

Empire Unified School District in San Diego County); board: five to seven members with president and vice president; administration: district superintendent and staff.

8. *Junior College District*　jurisdiction over the junior college or colleges serving a political subdivision with several elementary districts or even several high school districts; board: five members; administration: president or district superintendent.

9. *"No High School District"*　an elementary district that does not lie within any high school district and that therefore must contract for the secondary education of its pupils with an adjacent high school district.

10. *County District*　until recently, a descriptive term to distinguish elementary districts outside of cities and hence more directly under the county superintendent. The term is being broadened to cover unification of all schools within a county.

As may be expected, since school districts in California "growed like Topsy," they multiplied into a vast mass of small school districts, many with one-room schools. Local groups often resisted union schools and any sort of consolidation, despite the advantage that consolidation could bring. A time-worn American tradition in public education, particularly in rural areas, causes the taxpayer to keep his schools near his home and to keep as much control of the schools as possible in the local community. This tradition is still being held by Californians, who are suspicious of a district office outside their community and who are wary of sharing and pooling their local resources with other remote or even relatively near school districts. Many rural communities have clung to a one-room or small school with all of its disadvantages rather than consolidate and lose some local control. They do so in the name of democracy. There are state administrators and legislators, however, who would say that this is an interpretation of democracy that we can no longer afford.

The problem was first brought to a head during World War II, when California began to grow rapidly and when California governors and legislatures were struggling to find resources adequate to finance the public schools. During this time, school leaders were becoming keenly aware of the vast range of unequal educational opportunities afforded the children and youth of California. A cry was being raised by school districts in rural or poorer areas for some type of state equalization funds that would improve their scanty school services and correct their financial problems. Therefore, since June, 1944, the state government and the state department of education have been devising means to equalize educational opportunities in California school districts and to encourage, demand, and even "buy" the consolidation and unification of school districts in smaller districts. Thus, even today California is in the midst of a long war between state authorities and local districts.

State school authorities have won some battles. The tiny one-room school has all but disappeared. Smaller cities, which formerly had district elementary and secondary school districts, have unified under one board and one superintendent, as is the case with Coronado and Ramona in San Diego County. Whole counties, such as Plumas and Sierra, in the northern part of the state have worked toward unification of all the schools in the county with some success. Even such completely rural areas as the Mountain Empire area in San Diego County have merged several smaller elementary school districts with their union high school districts into a unified district with one board and one superintendent.

Radical suggestions, such as recommending one unified district for whole counties, have been tried successfully in the northern and interior "cow" counties, but these plans would be catastrophic in immense metropolitan areas such as Los Angeles County. So, with some battles won and many grass-roots areas still up in arms, the forces of consolidation are still far from complete victory. The complexity of the situation is demonstrated by the extensive legislation on school district reorganization.

The 1965 edition of the California Education Code devotes Sections 3001–3389 (about 45 pages of school law) to school district reorganization. The substance of the law is this:

1. Reorganization means "formation, annexation, transfer, uniting, unification, unionization, merger, division, transfer of territory or change of boundaries of school districts" (Section 3102).

2. The state board of education governs the statewide survey of feasible district reorganization and establishes standards for approving or rejecting reorganization plans.

3. The state superintendent of public instruction administers the program of reorganization, largely through the Bureau of School District Organization in the Division of Public School Administration.

4. County superintendents of schools establish county committees of school district organization and through the committees formulate county master plans for school district reorganization. These are submitted to the state superintendent and state board of education for approval and inclusion in the statewide survey.

5. The districts involved may plan, discuss, and ultimately vote in approved plans for reorganization.

6. As an enticement for unification, school districts voting for them receive $15 per ADA as a bonus in foundation programs for elementary or secondary schools.

If, as is entirely possible, state educational authorities should abandon enticements and rewards for the unification of school districts and instead take strong-armed legal measures, there would be economic, managerial, and some educational gains. But whether the people of California would accept forced centralization of school authority without some retaliation at the polls against elected officials is not yet known.

What is clear is that the battles for and against consolidation of school districts have been waged for over 20 years. The initial problems in 1944 were matters of economics—the costliness of myriads of small districts—and of equalized educational opportunities for all children. Small school districts sought to gain more state aid without much or any loss of their local autonomy. The legislature's position was strengthened by the statutes of 1959 on the reorganization of school districts; but since there was still much resistance to consolidation, the 1963 statutes revised and strengthened county master plans for school district organization to be administered by the state superintendent of public instruction. (See Education Code Sections 3001–3389.)

THE CALIFORNIA PLAN FOR SCHOOL DISTRICT REORGANIZATION

In June, 1944, Governor Earl Warren called a special session of the state legislature to secure additional state aid for public schools and teacher retirement. For additional state aid, the legislature voted $4.5 million as an equalization fund and a $20,000 appropriation for the California Commission for Post-War Planning. This latter appropriation was used by the commission to secure the services of George D. Strayer, professor of school administration at Teachers College of Columbia University. Strayer was to survey the state school system and make recommendations. As a result of the Strayer Survey, the Fair Equalization Law of 1945 was passed. It called for:

1. The distribution of elementary school funds on an equalized basis, the foundation stone of modern state apportionment.

2. County elementary school supervision for small districts, either paid for by the county or shared by the county and the district.

3. The creation of state and local commissions for school district organization.

In one way or another, these commissions and studies of district reorganization have continued, have made recommendations to the districts and to the legislature, and have made substantial gains in the consolidation and unification of small school districts. For the 20 years between 1945 and 1965 California's educational leadership, its state and county authorities, as well as its politicians and economists, have been putting increasing pressure on small, uneconomical, and more-or-less ineffective school districts to consolidate, "unionize," or unify.

As the state government sees it, the whole question is one of sound economics and equalized educational opportunities. If the constituents of local districts fear the loss of control over "their own schools," the legislators try to make the remedy more palatable. Therefore, the 1963 master plan for school district reorganization stresses optional reorganization of school districts by the electors, provides for a statewide survey of school districts under the state board of education, and offers some financial benefits to districts that choose to unify.

The various superintendents of schools in California are involved in this revolutionary approach to district reorganization. On the one end, the state superintendents of public instruction and the county superintendents are committed to district reorganization, which on the other end will eliminate the position of many district superintendents and their staffs.

Superintendencies in the State, County, and District Schools

The early superintendencies in California—state, county, and city—should be considered in the light of the development of these offices in the United States before 1840, for the first California lawmakers were following the tradition that they knew. This American tradition is not as old as we may suspect. In 1850, the experimental stage was not yet finished, so California merely furthered a continuing experiment.

The office of state superintendent of public instruction was created in New York in 1812 and abandoned nine years later by assigning the superintendent's duties to the secretary of state *ex officio*. Maryland and Vermont, having tried a state superintendency for a while, abandoned it after 1826. Only Michigan, among all the states, has had a continuing state superintendent since 1829. This was eight years before Horace Mann was appointed as Massachusetts' first secretary of the state board of education (actually as superintendent) in 1837. It was only 12 years before California's constitution was written. By 1850, there were nine *ex officio* superintendents and seven regular ones, including California's, in the United States.

Ellwood Patterson Cubberley discusses the state superintendency in its origin and notes that about a third of the states had county superintendents before 1850 and that less than 25 cities had city superintendents prior to that time.[7]

The nature of these superintendencies and development of their responsibilities in California are described on the following pages.

The State Superintendent of Public Instruction. This is a constitutionally established office in California, but it was left to the legislature to outline the superintendent's duties. In the mind of the lawmakers, it was a political office like that of governor, state treasurer, or secretary of state. For many years the candidates ran for the office on partisan tickets. If the superintendent was to be a leader, his leadership would have to be effective in the legislature, with school boards, and in local political subdivisions. Professional and educational leadership as it is known today had not yet evolved. The "clerical, statisti-

[7] Ellwood Patterson Cubberley, *Public Education in the United States* (Boston: Houghton Mifflin, 1919), ch. 6, pp. 166 *et seq.*

cal, and exhortatory" functions of the state superintendent, as Cubberley saw them, caused him to require, edit, and forward attendance and financial reports, to manage the state school fund, and to encourage desirable legislation for public education. It often seemed more important that candidates for the superintendency have legal, business, or political experience than that they have previous experience as teachers, principals, or local superintendents.

The names, professional backgrounds, and terms of the 21 men who have held this office in California are listed below:

1851–53   Judge John G. Marvin, attorney.

1854–56   Colonel Paul K. Hubbs, attorney and U.S. Consul in France.

1856–62   Andrew Jackson Moulder, Virginia teacher and college professor.

1863–67   John Swett, teacher and San Francisco school principal.

1867–71   Oscar P. Fitzgerald, Virginia journalist and California newspaperman, secured legislation for the creation of the University of California (March 12, 1868).

1871–75   Henry Nicholas Bolander, Prussian-born San Francisco teacher and principal.

1875–79   Ezra S. Carr, New York physician, professor of agriculture and horticulture at the University of California.

1879–82   Fred M. Campbell, former superintendent of Oakland city schools, state superintendent when the second constitution was adopted.

1883–87   William T. Welcker, U.S. Army officer and university professor.

1887–90   Ira Hoitt, San Francisco high school principal.

1891–94   James W. Anderson, Solana County superintendent of schools.

1895–98   Samuel Thorburn Black, principal of a Chico school and county superintendent, retired from the state superintendency to become the first president of San Diego State Normal School.

1898   Major Charles T. Meredith, Ventura County superintendent, appointed by Governor Budd to fill Black's unexpired term, three months only.

1899–1906   Thomas Jefferson Kirk, Fresno County superintendent.

1907–18   Edward Hyatt, first Riverside County superintendent in 1893.

1919–27   Will C. Wood, superintendent of Alameda City Schools, left the state superintendency to become a California bank commissioner.

1927–29   William John Cooper, San Diego city schools superintendent (1925–27), U.S. Commissioner of Education (1929–33), and professor at George Washington University.

1929–37   Vierling Kersey, principal and assistant superintendent of Los Angeles City Schools, returned to the Los Angeles City Schools when he left the state superintendency.

1937–45   Walter Dexter, former president of Whittier College.

1945–62   Roy E. Simpson, South Pasadena superintendent, had the longest tenure in the state superintendency.

1963–71   Max Rafferty, superintendent of Needles and La Canada schools.

As we survey this list, the names of Moulder, Swett, Carr, Hyatt, Wood, and Cooper loom large in the early and pre-Depression days. Andrew J. Moulder was a vigorous fighter for the expansion and better financing of schools in the pre–Civil War days. John Swett was the first superintendent with professional leadership qualities in the modern sense. Ezra Carr had an effective hand in the reframing of Article IX on education in the second constitution.

Under Edward Hyatt, the state department of education began to take on its present form of educational leadership. Will C. Wood developed the department further and saved the state system financially in the face of an economy-minded governor. William John Cooper moved on to the position of U.S. Commissioner of Education.

The state superintendency has rarely been an exceedingly desirable office. For the first 70 years (until 1913), candidates ran for the office on partisan tickets (Democratic or Republican) for two-year terms. Since 1880 the term of office has been four years. The state superintendent has never been more secure than his ability to be reelected, though since 1930 the incumbents have usually been reelected as often as they desired.

The office has never paid a fabulous salary. The legislators first tied the superintendent's salary to that of the secretary of state. In 1861, it reached $3,000 per year and was fixed there by the second constitution. It was increased to $5,000 in 1909 and to $10,000 in 1951. These figures are modest in comparison with postdepression and post–

World War II salaries of city superintendents. Even in 1966, when the state superintendent received $25,000, city superintendents' salaries had gone up to $45,000 or more per year.

Because the position has not been overly attractive from either a financial or a security viewpoint, it has often been difficult to find competent candidates willing to run for the office. The leadership aspects of the state superintendency, however, have grown tremendously since 1910, particularly since the 1930s. The office is no longer a purely political and fiscal position involved with statistics, reports, finances, and teachers' credentials.

The state superintendent is now the executive officer of the state board of education and an *ex officio* member of the board of regents of the University of California and the board of trustees of the California state colleges. And as director of education, he heads the California State Department of Education.

Although it is true that state superintendents after 1880 assumed leadership among county and district superintendents, their best claim to educational leadership has been through their development of the state department of education. Superintendents have shown their interest and leadership in truly educational matters by their expansion of the state department in the areas of instruction, kindergarten and primary education, and continuation and adult education. Furthermore, they have cooperated in federal programs of rehabilitation and vocational education and more recently in compensatory education. Finally, they have provided generously for junior high schools, junior colleges, special schools, and special education. The superintendent can best be judged by what he does for and in the state department, for that department is the surest channel of his leadership in the whole state.

The County Superintendent of Schools. The county superintendency in California began as a one-man business operation. The superintendent, elected on a partisan ticket, was held responsible for school records of statistics on schools, teachers, and students and for the fiscal management of tax receipts and school costs. In 1851, when this office was created, the county superintendent was the chief and frequently the only local manager-auditor of the schools in a given county. It was natural, therefore, that the county assessors were the first *ex officio* local school superintendents.

What was happening in the county office from 1851 to 1861 was a mere reflection of prevailing American school practice. Cubberley notes that by 1861 34 states, (that is, a great majority of the existing states) had created the office of the county superintendent.[8]

That the office had become a fiscal operation and a local arm of the state governments is clear from this brief summary in a USOE bulletin:

> As education developed into a movement of state-wide significance there grew up a need of some responsibility for education by the State. When the States began to collect information and data concerning education, someone was needed for its collection. As the need for common schools increased, the State needed someone to promote the interest of common education. The States also needed someone as an "organ of communication between the state superintendent and the several township boards of education," and to check up on local school officials. In some instances in the beginning of this office it was felt that someone representing the county as a whole, rather than each local unit independently, would see that the State requirements were more uniformly carried out. The gifts of school lands by the Federal Government had to be looked after, and as they were scattered over the county, someone was needed for this purpose. For such reasons the office of county superintendency was established, although in the beginning it was not created outright as such in all States.[9]

Professor Stuart Noble of Tulane University comments further:

> The office [of county superintendent] in some states grew out of the the earlier township superintendency; in others it came as a specialized function of various county boards having to do with the administration of land grants. Between 1830 and 1860 nearly all the states [had county offices] with the exception of the New England states, which continued to recognize the town as the unit of administration, established the office.

> The early duties had to do with the keeping of records, the apportionment of school revenues, and the settlement of disputes regarding district boundaries. It was some years before the duties of school supervision came to be assumed by the office. The county

[8] *Ibid.*, p. 160.
[9] N. William Newsom, *The Legal Status of the County Superintendent*, Bulletin No. 7, U.S. Office of Education, 1932, pp. 3–4. Quoted in Stuart G. Noble, *A History of American Education* (New York: Rinehart, 1954), p. 190.

superintendent was regarded as a political officer and was almost invariably elected by popular vote.[10]

In California before 1880, county superintendents of schools were record-keeping and fiscal officers whose only absolute prerequisite for the position was that the candidate, himself an elector, could muster enough votes to get himself elected for the two-year term. After 1855, the county assessors were no longer county superintendents of schools *ex officio;* after 1860, the county superintendents could appoint county boards of examiners, composed of teachers, to examine and certify teachers for one year.

Because the superintendents were not necessarily professionally trained schoolmen, the 1880 constitution offered them a professional board of four schoolmen. The superintendent himself was both the fifth member of the county board of education and its secretary. Gradually, but particularly after the turn of the century, professional schoolmen began to run for the county office. These men tended to hire professionally trained deputies and attendance officers.

After 1925, however, some county superintendents of California had become examples of the educational leadership that could be exerted from the county office. In San Francisco, where there was a combined city-county local organization, the superintendent exerted all the local educational leadership there was. The county charter of Los Angeles was changed to put the county superintendent and his staff on civil service, which made the operation an office of professionals interested in curriculum development and teaching aids.

The long tenure in office of able Los Angeles County superintendents did much to improve the status of the county superintendency throughout the state. Mark Keppel, who was the county superintendent there from 1902 to his death in 1928, was succeeded briefly by Hubert S. Upjohn, who in turn was followed by the popular Archie Roy Clifton. When Clifton died in 1942, his chief deputy, Clinton Conroy Trillingham, succeeded to the superintendency, which he held for the next 25 years.

By the mid-1930s, the position of curriculum coordinator in many county and city schools of California created interest in curriculum revision, coordinated the supervisory and instructional services, and gave a completely new look to the county offices. Trillingham, the original curriculum coordinator in California, was instrumental in or-

[10] *Ibid.,* pp. 190–91.

ganizing the work of the coordinators throughout the state. By 1938, the group included curriculum coordinators of large city districts, such as J. Richmond Barbour and Charles J. Falk of San Diego, and future county superintendents of schools like John Stephen Carroll of the San Diego County schools.

The coordinators' chief interest was curriculum development based on a sound philosophy of education and progressive methods of instruction. Many county coordinators were better equipped professionally than their superintendents, a fact which forced Californians to require more professional training for the superintendency itself. Concomitantly, there was concern for the salaries of county superintendents.

On November 5, 1946, a constitutional amendment ordered the legislature to prescribe the qualifications of county superintendents and to fix their salaries according to the legislature's classification of California counties (from Class I in descending order to Class VIII). The amendment also permitted changes in county charters to require elected county boards that would select and appoint their county superintendent. By the 1965 education Code,[11] all county boards consist of five or seven elected lay members, and, even where county superintendents are still elected, the credential requirements scaled by school law must be met.

State law now defines not only the professional qualifications of county superintendents but their salaries as well. The legislature has classified counties into eight classes on the basis of average daily attendance in the public schools. Each class was given a salary factor in 1963 for the purpose of computing the salary of the county superintendent. In each case, the salary of a county superintendent was computed by the factor multiplied by $7,789, considered to be the average of teachers' salaries in 1963. For example, the salary factor for Class I counties is 3.375, for Class VIII 0.750. Hence, the superintendent of a Class I county receives $7,789 × 3.375, or $26,287.88, and that of a Class VIII county is paid $7,789 × 0.750, or $5,841.75.

The following scale of counties will clarify the range of salaries.

Class	ADA	Factor
I	750,000 and over	3.375
II	140,000–749,999	3.092
III	60,000–139,999	2.717

[11] California Education Code, Part I, Division 3, Sections 601–708.

IV	15,000–59,999	2.249
V	7,000–14,999	1.780
VI	1,000–6,999	1.499
VII	100–999	1.124
VIII	under 100	0.750

A Class VIII county would represent a sparsely settled rural situation where only a few teachers (five to eight) are employed. Los Angeles is the only Class I county. San Diego is in Class II.

In the counties of the first three classes, the superintendent must have either a general administration credential (or a life diploma based thereon) or a new standard administration credential. The general administration credential requires that the holder has training for and some experience in elementary or secondary teaching, that he has had courses in both elementary and secondary education, and that he has had additional training in school supervision and administration, school law, and finance. The new standard-administration credential calls for seven years of college training, three on the graduate level. The candidate must have an academic major and minor, proven experience in teaching, and graduate-level specialization in the organization and administration of public schools, in school supervision, and in the legal and financial aspects of public education in California.

In counties of Classes IV through VII, the credential requirements for county superintendents become less stringent, as their salaries are less attractive and their responsibilities less extensive.

In this descending order, the credential requirements are:

1. A new standard supervision credential, which after two years of graduate work in education qualifies the holder for an elementary or secondary principalship.

2. An old-type elementary or secondary school administration credential originally designed for principals.

3. An old-type general elementary or general secondary teaching credential or a new type standard teaching credential, which requires only one year of graduate work with specialization in education.

A review of the county superintendency in California even over the past 75 or 100 years reveals a gradual, though ultimately remarkable, improvement in the professional qualifications of those in the key educational position. In the beginning, no professional qualification was necessary for the office, and the pay was very low. The first clerks and bookkeepers, who summed up attendance and financial records and doled out state funds to local districts, would never have imagined the possibilities of their office. But the best of them were zealous promoters of tiny school systems, some of which have grown to systems as large as some states.

As a result of new legislation from 1946 to 1963, the county offices in California, particularly those in the larger counties, have become models of professional services. This does not mean that the statistical, fiscal, budgetary, and bookkeeping responsibilities of the county office have ceased. The law still holds the county superintendent responsible for acting as an arm of the state government in these matters. But professional responsibilities in matters of curriculum, coordination, teaching aids, supervisory services, and other matters of educational leadership have been added to the county office. This has led to the expansion of the personnel and services of the county department of education, which we shall discuss later.

City and District Superintendencies.   In the early American towns, townships, and school districts, the school boards handled business matters. Teachers did the teaching, and often enough the local minister provided supervision. Rural areas required no more superintending than counties could give. In California, the shifting of operational responsibilities to district superintendents occurred for the most part after the Civil War. Even then the incorporated towns in rural areas followed an older city pattern.

There were city-school superintendents in the United States at least as early as 1826 (for example, in New Orleans) and in San Francisco by 1849. They served as operational managers or as executive officers of the boards of education. In the smaller California communities, the superintendency evolved gradually as the school board began to delegate its own managerial duties. The first step was to put the management of a school under one of the teachers, first called "the principal teacher" and then simply the principal. As schools multiplied in a village or city, it was not uncommon for the school board to assign one of the better principals to the job of "superintending" all the other schools of the district. Then, when the managerial duties in a district required full-time service, the superintending principal became a separate administration officer with rooms and clerks of his own. This occurred in San Diego in 1886.

As with county superintendents, district and city superintendents aspired to be more than business managers. They sought means of providing better instruction and better educational opportunities for the youth of their districts. They would, in due time, promote kindergartens, manual training, physical education, "domestic science," and up-to-date methodology. The city offices would then hire assistant superintendents, supervisors of music, art, and so on, and establish separate business offices, attendance bureaus, and other needed services. In effect, the expansion of the superintendent's staff amounted to the establishment of city departments of education, which have gained almost complete independence of operations.

The large city districts in California still file their October Reports with the county superintendent for transmittal to the state department of education, but they are no longer required to gear their curriculum to the county courses of study. These large cities are not under the county boards, and they do not enjoy the services of county departments of education; they must supply departmental services of their own for the schools in the city. Cities like Los Angeles, Oakland, and San Diego have "departments of education" and departmental services (administrative, supervisory, curricular, business, and personnel) as large as or larger than those of the county in which they are located. It is not our purpose to analyze the services that the many and varied cities provide for themselves. It is merely necessary to call attention to these services before we analyze the state and county departments of education.

State and County Departments of Education

As we have implied, the duties of school superintendents at all levels developed from simple tasks of record-keeping and supervision to the monumental responsibilities of the modern superintendency. If this is true in city districts, it is all the more true of state and county superintendents.

The effectiveness of California superintendents was first increased by a small staff of clerks and deputies, but as their responsibilities grew it increased by the creation of an entire department with a variety of divisions. The state legislature repeatedly sanctioned the expansion of state and county departments of education. At the local level, county charters contained sections on the county department of education. These sections dealt with the county board of education, the county superintendent, and his staff, particularly as they were related to the board of supervisors and other county offices.

On the state level, financial and attendance accounting, selection of state textbooks, and issuing teachers' credentials required specialists and deputies to the state superintendent. In the late 1800s, this was the beginning of a state department of education.

THE STATE DEPARTMENT OF EDUCATION

By 1913, the state department as it is known today began to develop in earnest. That year the legislature approved divisions of elementary schools, secondary schools, and vocational education to be headed by professional state "commissioners," who salaries were set at $4,000 per year, $1,000 less than that of their chief, the state superintendent. The legislature specified that these three commissioners (actually assistant superintendents) be appointed on a noncivil service basis to form a sort of cabinet for the state superintendent.

To reconstruct the situation in the state department at the time, it may be well to remember that Superintendent Edward Hyatt was elected to his first term of office on the Republican ticket in 1906. On August 16, 1907, the year Hyatt took office for his first term, the direct-primary amendment was passed as Article II, Section 2½, which details "the right of suffrage."

After this amendment took effect, elected state and county school officers were no longer nominated in political conventions but by direct-primary elections. Other state department staff members were not yet on civil service status. In 1913, however, the year the three top commissioners were approved, all state employees except the commissioners were put on civil service status by California's first civil service law. Superintendent Hyatt served two more terms as a nonpartisan state superintendent, which created more stability in the state office.

For the next 50 years after 1913, partisan politics had little influence on the state department of education or on its chief. It was no longer as necessary for the state superintendent to demonstrate leadership in his party as it was for him to prove himself an educational leader. That the state department of education was reborn or recreated during Governor Hiram Johnson's administration was fortunate for California, for progress was then in the air. California was not only garnering the best government and education practices from other states; it was developing a creative leadership of its own. California came up not only with direct primaries and civil service but with a teacher-tenure law and a state teacher-retirement system.

Superintendent Hyatt and his growing department were not slow to recognize the green light that signaled them into heavy educational traffic. The department bravely speculated about state aid for kindergartens, encouraged the development of junior high schools in California, opened vocational, adult, and continuation schools, and proposed cafeteria service in schools and special classes for handicapped children.

Obviously, the state superintendent and his staff were no longer mere bookkeepers and fiscal officers. Hyatt and his successors were developing a new leadership that was both progressive and expensive. No wonder then that Governor Friend William Richardson complained of the lavish expenditures on California schools. But even in Richardson's day, state aid was put on an ADA basis, school cafeterias were legalized, and normal schools became teachers' colleges. Under Richardson, Superintendent Will C. Wood managed to expand school services and state department personnel.

Each succeeding state superintendent after Hyatt had his own philosophy and objectives and guided and selected his staff according to his philosophy. California, in the mind of most of the superintendents, was a growing and progressive state that should be second to none in adopting progressive ideas, new educational services, and forward-looking policies in line with developing educational research.

Most state superintendents had come to believe that a desirable uniformity in the educational programs of the schools of California would be best achieved through democratic processes under the leadership of the state board and the state department of education. They were not opposed to some legislation on required or prohibited instruction in important areas, such as the teaching of U.S. history and government, nor to the prohibition of sectarian and racist instruction in public school classes. The prevailing philosophy, however, allowed considerable latitude for county boards and local school districts to handle these matters as best fitted local needs.

Under the direction of the state superintendents, the state department was alerted to the need for new types of schools, courses, and services. Under existing or expanded department personnel, these services among others were promoted and assisted in due season. Kindergarten services, originally permitted at district expense (1893 and 1909), became eligible to receive aid on an ADA basis in 1920. Junior colleges, formerly a thirteenth and fourteenth year of high school education, developed by state department encouragement in 1907 into a full-blown junior college system. Junior high schools or "intermediate schools," as they were first called in California, were legalized in the 6-3-3 school plan, or even in the 8-4 plan, where elementary districts were permitted to establish junior high schools for grades 7 and 8 in 1915 and thereafter. Adult and continuation education received considerable impetus from state department chiefs and staff in these fields, particularly after 1916. After the 1915 law permitting high school boards to contract with county libraries for library facilities, the state department's interest in school libraries was expanded. The California state librarian still functions as a division chief in the department of education.

The alert leadership in the state department supported and encouraged new and progressive practices initiated at the county and district level. Superintendents like Susan M. Dorsey of Los Angeles, Mark Keppel of Los Angeles County, John Sexson of Pasadena, Roy Cloud and Archibald Cloud of San Francisco and Redwood City, William John Cooper, Willard Givens, and Walter R. Hepner of Oakland, San Diego, and Fresno received state department support for experimental practices initiated at the county and district levels. The local experiments included the construction of more functional school buildings, establishment of new patterns of school organization (the 6-3-3 and the 6-4-4 plans), and development of instructional programs better fitted to pupil needs, such as improved social studies and citizenship training, special classes for atypical children, modernized supervision of instruction and additional guidance and health services.

The state department and local leadership, already deeply involved in CTA business, turned the association's interests from narrow concerns with teacher benefits to interest in state support for improved educational programs and to a concern for better teaching practices, curriculum revision, and improved auxiliary services to pupils.

The state department also made good use of the novel suggestions of the deans and professors of education in California universities and colleges. Stanford's dean of education, Ellwood Patterson Cubberley, for example, offered the ADA formula for state school apportionments and other improved administrative practices. Cubberley later brought to Stanford such experimentalists in social studies and curriculum revision as Paul R. Hanna, who trained a host of professional leaders in progressive education. Stanford-trained Hollis Allen, experimenter in school administration at Claremont, and Flaud C. Wooton, experimenter in educational philosophy and comparative education at Claremont and UCLA, are but two examples. UCLA's Merton Hill (junior colleges) and John Hockett (elementary education) and USC's Osmund Hull (school administration) and John Weersing (secondary education) are other professors who were used across the state.

Finally, if, as Superintendent Max Rafferty asserts, the schools of the state went progressive (or Deweyist) the initial basic step was taken under the superintendency of William John Cooper, who brought Helen Heffernan, as director of elementary education, and other progressives into the state department. About this same time (1928), San Diego's superintendent, Walter R. Hepner, appointed Stanford-trained Jay Davis Conner as director of elementary education. Conner, later San Diego's assistant superintendent, ended his career as associate state superintendent of public instruction in the 1950s.

In all these years, the state department was growing into a massive operation, and this was due in no small measure to California's increased cooperation with federal programs. Each succeeding state superintendent, from Hyatt to Rafferty, has committed the state department to cooperation with federal programs that increased federal dollar aid to education. (This federal aid from 1917 to the present is discussed in detail in Chapter 3.) Federal aid programs are the continuing cause of much of the recent expansion in California state department bureaus and personnel. A few examples will suffice to demonstrate this point.

The bureaus of agricultural, business, home economics, and industrial education were created originally to administer federal money available from the Smith-Hughes Act in 1917) through the George-Deen Act in 1937. Emergency federal aid during the depression increased the work of the state department bureaus. WPA building projects had to be worked into the state program, and the Federal Emergency Education Program expanded the adult and continuation school bureau extensively. Similar developments grew out of the NYA and the CCC camps. The Bureau of Rehabilitation Education grew out of the Veterans' Rehabilitation Act in 1920 and remained in the state department until 1965, when the state department of vocational rehabilitation took over the job.

The state department of education was vastly expanded after World

War I, the depression, and World War II. This tested the organizational skill of succeeding state superintendents; each emphasized the philosophical viewpoints to which he subscribed. In the long tenure of Superintendent Roy Simpson, the progressive movement in California education reached a peak and then began to taper off. When Simpson reached the age of compulsory retirement, Rafferty consolidated the views of critics of progressive education practices. The shift in public opinion, already noticeable in the last years of the Simpson administration, had necessitated changes in the department's personnel and in its very organization.

No single state superintendent is responsible for the recent and current organization of the state department of education. As has been said, the department grew rapidly after 1913, and it has kept abreast of the growth of the state and of the increased services demanded of it. It experienced spurts of growth in the late 1920s and in each decade thereafter. It is still growing, in order to keep abreast of such new federal programs as the Elementary and Secondary Education Act and compensatory education and related programs that require the disbursal of federal aid.

It will suffice to sketch the department's organization in the 1950s under the superintendency of Simpson and, for purposes of comparison, to detail the organization of Rafferty's department. (The current organizational pattern is found in Appendix IV.)

Under Superintendent Simpson there were six divisions, each headed by a deputy superintendent, an associate superintendent, or the state librarian: (1) Division of Departmental Administration (Deputy), (2) Division of Special Schools and Services (Deputy), (3) Division of Instruction (Associate), (4) Division of State Colleges and Teacher Education (Associate), (5) Division of Public School Administration (Associate), and (6) Division of Libraries (State Librarian).

The following 21 bureaus, headed by bureau chiefs, were arranged under the above divisions: (1) Administrative Services, (2) Adult Education, (3) Agricultural Education, (4) Audiovisual Education, (5) Business Education, (6) Educational Research, (7) Elementary Education, (8) Guidance, (9) Health, Physical Education, and Recreation, (10) Homemaking Education, (11) Indian Education, (12) Industrial Education, (13) Readjustment Education, (14) School Apportionment and Reports (ADA, October Reports), (15) School District Organization, (16) School Planning, (17) Secondary Education,

(18) Special Education, (19) Supplemental Education, (20) Surplus Property (from the U.S. government), and (21) Textbooks and Publications.

Under the above divisions and bureaus of the state department, consultants, specialists, supervisors, and technicians developed and improved a variety of special programs, such as child-care centers during the war, child welfare and attendance projects, and educational and rehabilitation programs for children and youth with physical, mental, or sensory handicaps. As a result, the Division of Special Schools and Services occupied a very important place in the department.

It should be noted that, while the Division of Special Schools and Services rated the second place in the Simpson organization, it is not implied that Simpson created these schools and services. He made every effort to expand this area, as we shall see; but the state schools for the blind and physically handicapped were established in the 1920s. Our reason for expanding on this phase of California education is to detail an area of state school services of which all Californians, including the Raffertys and Simpsons, are proud.

Simpson's enthusiasm for the development and achievements of special state schools and services is best illustrated by these excerpts from his 1953 report.[12]

Special Schools and Services

Whether measured by number of children served, improvement of organization, enlargement of scope, increase in funds expended, or improvement of the quality of service, the rapid development of the state program for the education and rehabilitation of its physically handicapped children and adults is one of the outstanding features of this eight-year period (1945–53).

The development and supervision of special classes administered by local school districts throughout the State have been carried on by the Bureau of Special Education in the Division of Instruction.

Services to Blind Children and Youth

California School for the Blind has a complete building for deaf-blind pupils, a program of prevocational training, a vocational placement officer, and a number of counselors.

[12] This report was made to the county, city, and district superintendents of schools at the California Association of School Administrators meeting in October, 1953. Copies were made available to the school administrators.

A visiting teacher program for preschool blind and their parents has been established. Over 400 such children are now being served.

The reader service to blind college students has been expanded. The number of blind pupils transferred to public high schools has more than doubled.

Services to Deaf Children and Youth

1. *California School for the Deaf* (Berkeley)
   Pupil enrollment is over 450 (1953).
   All old dormitories and school buildings have been replaced by modern structures.
   The ratio of teachers and counselors to pupils has been increased.
   The qualification requirements for teachers have been raised.
   A modern building for prevocational and vocational training has been constructed.

2. *California School for the Deaf* (Riverside)
   A new school was opened in January, 1953, when the enrollment was 225. It will eventually service between 450 and 500 pupils.

Services to Severely Handicapped Cerebral-palsied Children

1. *Residence schools at Redwood City and Altadena.* These two schools were established in 1946. They supply expert intensive medical treatment and individualized education to over 500 children, as well as social service and parent education to their families and training to professional workers. These State schools have contributed significantly to the development of more effective methods of treatment and education for brain-injured children.

2. *Diagnostic and Treatment Centers.* Through contracts with the University of California, the Children's Hospital Society of Los Angeles, and the Orthopaedic Hospital of Los Angeles, the Department of Education established three diagnostic and treatment centers which served more than 3,500 individual children between 1946 and 1953. This service entailed an aggregate of over 100,000 clinic visits.

Special Services to Adult Blind Persons

1. *Visiting teacher services to recently blinded adults*
   The field staff was increased to 25 in 1953.
   The area of coverage was increased to 23 counties in 1953.
   A program of in-service staff training has been developed.

The emphasis in teacher service has been shifted toward orientation for daily living in the home and community.

The separate programs offered by two Divisions within the Department have been combined for more effective administration.

2. *Orientation Center for the Blind*

Upon the recommendation of the Department, the Legislature established this new institution in 1951 to assist blind persons to achieve social and economic independence and to enable them to live full, productive, and normal lives. The program includes intensive training in techniques of daily living, travel, household arts, typing, Braille, and prevocational skills. The period of training is from three to nine months.

3. *California Industries for the Blind*

In 1945 the administration of the three existing workshops for the blind at Oakland, Los Angeles, and San Diego was transferred to the Department of Education. Since that time the Department has worked to gradually reorganize these facilities to bring them in line with modern concepts concerning the desires, needs, and capabilities of visually handicapped men and women. This is necessarily a slow process, but definite progress had been made toward the following objectives:

a. To restrict employment in these workshops, as far as possible, to blind adults who desire to be independent and who seek full-time work, but who are not able to secure remunerative employment in private business or industry.

b. To select for production articles in the making of which blind persons working at the shop can equal the quality and approach the quantity output of an average sighted worker.

c. To select for production articles for which there is a relatively constant demand in the competitive market.

d. To develop long-term assembly contracts with well-established private industries.

e. To establish and maintain for the California Industries for the Blind a reputation for high-quality production and for dependability.

f. To develop cooperation and mutual confidence between the management and the workers in each shop.

g. To develop an alert and effective sales organization throughout the state.

The above excepts from Simpson's report are extensive, not only because they express his personal interests but also because they delineate some of the important and continuing functions of the state department of education.

The quotations also afford us the opportunity of paying tribute to the man who served as state superintendent and chief of the California state department of education for nearly 18 years, longer than any previous state superintendent. Appointed to the superintendency in 1945 on the death of his predecessor, Walter Dexter, Simpson left the superintendency of the South Pasadena schools to round out Dexter's term of office. On his own merits, Simpson was elected and re-elected to four four-year terms of office, which were finished as he approached the state compulsory-retirement age of 70 years. Simpson went into retirement with more than 20 years of public school administration and many more years of teaching behind him. Simpson, a Republican, was appointed to the state superintendency by a Republican governor; but during his long tenure of office he carefully avoided official involvement in partisan politics. During his last term in the state office, the superintendent was made aware of a shift in public and legislative attitudes toward schools and public education. Experimentalism seemed to have lost favor, as became apparent by the passage of the Fisher Act and drastic changes in the requirements for teachers' credentials. Staunch progressives in the state department were protected by their civil service rights, but Jay Davis Conner, the associate superintendent and a staunch progressive, left the department for educational work abroad. Evidently, a new day had dawned in California education. The *Phi Delta Kappan* has identified the change as California's conservative revolution. (See Appendix V.)

Max Rafferty, who succeeded Simpson in 1963, has campaigned and written frequently against the philosophy of education that had permeated California schools and the state department of education. Rafferty has since been reelected, in 1964, by a great majority of California voters. In January, 1968, he began his sixth year in the state superintendency.

The California state department of education, like many other essential government agencies, has developed into a vast bureaucracy. The positions of the departmental employees are protected by their civil service status. Moreover, a considerable number of the department's activities (for example, the fiscal and record-keeping aspects and the issuing of teaching credentials) are defined by law. Besides this, the state department of education operates under the California state board of education with the superintendent functioning as the director of education and the chief of the whole department. Finally, the department has experienced only one top administrative change since 1946. As a result, there has been considerable stability in the department and its operations. But that the department is still growing is evidenced by the inclusion of the Foreign Language Placement Project (S-003-0060) and by the creation of the Division of Compensatory Education (S-007-000).

The department is spread across the state, with its principal headquarters in the State Education Building in Sacramento and its regional headquarters in Oakland, Fresno, and Los Angeles. Regional and area supervisors are spread still further. Their offices are in Chico and San Luis Obispo, at UCLA and UCR, and in San Diego. The division of libraries is in the State Library in Sacramento and at the Sutro Library in San Francisco. State warehouses are operated in San Francisco, San Leandro, and Los Angeles. State special schools are located in Berkeley, Riverside, Los Angeles, San Francisco, and Vallejo. Finally, attention should be called to the fact that the State Libraries (S-004) and the State Teachers' Retirement System (S-014) operate as divisions in the state department of education.

All in all, this is a massive operation, the detailed functioning of which is eased somewhat by the fact that the 58 county departments of education operate as local arms of the state government.

COUNTY DEPARTMENTS OF EDUCATION

The development of the county superintendency, as outlined earlier, makes it patently clear that the county departments of education developed out of the expansion of the county superintendent's responsibility.

Before 1880, when the state system was highly centralized, the county superintendent was the state superintendent's "man Friday" at the local level. He kept all educational data on finances, enrollments, and teachers. He visited the schools through the county and guided district school board activities. In the many rural counties of California, he was the only superintendent at a time when "superintending" was interpreted literally. The county superintendents and their deputies were managers—inspectors with the right of direction over school activities.

The second constitution strengthend the hands of the county offices, which were now to select authorized textbooks, formulate county courses of study, and certify teachers. The structure and duties of the county departments of education were written into county charters. The departments worked under and with the county boards of supervisors.

In a state so vast and varied as California, it was inevitable that county departments of education would appear in every imaginable variety. The variation in county departments remains down to the present. In remote rural and mountain areas, the so-called cow counties, there could be and still are as few as a half-dozen schools. These are the areas in which one-room schools persisted down to very recent times and in a few cases continue to exist.

Sierra County in 1966 had six elementary schools, one with only 17 pupils, and three high schools, one with 24 pupils; the total school enrollment was 799. Its pupil census and its terrain are such that the one school district in the county is the Sierra-Plumas Unified District, which draws some pupils from Plumas County, Sierra's neighbor to the north. The district superintendent, business manager, and supervisor of instruction serve all of Sierra County in their several capacities. This is a good example of the consolidation of services for a whole county.

San Francisco, at the opposite extreme, with a compact metropolitan population of 740,360 in 1960, has long had a combined city-county government. There is a mayor and a board of supervisors, a city-county board of education, and a city-county superintendent. The department of education, as well staffed as that of any city, serves both the city and the county. This is unique in California, though it is not uncommon in other states.

In California, between and beyond the extremes of Sierra County and San Francisco, there are a great variety of county department patterns. Los Angeles County with a population of over seven million is an immense organization in the state's most populous area. For many years the Los Angeles County charter has kept its county superintendent and the department of education staff on a civil service basis, which has given the county's education program considerable stability.

Large rural counties, such as Kern and Imperial, have maintained strong county offices, but the models of good county-school organization can be found perhaps chiefly in the heavily populated, partially urban counties, like Alameda, Fresno, and San Diego.

Perhaps the most ideally organized, housed, and located county superintendent's office in California or in the West is that of San Diego

County. In 1966 the county population was estimated at 1,224,000—670,000 of which lived in the city of San Diego. The county department of education, which is chiefly responsible for schools outside the city, was once a tight little organization housed in a few rooms of an old and inaccessible county courthouse. As expansion was required, the county services were scattered throughout the city, until in 1961 a model educational center was established on property easily assessible to all freeways that lead out into the county. So now in one location, the 51 school districts of San Diego County have access to all county-school services. The department of education is organized as follows:

1. County board of education of five members elected for four-year alternating terms of office.

2. County superintendent with nine deputies, three of whom are assistant superintendents and division chiefs.

    a. Special services division headed by an assistant superintendent and deputy who have responsibility for these sections:

        (1) Administrative

        (2) Teachers' credentials and county teacher certification

        (3) Production of audiovisual, instructional, and public relations material

        (4) Special schools and classes, in charge of county special schools at Rancho del Campo High School, Juvenile Hall, Hillcrest Receiving Home, and Sierra Vista High School. In addition to these school services for delinquent children and wards of the court, the section provides special teachers in various parts of the county.

    b. Business services division, with responsibility for these sections:

        (1) Accounting, in charge of accounting, commercial warrants, data processing, mail, payroll, teacher retirement, county schools' service fund

        (2) Administrative

        (3) Legal

    c. Curricular services division, with responsibility for these sections:

        (1) Audiovisual

        (2) Community educational resources

        (3) Curriculum coordination

        (4) Pupil personnel, or guidance

        (5) Library

The county department of education has a resident staff from the county's department of public works. It also cooperates with the county purchasing department to enable school districts to purchase materials and supplies at quantity prices.

Guidelines for county departments of education are found in the Education Code and in each county charter. Most counties describe their organization in the county-school directories.

CITY DEPARTMENTS OF EDUCATION

The charters of California cities have sections devoted to the department of education. The charters designate for example the size, election, and recompense of members of the board of educators and the overall organization of the city system. They do not generally detail the district's control organization or its administrative, curricular, personnel, health, and guidance services. These central services, housed at the "board rooms," in the "central office," at the "superintendent's office," or in the "education center," can be compared readily with the state and county departments of education.

In large California cities such as Los Angeles, San Diego, San Francisco, Oakland, and Sacramento, the city's central services are as complete, or are even more complete, than services available in large county departments of education. The central services of the large cities are self-contained and independent of county services. In smaller districts, the district provides some of its own services and relies on, or contracts with, the county department for other needed services. The cities of Los Angeles and Claremont in Los Angeles County would be apt examples of widely differing district services. All of California's more than 1,400 school districts offer some central administrative, financial, and personnel services. The larger districts outline departmental services in the city-school directories, the most convenient guides to the types and amounts of central services a given city or school district offers. Finally, it may be of interest to note that the cities of California are classified in the California Government Code, Title IV (Government of Cities).

THREE

FINANCIAL SUPPORT

AND FISCAL MANAGEMENT

In California, as in most other states, the support of public education has been a continuing and often crucial problem. Unlike other states, however, California has experienced a succession of population explosions. A little over 160 years ago, California opened its history with a population of just over 100,000, exclusive of Indians. It has now become the most populous state, approaching the populations of Canada or of Belgium and Holland combined. California's burgeoning population[1] provided these staggering enrollments in the fall of 1966:

Elementary grades (K–8)	3,087,335
High schools (9–12)	1,147,832
Junior colleges (13–14)	284,204
Special classes and adults	771,348
Total	5,290,719

This massive enrollment represented an increase of 3.4 percent over the fall of 1965, and the state looks for six million by 1973. The increasing demands of public

[1] Recent population data are detailed in the Conclusion.

schools on state revenues and on revenues produced by school district taxes on real and personal property can be judged by the following data.

In 1964–65, the total cost of public education exclusive of that of the University of California and the California State Colleges amounted to $2,145,843,086.36.[2] Of this sum, the state provided $932,-136,262. Federal aid for these school purposes provided another $70 million (a little over 3 percent), and the remainder was produced by district taxes. In 1965–66, state aid had increased to $993,893,792.[3]

There was hope for $1,229,113,588 in state aid in 1966–67 and $1,-754,000,000 in 1967–68, but the exact data will not be available until after the compilation of the October Reports of 1967 and 1968.

In 1963–64, when all revenues were included, the state bore 42 percent of the cost of education, the school districts 55 percent, and the federal government 3 percent. Though the percentage of federal aid has increased and state aid has varied from year to year, it is generally assumed that the state has paid an average of about 40 percent of the cost of education for the past several decades. There is evidence, though, that the percentage of state aid is decreasing. The U.S. Department of Health, Education, and Welfare reports it as "approximately 37 percent of the non-Federal revenue" for 1966–67.[4]

In the eyes of local school authorities and those who pay school district taxes on their real property, the state is often considered not to be paying its full share of school costs. Yet, for every student in average daily attendance, the state provides an annual foundation program of $249 (K–grade 8), $339 (grades 9–12), and $600 (junior college), with supplemental aid provisions that may reach $331.50 (elementary grades) and $426.50 (high schools). These foundation programs, as we shall see later, were increased considerably by the state legislature in 1967.

The legislatures and the governors have noted, of course, that 42½ cents of every dollar that the state spends is used for public education

[2] California State Dept. of Education, *Average Daily Attendance and Selected Financial Statistics of California School Districts—1964–65* (Sacramento: Bureau of Educational Research of the Department, March, 1966).

[3] California State Dept. of Education, *School Fund and Educational Statistics for the Fiscal Year Ending June 30, 1966,* Book 2 (Sacramento: Bureau of School Apportionments and Reports of the Department, June, 1967).

[4] Bureau of Elementary and Secondary Education of the Division of State Agency Cooperation, U.S. Dept. of Health, Education, and Welfare, *California Public School Finance, 1966–67* (March, 1967).

and that, in 1967–68, 54 cents of each dollar may be required. This is, indeed, a far cry from early state-support programs; in 1858, Superintendent Andrew Moulder had but $284,183.19 to offer in state aid for all the public schools in California.

The State School Fund

In 1849, there were Californians who believed that the sale or rental of public lands would support public schools indefinitely. It should be remembered that 500,000 acres were soon to become available by a direct federal grant and that 5,534,293 acres were yet to be derived from sections 16 and 36 of each California township.[5]

Mere inklings of so lush a resource led some cautious forty-niners to suspect that the state school system could not use so vast a resource effectively. So, if there was general agreement in the constitutional convention of 1849 on the need of a state school fund, there was no consensus on how much of the income from the sale of public lands should be used for schools. California has always had its share of generous and reluctant supporters of public education, even in its first constitutional convention. Some cautious delegates recommended a proviso in Article IX of the constitution to permit the legislature to use the state school fund from the sale of public lands for other than school purposes. They felt that the state might have other and better uses for all that money. Attorney Winfield S. Sherwood favored the proviso on the grounds that the school fund would deprive the state of much unmined gold.

To this objection, M. M. Carver, a Sacramento farmer, replied:

> Now, sir, if we can locate in the gold mines and procure a fund sufficient to educate our children without calling upon the parents to do so, we should do it. I am decidedly in favor of placing every farthing that we can, and securing it by constitutional provision, in the hands of this community for the purpose of educating our children. Nothing will have a greater tendency to secure prosperity

[5] Judge Marvin, California's first state superintendent, estimated that the state had 500,000 acres of land by direct federal grant and 5,880,320 acres in sections 16 and 36 of each township. Moehlman gives the more exact figure of 5,534,293 acres in sections 16 and 36. See Arthur B. Moehlman, *School Administration* (Boston: Houghton Mifflin, 1951), p. 462.

to the State, stability to our institutions, and an enlightened state of society, than by providing for the education of our posterity.[6]

As other delegates countered with intentions to limit the state school fund, Robert Semple of Sonoma, the president of the convention, protested: "I ask you whether you have ever seen a school fund sufficiently large to answer every purpose, or secure too great a spread of knowledge?" [7]

The motion was rejected, but Semple succeeded in getting Botts's limiting proviso out of the constitution by presenting this forward-looking viewpoint:

> I think that here, above all places in the Union, we should have, and we possess the resources to have, a well-regulated system of education. It is the duty of the members of this House to unite together and secure the reputation, character, and ability in our public teachers which can only be obtained by a liberal and permanent fund. It is the basis of a well-regulated school system that it shall be uniform throughout the State; that any surplus fund collected in one district shall not be appropriated to that district, but that the aggregate fund from all the districts shall be appropriated strictly to school purposes, and distributed equally throughout the State. . . . Education, sir, is the foundation of republican institutions; the school system suits the genius and spirit of our form of government. If the people are to govern themselves, they should be qualified to do it; they must be educated; they must educate their children; they must provide means for the diffusion of knowledge and progress of enlightened principles.[8]

Semple also proposed that fines collected by the state be put into a fund under the control of the state superintendent (or as he said, "school commissioner"), who would have control over the entire system and distribute state aid to local districts on a prorated basis.

The result of this discussion was a constitutional directive to the

---

[6] The discussion between Botts, Carver, and Semple, who were opposed to the proviso, and Sherwood, who defended it, is reported by Roy Cloud in *Education in California* (Stanford, Calif.: Stanford University Press, 1952), p. 21. Cloud notes that J. Ross Browne, a shorthand reporter, was employed by the convention to make a verbatim report of the convention's proceedings. The transcript was printed in Washington, D.C., in 1850.

[7] *Ibid.*

[8] *Ibid.*

state legislature to create a state school fund by the sale and rental of public lands. The 1851 and 1852 legislatures complied with the directive, albeit with some reluctance. In its first major attempt to dispose of public lands, the 1853 legislature offered 232,000 acres of land at two dollars an acre but only in tracts of 160 to 320 acres. The demand for this land was good at the time, so the sale produced $463,-000, which, lent at 7 percent interest, produced $32,410 in one year. This latter sum, which was made available to local school districts, provided a modest amount of state aid, but there were as yet only a few school districts in California. If more schools and more school districts were to be established as rapidly as needed, greater financial resources would be necessary. Since public land could not be put on the market or sold rapidly enough to meet the financial requirements of a growing school system, it seemed wise to the legislature to levy a state school tax for rapid and regular revenue. Besides, the legislature sanctioned county and school district tax levies within limits and then increased the maximum tax rates for these local political subdivisions. But all the while there remained much public land that could have been sold.

In 1861, State Superintendent John Swett berated the state legislature in these words: "After many years of impractical legislation, in which each successive Legislature tinkered on a township land bill, a plain practical law was passed, under the provisions of which, in less than a year, nearly 200,000 acres were sold, and the proceeds applied to the State School Fund." This "plain practical law" was introduced by John Conness, assemblyman from El Dorado County in 1861. It was not only effective in 1861, as Swett noted, but it eventually made possible the sale of five million acres of public land and the creation of a perpetual school fund.[9]

The immediate results of Swett's complaint were modest, but the ultimate effect was excellent. Under the Conness Act, the rest of California's five million acres of public land were eventually sold, and, since only the interest on the receipts were used for state aid to schools, the capital in the perpetual fund eventually reached $10 million. In fact, the entire perpetual school fund of $100 million was such a lush resource in the depression year of 1933 that Governor James Rolph proposed that it be taken from the schools and used by the state for other emergency measures.

[9] *Ibid.*, pp. 38, 176.

In the 1850s and 1860s, however, there were no such lush cash resources for public education. Moreover, succeeding legislatures were always tempted to sell public lands cheaply and even to use them as subsidies to railroads and other corporations that the growing state wanted and needed. Therefore, when the state lacked ready cash for schools, the legislature resorted to various state school taxes.

School Taxes—State and Local

Taxation, in the final analysis, is the surest and most regular source of revenue for any government. If self-evidently the chief purpose of taxation is to keep an effective government in operation and if, as in California, public education has been considered a major responsibility of the government, then school taxes are inevitable. Despite federal windwalls in the way of early land grants and later dollar aid, the California legislature from 1852 levied state school taxes and authorized county and local district taxes for educational purposes.

Over the years new taxes were created or permitted and then sometimes abandoned in this interesting sequence:

1852 A state school tax of five cents on each $100 assessment was enacted temporarily until the sale of public lands would provide needed money. Incorporated towns and counties were permitted to levy a school tax of not more than three cents.

1853 The limitation on county school taxes was raised five cents and incorporated city taxes to twenty-five cents.

1859 The county school tax limitation was raised to twenty-five cents.

1866 The state school tax was increased to eight cents. County school taxes were limited to thirty-five cents; but each county was required to raise at least three dollars per census child.

1874 The state school tax was made automatic in this way: The state controller was required to make an estimate in August of the amount of money required to provide seven dollars for each census child (5 to 17 years of age). After certifying this estimate, the state board of equalization was required to fix the *ad valorem* tax rate so as to meet the estimated costs. The legislature was then required automatically to set the tax levy needed to meet these costs.

1880 The new constitution created a poll tax of two dollars or more levied on each male citizen over 21 years of age. The money was to be deposited in the state school fund.

1887 A levy of one cent per $100 assessed valuation of taxable property was approved for the support of the University of California.

1903 An *ad valorem* tax of about one and a half cents (to be fixed each year by the legislature) was levied for the high schools of the state.

1910 A constitutional amendment provided for the separation of state and local taxation and for the taxation of public service corporations. Section 14 of the amended Article XIII read in part: "Out of the revenues provided from taxes . . . in this section, together with all other state revenues, there shall first be set aside the moneys to be applied by the state to support the public school system and the State University." [10]

The 1910 amendment for all practical purposes put an end to special *ad valorem* school taxes, thus transferring state school support to the "general fund"—that is, to the general revenues of the state as applied to the school fund. The state school *ad valorem* tax was discontinued largely because of widely different methods of assessment by the many county assessors. The gross receipt tax on public service corporations, on the capital stock of banks, and on the assessed value of their franchises was a partial substitute for the state tax for schools.

1914 On November 3, a constitutional amendment was adopted that included these provisions in Section 12: "No poll or head tax whatsover shall be levied or collected in the State of California."

In 1910 the unpopular poll tax alone had produced $687,953 and it would have brought $820,000 into the school fund in 1915. Besides, the receipts from inheritance taxes were down to $250,000 in 1915. Consequently, there was much pressure on the legislature from the CTA and school officials to provide other new money for these losses.

After 1920, state aid for public schools was taken from the general fund. In the lush years after 1923, when state resources were adequate, the financial war of economy-minded Governor Richardson had to be

[10] This in effect foreshadows "fixed charges"—that is, the first charge upon the funds of the state treasury, which were specifically written into the constitution by the amendment of November 2, 1920.

ended before adequate state support was restored. After the major battles were over, there were a few lush years during which local school districts bonded themselves to the hilt. Then the depression created panic. Counties and school districts were going broke and the state lacked funds to increase state aid for the support of local school districts.

School Finance
from 1930 to 1945

On October 24, 1929, the worst stock market crash in our history initiated years of depression. The economy of the entire country was shaken to its foundations, and it was inevitable that the financing of public education would need revision. Vast numbers of unemployed sought welfare aid from the counties of California, thus reducing one major source of school funds. Local school districts reduced teachers' salaries and canceled building and maintenance programs.

Before the depression struck California, the California Taxpayers Association had proposed the county-unit system of schools (one governing board for each county) as an economy measure, but this bill failed. In 1932, Proposition Nine proposed new sources of state revenue —for example, tax on stock transfer, natural resources, retail sales, and income. This would have provided new money for the state school fund. The CTA was for it, but the proposition failed.

In 1933, the state treasury with no new revenues recorded a deficit of $9,500,000, and the worst was yet to come. As a result, these school measures, detrimental to school finance, were proposed: (1) the elimination of the $100 million perpetual school fund; (2) the elimination of all fixed charges, of which education is one; (3) the reduction of county responsibility for school aid; (4) a 20 percent reduction of state and county allocation for schools; and (5) a reduction of $12 million in state school apportionments.

Since these and some other school finance measures failed and since counties were hard pressed by welfare cases, the Riley-Stewart Amendment of 1933 relieved both counties and schools by abolishing county-school taxes and by providing increased state aid from the state's general fund. This amendment, which was passed by a large portion of the electorate, made these changes in the constitution:

1. In Article IX, it transferred to the state the support that counties had previously granted to schools. Since the former county portion of school support was now to come from the state's general fund, county taxpayers were relieved of school taxes on their real property.[11]

2. In Article XIII, the amendment required that sufficient funds from the state's general fund be set aside to supply each county with the amount it needed for local district apportionment. School apportionments were again given the right of first claim on funds in the state treasury.

Through the enactment of the Riley-Stewart Amendment of 1933 and subsequent amendments and statutes including the Fair Equalization Law of 1946, the state government accepted responsibility for about 40 percent of the cost of public education through the state. This money is taken annually out of the state general fund as a fixed charge. Most of the remaining 60 percent of school costs comes from property taxes levied by local school districts. County-school taxes have been effectively eliminated.

The Evolution of State Apportionments— The Five Plans

Adequate support of public education by the state is not merely a matter of securing adequate funds. It also involves the state's method of apportioning these funds to local school districts. In California, the evolution of apportioning practices has resulted in five fairly distinct plans.

Plan I (1850s to 1880). The state school fund was apportioned to counties on a population (census) basis. The amount of state income depended on sales and rentals of public lands, and whatever money came in was distributed by the state superintendent's office. These funds were used largely to pay teachers. School buildings and equip-

---

[11] Before the amendment, the state had apportioned $30 per unit of ADA in elementary and secondary schools, on the condition that county taxes (or city-county taxes, as in San Francisco) would provide an additional $30 per unit of ADA in elementary schools and $60 in secondary schools. Now, with these county taxes abolished, the state began to provide $60 for elementary ADA and $90 for secondary ADA units. Junior college classes were considered secondary, and as yet there was no state aid for kindergartens.

ment were to be paid for locally from county taxes (25 cents per $100 assessed value after 1859) and from township (district) taxes. The only state-supported schools were elementary; if a city offered educational opportunities beyond the elementary and grammar grades, it did so at local district expense.

State apportionments after 1874 were raised to seven dollars per census child between ages 5 and 17. In theory, these apportionments were for elementary schools only, but the concept of elementary education was gradually moved to include grammar grades, a quasi-secondary education. Thereafter, elementary schools proper were considered primary grades. The apportionment of state school funds for secondary education proper was a moot question until 1903.

Plan II (1880 to 1910). This plan came after the second California constitution and the impact of the Kalamazoo Case for free high school education. The state school fund was still derived from the sale or rental of public land, a state school tax, and a two-dollar poll tax. State apportionments were made on a child-census basis until 1905, when the legislature gave consideration to the number of teachers a district employed—an incentive to smaller class sizes. In 1905, $25 was allotted for each census child and an additional state aid of $550 for each teacher employed, unless a teacher had fewer than 20 pupils. County taxes remained the major source of public school support, but, since counties varied in taxable wealth, educational opportunities varied widely in different counties.

The Municipal Corporation Act of 1883 permitted municipalities to tax for schools, and in 1903 the state supreme court reaffirmed the independence of the city-school district from the city itself. School districts were becoming quasi-corporations with taxing and bonding rights.

Plan III (after 1910). A major source of state money was the taxes derived from public service corporations (railroads and so on). Constitutional Amendment No. 1 in 1910 provided that the first call on this money was to be for the public school system and the state university. Poll taxes were repealed in 1914, when the CTA proposed an ADA allotment of $13 to $18 per pupil, but the proposal failed. Before the ADA principle was adopted in 1920, state apportionments continued on the pupil-census and teacher-unit basis. County taxes were still a major source of revenue, and district tax rates set by district boards supplied the remaining income for school costs. In the school year of 1919–20, state elementary school apportionments were $19.33

per pupil and county apportionments were $24.70 per pupil in daily attendance averaged during the previous year. State high school apportionments were $15, and the county's share was $60 per pupil enrolled. Local district taxes made up the difference in school costs.

Plan IV (after 1920). Average daily attendence, as counted in the previous year, became the standard of all school apportionments.[12] The 1920 law provided $30 per unit of ADA from state funds for all elementary and secondary levels. The law required the county or city and county to provide no less than an additional $30 per unit of elementary ADA and no less than $60 per unit of secondary ADA. A basic $60 (state and local) was provided for all elementary pupils, $90 per secondary pupil. State ADA gradually increased to $30 (elementary) and $60 (high school), and then to $60 (elementary), $90 (secondary), and $120 (junior college) in the 1930s.

It was necessary to increase state aid after the depression began because the welfare programs of California counties used up the county resources that had formerly been used for schools. Thus the current system of supporting education began, with money provided by district taxes and state aid and with some county services to smaller and poorer districts. But there was no fair equalization program for impoverished districts and for districts with special problems such as extensive transportation of pupils, special programs, or the unwillingness of the electorate to tax itself reasonably according to its ability to support its schools.

Impoverished districts and districts overburdened with the children of military and war-related personnel multiplied so rapidly in California during World War II that Governor Earl Warren created the California Commission for Post War Planning in 1944 to study the problem and make recommendations for better state financing of education. The commission secured the services of George D. Strayer of Columbia University, who produced the well-known Strayer Survey. The survey recommended important changes in the organization of California school districts, chiefly through consolidation, the reorgani-

[12] Elwood Patterson Cubberley, former superintendent of the San Diego City Schools and later dean of Stanford University's school of education, had long urged the average-daily-attendance principle of apportioning state funds to local districts. Under this principle, which was adopted in 1920, if a pupil was in regular attendance during the previous year he earned one unit of ADA ($30 in 1920). For a pupil in irregular attendance (say one who attended 120 days in the 180-day term), a computed proportion of the ADA unit was allotted (in the example, 120/180, or two-thirds of the $30, that is, $20).

zation of the state department of education, and improved financial support for public passage of a constitutional amendment (No. 9 in 1944) and of the Fair Equalization Law of 1945.

> Amendment Number 9 proposed that the $30, the amount trans-
> ferred from the county taxes to the State under the old 1933 amend-
> ment, should be increased to not less than $50 per year per unit
> of average daily attendance. With the passage of the amendment
> the States would have to contribute a minimum of $30 plus $50,
> or $80 altogether for each unit. The funds so provided were to be
> allocated on a semiequalized basis for elementary schools.[13]

The Fair Equalization Law, suggested by the Strayer Survey, provided these financial improvements, among other administrative reforms:

1. The distribution of the elementary school fund on an equalized basis (see Proposition No. 9).

2. The provision of a fund to support county elementary school supervision for school districts of under 900 units of ADA.

3. A minimum teachers' salary of $1,800 and an increase of the state superintendent's salary from $5,000 to $10,000. (It has since been increased to $25,000.)

4. Permission for local district tax levies to support child-care centers.

5. Provisions for the establishment of schools and training centers for spastic children, blind children, and children with speech disorders and other physical or mental handicaps.

The fair equalization of educational opportunities and costs was brought to further fruition by Proposition No. 3 in 1946 and by improvements in the laws of 1963, 1964, and 1966. This brings us to the fifth and latest plan for the financing of public education in California.

Plan V (since 1946). Current plans for the equalized apportionment of state school funds are as follows. The constitutional amendment called Proposition No. 3 was passed on November 5, 1946, with a record vote of 1,772,370 in favor and 610,967 against. It established these basic requirements:

[12] Cloud, p. 202.

(1) a minimum salary of $2,400 a year for teachers; (2) State aid for kindergartens as part of the elementary school system; (3) State support of public education on the basis of $120 per year per pupil in average daily attendance in the kindergartens, elementary schools, high schools, and junior colleges; (4) a minimum apportionment of not less than $90 per pupil for all districts, with no district receiving less than $2,400 a year (apportionment by the legislature by a system of equalization of the difference between the $90 guaranteed by law and the $120 guaranteed by the constitution); (5) the right of school district trustees to fix the amounts needed for their school district and a mandatory law that County Boards of Supervisors would fix a tax rate to raise such amount; and (6) continuation of the California constitutional guaranty giving public education first call upon all revenues of the state.[14]

It must be remembered that the 1946 constitutional amendment is merely the foundation upon which subsequent legislation for fair equalization of the costs of education has been built. The constitutional guarantees of 1946 remain, of course, as do the basic state aid of $120 per unit of ADA and the minimum teachers' salary of $2,400 per year. However, the legislature has established higher legislative guarantees—for example, $125 in basic aid and $4,500 as a minimum salary for teachers. During the past two decades, the legislature has developed a complex system for the sharing of cost.

Currently, the state guarantees basic state aid ($125 per unit of ADA) to all districts regardless of their wealth. The constitution further guarantees sufficient state aid so that the combined state and local support will never fall below $180 per unit of ADA. This is the constitutional minimum for the foundation program. Each year, however, the legislature establishes more generous foundation programs for each school level—elementary, secondary, and junior college. The state thereby commits itself to giving extra assistance to poorer districts and districts with special problems, so that even these will have sufficient funds to meet the minimum defensible costs—that is, the foundation programs at each level. Then, lest a school district fail to bear a reasonable share of the foundation program, the state establishes criteria based on the ability and willingness of the district to produce adequate property-tax revenues.

It is as though the state were saying to all local school boards: "We must have an adequate finance for all the children and youth of

[14] *Ibid.*, pp. 228–29.

California. The legislature will set minimum defensible expenditures for each school level each year. Together we can meet these levels of costs. The state will do its full share, if the local districts carry a reasonable share of the costs. Furthermore, the state has supplementary aid programs for school districts with special problems such as a limited tax base, small but necessary schools, or transportation problems. Finally, to encourage some special education or more economical district organization, the state will provide additional aid for excess cost programs and bonuses for the unification of school districts."

It will be understood that this basic concept is an outgrowth of the 1946 Fair Equalization Law, which has been improved repeatedly for the past 20 years. Indeed, the legislative changes of equalized state aid have been so frequent in recent years that people concerned with public school budgets often need to be alerted to revisions by the state and county departments of education[15] and by research reports of professional organizations.[16] The 1966 CTA report specifies that the major feature of Senate Bill No. 12 (Special Session, 1963), Assembly Bill No. 145 (Special Session, 1964), and Assembly Bill No. 52 (Special Session, 1966) are included in the report. But there is still a later revision in Assembly Bill No. 272 of January 30, 1967, which amazingly was amended eight times between March 6 and August 4, 1967.

Frequent revisions of the already complex equalization law pose problems for budget officers and professors of school law and finance who are training superintendents and business managers for California public schools. So far as this book is concerned, we must be content with an explanation of the principles of equalized state aid and the basic aspects of the law, though dated examples will be used to illustrate the law's application. The complete law can be obtained from the most recent edition of the code and from copies of such bills as Assembly Bill No. 272. Appendix Three gives an outline of state school finance as it appears in the code.

As a beginning, the principal parts of the equalization program—basic aid, equalization aid, the foundation program, variations in local property tax assessments (the Collier factor) supplemental support, and excess cost programs—need clarification:

Basic Aid.   As already indicated, basic aid is $125 per unit of ADA

[15] See the *School Business Services Guide,* 1966 Edition of the Dept. of Education (San Diego County), ch. 14, "School District Budgets."

[16] See *State Apportionment to California School Districts,* Supplementary Research Report No. 54 (July, 1966), distributed by the Research Department of the California Teachers' Association.

across the board—for all levels and all districts throughout the state.

Equalization Aid. Of course, equalization aid is additional state assistance for districts with special problems such as an inadequate tax base, inadequate transportation, and the like. Obviously, small districts with small but necessary schools have the problem of offering educational opportunities that will compare favorably with those offered in large or wealthy districts.

The 1967 law provides extra aid for elementary districts with one elementary school (kindergarten–grade 8) whose enrollment is less than 101. If the school has less than 26 pupils and only one full-time teacher, it receives $8,175. Schools with less than 51 pupils and having at least two teachers receive $16,350; less than 76 pupils and three teachers, $24,525; less than 101 pupils and four teachers, $32,700.

Elementary districts with up to 901 ADA may compute their foundation programs at $327 per unit instead of the named $263.14. As we shall see later, there is further specialization aid (supplemental aid) for school districts with smaller amounts of assessable property. Since January 30, 1967, elementary districts receive a bonus of $20 per unit of ADA if they unify or consolidate. The earlier bonus was $15.

Equalization aid for small but necessary high schools has also been improved by the 1967 law. This aid is based on pupil enrollments and a minimum full-time teaching staff as follows:[17]

ADA	Teachers	State Aid
1–20	3	$ 41,400
21–40	4	49,500
41–60	5	57,600
61–75	6	65,700
75–90	7	73,800
91–105	8	81,900
106–120	9	90,000
121–135	10	98,100
136–150	11	106,200
151–180	12	114,300
181–220	13	122,400
221–260	14	130,500
261–300	15	138,600

These small high schools receive, in addition to the sums listed, $472 per unit of ADA. Furthermore, if a high school district has less than $25,000 of assessed valuation behind each unit of ADA, it receives

[17] *Ibid.*, p. 8.

a supplemental support based on the district tax effort over 80 cents per $100 of assessed valuation. For every one cent raised above the 80 cents, an additional $2.50 per unit of ADA may be added.

Foundation Program. As the name implies, the foundation program is the basic financial effort to provide for the minimal defensible costs of operating good schools at all grade levels. This effort includes state aid (basic and equalization aid) and state-required local effort to produce school funds by taxation. There is a foundation program for each level—elementary, secondary, and junior college, and there is a constitutional guarantee that the foundation program will never fall below $180 per unit of ADA. The legislature also establishes higher foundation programs for each level each year. Examples of increase in the foundation program for elementary schools follow:[18]

1962–63	$201.36	(plus 0.40 gifted)
1963–64	208.44	(includes gifted)
1964–65	220.83	(includes gifted)
1965–66	235.64	(includes gifted)
1966–67	263.64	(includes gifted)
1967–68	337.00	(includes gifted)

An idea of the component parts of the foundation program can be gained from this breakdown of the program in 1964–65, when the elementary schools were guaranteed $220.83 per unit of ADA:

Basic and equalization aid	$180.00
County supervision	1.60
Regular transportation	4.00
Special education and transportation of special pupils	9.63
County services	3.06
Mentally gifted	.80
Additional equalization aid	21.79
Total	$220.88

As already indicated, the elementary foundation program in 1967 is $263.64. The secondary program is $387.00. Both can be increased by $36 per unit, if and when districts are unified. Although the junior college program was increased by $88 in 1967, making it $628, the complexity of arriving at average daily attendance makes this a special problem. Since the computation method does not change with the rates, a page out of the 1966 county guide will clarify the problem:

[18] *Ibid.,* p. 2.

Separate computations are required for (a) resident students, other than adults; (b) nonresident students, other than adults; (c) resident adult students; and (d) nonresident adult students:

a. For resident students, other than adults, the foundation program is $600 per ADA less the computation of a local rate of twenty-five cents on each $100 of assessed value.
b. For nonresident students other than adults only the basic aid of $125 per ADA is allowed.
c. For resident adult students the foundation program is $490 minus twenty-four cents times the assessed valuation per resident student, other than adults, with a maximum of $230 per unit of ADA. Should the computation result in basic aid of $125 per ADA, the district will receive either the amount produced by the current or previous year's ADA, whichever is less.
d. For nonresident adult students—that is, adults not residing in the district and not residing in any district maintaining a junior college—the allowance is $125 per unit of ADA.[19]

Obviously, therefore, the 1967 foundation program for junior colleges ($628) was used for residents only and not adults, as the law defines them.

Moreover, as may be expected, there are small and large junior colleges, so the state provides a small junior college formula for junior colleges of less than 1,001 ADA. This formula, like those for small elementary and secondary schools, is based on ADA and teachers employed:[20]

ADA	Certificated Employees	State Aid
1–150	12	$169,000
151–200	15	220,000
201–300	18	271,000
301–400	21	322,000
401–500	24	373,000
501–600	27	424,000
601–700	30	475,000
701–800	33	526,000
801–900	36	577,000
901–1,000	39	628,000

[19] *School Business Services Guide*, p. 15.
[20] *Financing California Public Schools* (Los Angeles: Research Office of the California Teachers' Association, Southern Section, 1967), p. 39.

The whole concept of the above foundation programs is based on a stipulated local effort. In computing equalization aid for elementary schools, this stipulated local effort is the amount a one-dollar tax rate times each $100 of assessed valuation would raise. This amount is then deducted from the computed foundation program as a method of equalization. If this reduction of the foundation program should result in a figure less than $125 times the ADA of the previous year, then this "basic aid" becomes the amount of state aid for the current year. (The minimum under this program is $2,400 for a school district employing but one teacher.[21])

Variations in Local Property Tax Assessments—the Collier Factor.[22] Since the percentage of property values used for assessment purposes varies from county to county, the state has tried to equalize the assessment of tangible properties to this end, the state board of equalization annually determines the relationship between the total assessed value of the tangible property on the county's current local roll and the board of equalization's estimate of the full cash value of locally assessable property in the county. The ratio obtained from this process is divided into the ratio for the state as a whole and results in a current-year factor. When the current year is averaged with the certified factors for the two preceding years, the three-year-average modification factor (referred to as the Collier factor) to be used for the fiscal year is obtained.

Example: a. Ratio of county assessment to full cash value: 23.9 percent
  b. Ratio of statewide assessment to full cash value: 21.8 percent
  c. 21.8/23.9 = 0.91 current-year factor
  d. 1963 certified current-year factor   0.97
  1964 certified current-year factor   0.92
  1965 certified current-year factor   0.91

  Total   2.80
  Three-year average   0.93

The three-year-average factor is used in modifying the locally assessed secured and unsecured valuations in preparing estimates of state apportionments. To this modified amount is added the state-

---

[21] *Ibid.,* pp. 9–10.
[22] *Ibid.,* pp. 6–7.

assesed utility-roll valuations, which is not subject to the modification process, to obtain the total assessed valuation.

When the school district has attained its modified assessed valuation and measured its ability to raise funds, the foundation program becomes the sum of basic aid, realistic local tax support, and, finally, state equalization aid—the last necessary to supply the district with funds required to reach the stipulated foundation program. But this is not yet the end of state aid, for the state wishes to encourage special programs for regular and exceptional children and district unification. It has extra money to use on these two areas, and it can supply supplemental aid for some school districts.

Supplemental Support. For those elementary districts whose adjusted assessed valuation is less than $11,000 per unit of ADA, additional equalization aid is available under the supplemental support program, scaled to the amount of local tax effort in excess of the eligibility one-dollar rate. For each cent of tax above one dollar, an additional $1.10 per unit of ADA is granted up to a given maximum. No summer school ADA is allowed in this computation. The total state aid then becomes the sum of basic aid plus equalization aid plus supplemental aid.[23]

Excess-Cost Programs. In order to encourage special education for exceptional children and programs of driver education, the state has additional aid for districts offering such programs. It also gives additional assistance to districts with special transportation problems. Examples of these excess-cost programs follow:

1. Programs for exceptional children (K–grade 14).

   a. Mentally retarded (up to $435 per ADA)

   b. Severely mentally retarded (up to $795 per ADA)

   c. Physically handicapped (blind, deaf, orthopedically handicapped, aphasiacs, and the cerebral-palsied (up to $1,018 per ADA)

2. Driver-training programs (actual cost up to $50 per pupil).

3. Mentally gifted (up to $40 per pupil).

4. Regular pupil transportation over normal transportation costs. Example: Julian Union High School District, which usually serves from 125 to 150 students in all grades, has transported these

[23] *Ibid.,* pp. 10–11.

pupils in an area that is larger than Rhode Island. This clearly presents a special transportation problem.

Obviously a complex equalization law such as this presents a problem of interpretation for school administrators and teachers and especially for the general public. The California Teachers' Association has publications that explain the law both briefly and in considerable detail.[24]

School Bonds and Bonded Indebtedness

Though school-bond elections in California generally bring out a sizable opposition, as they do elsewhere, few citizens would be willing to subscribe to the alternative, which is to build new schools and improve old ones out of the current operational budget. Yet even in the best of times, as in the lush 1920s, school budgets have seldom been so large that they could accommodate an extensive building program on a pay-as-you-go basis.

It is therefore a generally accepted principle that since many generations use a school facility, each generation should pay its share of the costs of that facility. This principle is so old and well established that we are amused by the early California practice of providing schoolrooms and schoolhouses without going into debt for them.

During the first 30 years of California's educational history, the building and maintenance of schoolhouses was a local obligation. All state aid and half of the county aid was to be used for teachers' salaries. Therefore, district boards built schoolhouses, primitive or substantial, when they could find tax money or when a public-minded citizen could be found to donate property or building material. As late as 1882, for example, John Russ, a San Diego lumberman, donated the material for the building of Russ School, which later became Russ High School and, finally, San Diego High School.

At an even earlier date, when a local board could not find the finances to build a school, it rented schoolrooms or even a complete

[24] Southern Section, *Financing California Schools* (Los Angeles, 1959), p. 7; and The CTA Research Bulletin No. 54 on State Apportionments to California School Districts (July, 1966).

building. Finding these procedures impractical, district boards often obligated the district beyond what it could afford. Since schools were a public service for which the public would eventually pay, school boards became careless about whom they owed and for how long. This practice was apparently so widespread that it merited legislative censure. The following laws were enacted to limit such free-wheeling school-board actions:

1. An 1859 law required that school funds raised for a given year be used exclusively for the support of schools during that year.

2. An 1863 law permitted district boards to accumulate or collect money to be placed in a school building fund.

3. The second constitution (Article IX), while it still forbade districts to spend beyond their annual income, sanctioned school bonds for improvements, provided the interest on such bonds could be met comfortably out of current taxes.

One California school district, however, had jumped the gun on this constitutional provision, as Roy Cloud relates in this amusing and important anecdote:

> The present method now commonly used for raising funds with which to construct school buildings for California school districts did not receive legal sanction until 1878. Before that time tax levies were made or contributions were solicited, and funds so secured were used to build schoolhouses. The first volume of the Orange County History Series, published in 1931, in describing the City of Anaheim, has this interesting account of the raising of the first bonds:
>
> "The school was maintained in the building of the Water Company until 1869 when a new building was erected. As the community grew this little schoolhouse became inadequate and in 1877 Professor J. M. Guinn, who had been the principal of the Anaheim schools for eight years, drafted a resolution authorizing the district to incorporate and issue bonds to the amount of $10,000. The bonds were sold at par and the building was erected."
>
> When the new Constitution of California was adopted in 1879, Article XI, Section 18, gave school districts the constitutional right to issue school district bonds. And the law permitting the

school districts of the State to incur bonded indebtedness for the building of schools was passed in 1881.[25]

So while the constitution opened the door to bonded indebtedness, it cautiously required "the assent of two-thirds of the qualified electors of the district voting at an election held for that purpose." The 1881 legislature further restricted the bonding rights to larger districts, which were cities of considerable size. Only in 1887 did the legislature extend these bonding rights to cities of the fifth class and to school districts partly within and partly without such cities.

The right to bond themselves was gradually extended to all school districts, with definite legislative limits. It has become standard practice for school districts to bond themselves for buildings and capital improvements. Most school districts now budget money for interest and for the amortization of school bonds.

Interest rates on school bonds has gone down considerably, particularly since they have become tax exempt. Interest on school bonds had been as high as 7 percent, but between 1910 and 1930 6 percent was the going rate. In recent years, it has been possible to sell school bonds at 3 percent or slightly more. Bond issues are, of course, more easily passed in prosperous times. During the 1930s, it was almost impossible to get a two-thirds majority in favor of school bonds. Although school-bond issues were passed more easily after World War II, there has been some agitation and at least one proposal for a constitutional amendment to reduce the required vote to a 60 percent majority.

It is not within the scope of this study to detail the many pages of California constitutional and statutory law on school bonds. Students may pursue the subject independently in two distinct sections of the state Education Code, for there are currently two different types of school bonds. The oldest and most familiar type is the bonding program of local districts. The other is a state school-bond program growing out of the state school-building-aid bond laws from 1949 to 1960.

This newer type of state school bond is an outgrowth of a certain type of population explosion peculiar to California. Since the first days of World War II, there have been sudden influxes of people into areas of the state where sufficient housing, schools, and other community facilities have not been available. Because the school districts in these areas are often unable to cope with the situation, it has become the policy of the state to bear a proportionate share of the con-

[25] Cloud, p. 81.

struction cost of school buildings. For this purpose, a state school-construction fund was established in the state treasury. The first money for this fund was raised in 1949 by a $250 million state school-bond issue. It was to be lent without interest to school districts that the governor had declared "state projects"—that is, districts affected by an influx of population such as those adjacent to military bases. The districts in these state projects may use state bond money to purchase school sites, furniture, and equipment and to plan and construct school buildings. Besides lessening school problems, this program can also provide needed jobs in local areas. Therefore, the program involves the state allocation board of the Construction and Employment Act, the director of general services, and the director of education, who is the state superintendent.

The extensive and detailed legislation (165 pages of it) on state school-building bonds is recorded in Chapters 5 and 8–15 of Division 14 of the Education Code (see Sections 18901–19905). The many pages include the state school-building-aid bond laws of 1949, 1952, 1954, 1957, 1958, and 1960. The laws include housing aid for reorganized school districts, as an incentive to district reorganization, and aid for the housing of exceptional children. Finally, Division 14 is concluded with the Junior College Tax Act of 1961, which supplies relief grants to junior college districts for payment and redemption of outstanding district bonds and for the purchase and improvement of junior college sites.

Before the advent of state bond programs, money was raised through local bond issues. State interest in and control of local school district bonds is described in the state Education Code, Division 16, Chapter 7. To outline the scope of the state's interest and to give reference for further study, it seems of value to list the 10 articles under Chapter 7, "Bonds of School Districts" (Sections 21701–22152).

Article 1

Purposes for Which School District Bonds May Be Authorized; Authority for Elections; General Limitations on Bonded Indebtedness; Validation of School District Bonding (Sections 21701–21708).

Article 2

General Provisions for Bond Elections of School Districts (Sections 21751–21757).

Article 3

Issuance and Sale of Bonds of School Districts (Sections 21800–21814).

Article 4

Required Form of Bonds of School Districts (Sections 21811–21853).

Article 5

Registration of Bonds of School Districts (Sections 21901–21905).

Article 6

Cancellation of Unsold Bonds of School Districts (Sections 21951–21955).

Article 7

Purchase of Bonds by the Issuing School (Sections 22001–22002).

Article 8

Method of Payment of Bonds of School Districts (Sections 22051–22056).

Article 9

Tax for Payment of Bonds of School Districts (Sections 22101–22104).

Article 10

Tax for Payment of Bonds When School District Is Located in Two or More Counties (Sections 22151–22152).

This then is the history and present status of school bonds in California. There remains still one major source of public school support, namely, the U.S. government.

Federal Aid for California Education

The Constitution of the United States included no plans for a national school system. Federal control of public schools was suspect. Yet as early as 1787 the Continental Congress declared that "religion,

morality, and knowledge being necessary to good government and
the happiness of mankind, schools and the means of education shall
be forever encouraged."

Since 1785, encouragement by the federal government has taken
the form of land grants for public schools (over 115,000 square miles
of federal lands for all the states) and for higher education in agriculture and the mechanical arts (a total of 11,315,665 acres). Furthermore, many billions of dollars in loans and outright gifts from the
federal government have supported education in the several states.
Had it not been so, many of the state school systems and state
universities would be vastly different, if, indeed, they would exist
at all.

In no small measure, California has what was developed in its
schools and colleges because of federal assistance at the right moments in California history. It is our purpose to detail California's
debt to the United States for this assistance.

Federal Land Grants. Federal land grants for California's public
schools began in 1850. Gifts of over five and one-half million acres
have been discussed elsewhere. Suffice it to say that these were direct
grants (500,000 acres) and township grants (sections 16 and 36 of
each California township) and that the lands produced over $10 mil-
lion of good American money when it was needed most during the
period 1851–80.

Though it is not well remembered today, the original Northwest
Ordinance land grants from 1787 included lands for "seminaries of
learning"—that is, for higher education. In pursuance of this principle,
the Congressional Act of 1853 made another 46,000 acres of public
land in California available for higher-education institutions, all of
which were private schools in 1853. Unfortunately, the state legislature
sold the land at $1.25 per acre and put the resulting $57,000 in a
higher-education fund. Its best result was to encourage the early establishment of a state university, though this was not seriously contemplated until 1865. In the end the money was used for the establishment of the first California state normal school.

Morrill Act (1862). The first Morrill Act was passed by the Congress to encourage higher education in agriculture and the mechanical
arts. It provided 30,000 acres of public land for each member of congress (senator or representative)—150,000 acres for California. Lest
the state lose this land altogether, the 1865 legislature passed "An Act
to Establish an Agricultural, Mining and Mechanical Arts College,"
but the state superintendent, John Swett, opposed "a mushroom uni-

versity." The University of California did eventually get the land or the benefits from it, and at a time when it could very well use it.

Dollar Aid for Land-Grant Colleges. The determined and persistent Vermont senator Justin Morrill pushed his almost private cause of developing land-grant colleges by the second Morrill Act passed in 1890. This act provided for an annual appropriation of $15,000 for each land-grant college such as the University of California. This annual grant-in-aid increased to $25,000 per year until the Nelson Amendment brought it up to a maximum of $50,000 per year in 1911. These appropriations, of considerable help to the University of California, continued to 1935 when the Bankhead-Jones Act gave flat annual grants of $20,000 to each land-grant college and apportioned $1,500,-000 to them on the basis of state population.

The University of California has received many millions of dollars in federal aid in the past three-quarters of a century, more than any other land-grant college or state university. It has been of tremendous value to the state and federal governments and national defense programs. The campus at Davis is the center of a vast program of agricultural research and experimentation for California vineyards and other extensive agricultural enterprises. The university developed the first cyclotron and has continued atomic and nuclear research. Many national defense projects have been carried out on its campuses. Continued and expanding oceanographic research and assistance to California fisheries have the center at the Scripps Institute of Oceanography on the San Diego campus.

Federal aid has long been a major source of income in the university budget, though the state also has been generous. In addition, there have been substantial endowments by influential and wealthy friends.

Smith-Hughes Act (February 2, 1917). This act opened a 20-year series of congressional measures and federal dollar aid for every type of vocational and agricultural education in secondary schools. During World War I, it purported to encourage vocational education programs in the high schools and junior colleges of the nation, particularly in trade industries, agriculture, and home economics. The act committed the federal government to reimbursing school districts for vocational teachers' salaries, for the salaries of supervisors and directors of programs in these areas, as well as for the training of vocational, agricultural, and home economics teachers.

The Smith-Hughes Act was the first of a series of acts that successively increased federal appropriations:

1. Smith-Hughes (1917–26) initially provided $1,700,000 per year but increased this to an annual contribution of $7,200,000 by 1925.

2. George-Reed (1929) provided $2,500,000 in additional annual appropriations to 1934.

3. George-Ellzey (1934) provided $3 million annually for three years.

4. George-Deen (1937) extended the aid to distributive occupations and provided $14,483,000, which raised the total vocational education aid to $21,785,000.

To assure California of its share of annual appropriations and to develop leadership in much-needed types of education, the state department of education in and after 1920 appointed directors, bureau chiefs, and staffs to promote vocational programs and handle state-federal cooperation in vocational, agricultural, and home economics education. The state department still maintains sizable bureaus of agricultural, business, home economics, and vocational education (see Chapter 2.) The impact of this federal aid was tremendous, even apart from the money it brought to California. Whereas there was little vocational education before 1917, no high school of repute is now without classes in industrial arts, business education, or home economics, and few rural high schools lack agriculture laboratories. Even when the shops were turned into industrial arts laboratories, apprenticeship programs were established in junior colleges. Vocational schools like the Frank Wiggins Trade School in Los Angeles are again coming into vogue at the high school level.

Vocational Rehabilitation. The Smith-Sears Vocational Rehabilitation Act of June 27, 1918, ultimately provided $591,494,000 for medical aid, vocational readjustment, and rehabilitation for veterans of World War I. This and the $11,672,112 appropriation in 1945–46 enabled California to match federal funds dollar for dollar in a program of vocational rehabilitation. The vocational rehabilitation program was expanded from veterans' services to the victims of industrial accidents and poliomyelitis and to the blind and other handicapped persons. Until 1965, the state department of education was the chief state agency cooperating with the federal government; since then the state department of rehabilitation has taken over these responsibilities. It is doubtful whether rehabilitation would have started when it did had it not been for substantial federal aid in this worthy project.

Emergency Aid to Education—1934–1943. The depression of 1929 had no real effect on California schools until 1931, but the state was also late in overcoming the difficulties of severe economic breakdown. California did not experience as many collapses of submarginal rural school districts in 1930 as the states of the Middle West did, but, as we saw earlier, county welfare needs diverted county aid from school districts and curtailed the educational program.

California really began to share federal emergency funds for youth and education in 1933 and continued to draw heavily on federal emergency resources until 1943, when the Works Progress Administration was finally abolished. The types and amounts of federal assistance to various aspects of California education are briefly described here.

The National Youth Administration, besides providing many millions of dollars in student aid for work experience, health services, testing, and guidance, also fathered the California Youth Authority, which is still in effective operation. CCC camps spread through the state. After giving a valued service to a lost generation of youth, the camps were later used for school camping and other continuing educational activities.

The Works Progress Administration, besides improving school and college buildings and grounds, was the immediate cause for the creation or expansion of these California educational projects and continuing programs. The nursery school movement, started during the depression, is still in operation in some of its aspects. The San Diego State College Laboratory School was established with WPA help. Adult education programs (day and evening adult schools and high schools) were firmly fixed in the state school system under the direction of the then small state bureaus of adult and continuation education. While California had long experimented with evening schools, adult literacy education, and Americanization classes for the foreign-born, adult education, as it is now known in California, came into its own with the Federal Emergency Education Program (FEEP). FEEP and its counterpart, the State Emergency Education Program (SEEP), were a major factor in all types of adult education, the reestablishment of a foundering junior college system, and such curricular development and social-civic programs as we shall now outline.

Curriculum laboratories and libraries in city- and county-school districts and in California colleges were among the new and effective innovations financed entirely by federal emergency funds. Money provided by the FEEP created jobs for curriculum consultants and co-ordinators, jobless writers and artists, librarians, typists, printers, and the operators of duplicating equipment. Curriculum libraries and laboratories are commonplace today in city- and county-school organization and in the schools of education of California colleges and universities. The initiation and development of many, if not most, of these can be traced to the availability of federal emergency funds.

Adult social-civic forums, lecture series in adult schools, institutes of government, and public affairs forums were initiated under the FEEP. A considerable number of these continued in public schools and colleges after emergency funds were no longer available.

Other emergency programs of a less permanent nature were developed for the first time in California. These include workers' education, parent education classes, avocational education, school hot lunches for needy pupils, and the effective use of surplus commodities in school cafeterias.

If a national catastrophe can ever be counted as a great blessing, the depression and its resultant federal aid was most certainly the greatest boon that California education ever received, even apart from the exact number of federal dollars that were pumped into the state. To specify the actual number of dollars that California received would challenge a considerable team of research workers. Suffice it to say that California received its full share of these federal emergency funds:[26]

Emergency Aid for the Forty-Eight States and Territories

$ 167,000,000	Expended by the National Youth Administration for scholarships
467,000,000	NYA money for wages
2,969,000,000	For CCC camps and work projects
662,895,000	For dependents of CCC-camp members
13,000,000,000	For WPA programs
120,169,087	For school buildings and libraries
$17,386,064,087	Total

[26] These financial data and the data on types of federal aid to education are developed in greater detail by Arthur B. Moehlman of the University of Michigan, to whom the author is in considerable debt. See Moehlman, ch. 33, "Federal Interest in Public Education," pp. 460–71.

National Defense Education. Before all federal and state emergency funds were used, the nation was faced with a massive national
defense program to protect itself and its allies against the Berlin-Rome-
Tokyo axis. California's geographical position, its actual and potential
naval, marine, and army bases, and its shipbuilding and aircraft-build-
ing potentials put it in the center of the picture.

Few people, Californians least of all, realize how the extensive
economic and educational readjustments California made to counteract
the depression gave the state the experience and the will to share fully
in the new era of national defense and defense education. The federal
government, however, was quick to exploit the situation and to shift
gears from emergency aid to new types of assistance and encouragement for state participation in national defense.

During the depression, California had received not only its full share
of the much-maligned "Okies" and "Arkies" but also a surplus of poorly
trained white and black workers from the Deep South and a significant
influx of immigrants from the Northeast and Midwest in search of job
opportunities in a propitious climate. Here, then, was a deposit of human resources ready for training and redirection. They lived in federal
housing projects on or near military bases or in war-production centers. California school districts, urban and rural, soon found themselves
with a surplus enrollment, for which they received state aid but no additional local revenues because the housing projects paid no property
taxes.

California has occupied a key position in World War II, the Korean
War, and the Vietnam involvement. It has likewise taken a great part
in the college training of the veterans of these wars. The high points
of federal assistance in defense education are as follows:

1. *National Defense Training.* California had a full share of federal
support for the part-time and full-time training of war workers and
military personnel in its high schools, adult and vocational schools,
junior colleges, colleges, and universities in 1940–44. Because of its
strategic position, it produced at least its fair share of the 6,850,000
war workers and the 3,315,000 workers in food production.[27]

2. *In-lieu-of-tax Benefits.* Because local school districts received no
property taxes for the education of dependent children living on military reservations or in military and defense housing projects, the fed-

[27] *Ibid.,* p. 471.

eral government began in 1941 to reimburse school districts for the additional costs of current operations caused by increased enrollment. In one way or another, the federal government has continued this type of reimbursement, though Congress has been repeatedly annoyed by these in-lieu-of-tax payments. School districts in national defense areas continue to make an accounting of federally connected children in their schools.

3. Lanham Act (1941–49). As soon as defense housing projects were begun, it became clear that the school-building needs on or near these projects would require federal aid. This was the purpose of the Lanham Act, passed in 1941. It provided for the construction, maintenance, and operation of schools, child-care centers, and recreation centers in housing projects. The initial in-lieu-of-tax money also came from funds provided by this act.

In general, the type of school buildings constructed under the act was to match the type of housing—that is, where the housing was temporary, temporary schools, often of plywood on concrete slabs, were constructed—but permanent school buildings were approved for permanent housing projects. In the end, the temporary school buildings were used as long as possible and then replaced, when necessary, by the school district. The permanent schools were eventually sold to the local districts by the federal government. As in the case of all war surpluses, the selling price was set at a very considerable discount from its actual cost.

4. Education of War Veterans. It is fair to note than many California state and private colleges could not possibly have been what they are today had it not been for the GI Bill of Rights (the Serviceman's Readjustment Act of 1944—Public Law No. 346) and Public Law No. 16 for the vocational rehabilitation of veterans.

College enrollment had decreased markedly, if not catastrophically, during World War II. The decrease of enrollment, particularly of men, pushed some private colleges to the brink of bankruptcy. As an example of what it did to public colleges, San Diego State College, which in 1966 enrolled 18,500 undergraduate and graduate students, saw its prewar enrollment of 5,000 undergraduates drop to about 2,000. The $11 billion made available by the GI Bill of Rights from 1942 to 1950 was therefore a godsend to this and to many of the California colleges.

When California began to acquire its share of these federal funds, the fantastic upward trend of college enrollment began. The education and vocational rehabilitation of veterans put many worthy private colleges back on their feet, and the ballooning of enrollments on the campuses of the state colleges and the university continued steadily for the next 20 years. Junior college enrollment also expanded massively between 1946 and 1966, and the 1966 enrollment in the 18 California state colleges has practically doubled. The growth is due in no small measure to the initial explosive impact of the need to educate war veterans.

The easy availability of money for veterans' education attracted the attention of unscrupulous hucksters. Many veterans were fleeced by bogus colleges, vocational schools, and so-called diploma mills. The situation was so bad with the latter that Assemblyman Sheridan Hegland initiated a bill to outlaw the numerous privately operated and very profitable diploma mills. The bill (Education Code 29012-29022), which was easily passed by the legislature and signed by Governor Knight on April 9, 1958, not only eliminated abuses in the use of federal funds for college education but also prevented bilking of prospective college students by unscrupulous owners of private "colleges" and "universities." Many of these institutions had few physical facilities, untrained staff members, and no reasonable standards for accreditation.

Federal funds for education (1958–67).   Federal aid for education in the broadest sense means general, across-the-board support for at least all public schools in the United States. Because of its value in the equalization of educational opportunities, the National Education Association and other organized groups have lobbied repeatedly but unsuccessfully for general support from the federal government. Some special-interest groups would have extended general federal aid to private schools. Congress, however, has never in its long history passed a law giving such general support to the schools of the nation. Owing to the reluctance of Congress to provide general aid to all the schools of the nation, the most recent federal aid has been tied to national defense, improved international relations, and the war on poverty, as has the National Defense Education Act and the Elementary and Secondary Education Act.

Even after the legislation of 1958 and 1965, federal aid has been designated for particular purposes—for example, for vocational education, science education, the children of low-income families, or those in federally impacted areas. In the last years of the Eisenhower Administration, in the thousand days of Kennedy, and especially during Johnson's Administration, there has been a broadening of specified areas for which federal aid is offered. Since 1958, Congress has passed laws affording federal assistance to public and private education at home and abroad in areas previously unknown in our national history.

1. National Defense Education Act (1958). New federal money for education, of which California has had its full share, has been appropriated under the National Defense Education Act of 1958 (NDEA). The two billion dollars for the first four years of this act have provided a new and expanded educational program in science, mathematics, and foreign languages. Had it not been for the Sputniks of 1957, the interest of Congress in the advancement of scientific and mathematical education might not have been so great. The NDEA also expressed the nation's intent to "keep up with the Russians" in learning and teaching certain foreign languages and in some aspects of counseling, guidance, and vocational education.

After 1958, NDEA institutes and counseling services developed with great rapidity on college campuses and in schools of education throughout the state. In its enthusiasm for foreign language instruction by the audiolingual method in language laboratories, the state legislature and state boards went Congress one better. The legislature required that all elementary pupils be required to take several years of Spanish. At the same time, foreign language entrance requirements were established for state colleges, and 50-unit foreign language major requirements became commonplace. NDEA institutes for teachers of Spanish and other foreign languages spread across the state.

2. Student Loans and Educational Grants. When Public Law 85-864, the National Defense Education Act, was passed in 1958, these two purposes were specifically stated: (1) to identify and educate more of the talent of our nation and (2) to insure trained manpower of sufficient quality and quantity to meet the national defense needs of the United States.

To implement the first of these goals, Title II of the act provided for the establishment of National Defense Student Loan Funds (NDSL), from which needy students may borrow on reasonable terms. During his undergraduate work, the eligible student who maintains good class standing and carries at least one-half of a normal full-time academic class load may borrow up to $5,000 to be repaid over a 10-year period, unless payment is deferred for service in the armed forces, the Peace Corps, or VISTA. Graduate and professional students may borrow up to $10,000.

Obviously this has been a great boon to California students and colleges; but, lest the NDSL fail to meet all student needs, a similar college work-study program (the CWSP) was included in the Economic Opportunity Act of 1964, as were educational opportunity grants.[28]

3. *Training for the Peace Corps.* This favorite and most successful education project of President Kennedy opened the door to the training of many Peace Corps candidates in California colleges. These three training programs at San Diego State College are worthy of notice: (1) Peru urban community-development project (1964), (2) a similar training program for Colombia (1965), (3) rural education project for Jamaica (1966).

4. *The Elementary and Secondary Education Act (Public Law 89-10 April 11, 1965).* To explore the educational outcomes of this act, particularly in California, amounts to indulging in prophecy. Nevertheless, some initial outcomes and some valid expectations deserve mention.

It has already been noted (in Chapter 2) that the state department of education in California has been expanded to handle the many requests for compensatory education programs in local school districts (see Title V of the act). The state office, headed by Wilson C. Riles, has been swamped with requests for Title I funds—that is, for assistance to districts with low-income families and such teacher-training programs as Operation Head Start. Title II is already bringing federal dollars to the state to provide needed library resources, textbooks, and instructional aid for public and private schools of the state.

Perhaps the chief California problems in handling federal aids are channeling these vast new resources to the places where they are needed most and administering the program in an atmosphere free of political, group, and local pressures.

Finally, an annual report of a single California college gives a clue to the vast scope of new federal aid. Besides indicating its part in many of the above-mentioned programs, the college spells out its use of federal funds in these areas:

1. National teacher-corps training program (summer, 1966).

[28] See Office of Education Bulletin 55001, *Federal Aid for College Students* (1967).

2. Prospective teacher-fellowship program (September, 1966, through August, 1968).

3. Counselor-advisor university summer education (CAUSE: summers, 1964 and 1965, and the academic year of 1965–66).

4. Vocational rehabilitation counselor training (1966).

5. Veterans' administration counseling center (1961–67).

6. International teacher-development program (1960–64).

7. Cooperative college extension program with USN extension service (Pacific Fleet).

8. AID contracts with staff placements in Brazil (secondary education development), Jamaica (elementary and secondary education development), and on campus (graduate programs for Vietnamese exchange students).

9. Training of research personnel to evaluate federal aid program (proposed project).

10. Proposal for an institutional assistant grant from Title V of the ESEA.

In 1947, an educational officer with the military government in Germany remarked: "I'll never know whether we did an effective job unless I see the effects on this system ten years hence." In 1957, he was satisfied that a job had been done well. Similarly, time alone will allow us to assess the effectiveness of the federal aid given to California education in the 1960s. However, one thing is certain now: For what it is and what it may become, the educational system in California owes a tremendous debt to the federal government.

THE INSTRUCTIONAL PROGRAM

It would be tedious, not to say meaningless, to detail the curricular developments in California schools over the entire 118 years of the school system's history. It does, however, make sense to examine current local and state controls of instructional programs in the light of the varying educational goals established in the past. That California educators and the government agencies for which they worked progressively changed their educational goals and objectives is not difficult to establish. Indeed, the educational history of this state falls into five fairly well defined periods.

1. The era of imitation (1850–80), when the chief goal of Californians was to create schools and instructional programs on the western frontiers that would compare favorably with educational programs east of the Rockies.

2. The textbook era (1880–1910), when uniform state and county textbooks were in effect the whole curriculum.

3. The developmental period (1910–30), during which the new educational leadership in the state department of education was encouraging new types of schools (junior colleges, junior high schools, vocational and continuation schools) and new types of instruction for them. It was an era of experimentation.

4. The postdepression era (1930–46), when most curriculum development occurred in local school districts and in county programs.

5. The postwar era (1946–present), characterized by attempts to equalize educational opportunities through the state, by a shoring-up of academic programs, and by renewed state interest in curriculum control.

That there was some overlapping of goals and transitional stages between these periods will be evident in the following analysis of the major trends in defining California's educational goals and in curriculum development down the years.

Eastern Seeds in Western Soil— The Era of Imitation (1850–1880)

The framers of California's first constitution, as well as its pioneer legislators and school board members, had as their first and chief goal the establishment of a school system that would offer instruction as good and extensive as that offered in the East and Middle West. Most pioneer teachers and board members had fond memories of school programs east of the Rockies. Specifically, they were trying to transplant eastern educational opportunities to California:

1. A complete system of elementary or common schools that stressed literacy in the English language (the 3 R's), some geography, and, where possible, some American history. Early Californians spoke bravely of grammar grades (quasi-secondary education) and high schools for college preparation, though in the 1850s and 1860s these courses were never thought of as being universally available nor entirely free.

2. The earliest courses of study involved the mere naming of subject areas for the different grades. It was presumed that prepared teachers and the available textbooks would give content to these subjects. The 1851 legislation sought to assure itself of proper instruction by requiring local boards to examine prospective teachers on their ability to

teach the subjects of a given grade. As in the East, California school boards were also concerned with moral education as it was reflected in Bible reading and prayer.

3. The textbook was already in great measure the content of the curriculum. Hence, to assure itself of a uniform course content, the legislature in 1860 authorized the state board of education to adopt a state series of textbooks and to enforce their use under the penalty of forfeiting state aid if the approved textbooks were not used. That there was need for uniform textbooks is evidenced by the casual manner in which early California teachers secured at least one book to guide their teaching. Many brought their own books from the East, while others picked up a textbook at an occasional sale in California cities.

On December 4, 1848, for instance, the San Francisco *Star* advertised slates and pencils and a few schoolbooks for sale: arithmetics, grammars, spelling books, dictionaries, children's small geographies, primers, music books, and astronomies. These books, printed in the East, were the seed stock used by American pioneers for the sowing of a Yankee curriculum in the new California schools.

4. The bravery with which pioneer school boards set out to establish eastern schools in western soil is evidenced from the early efforts in San Francisco. In accord with what they remembered of eastern traditions, the members of San Francisco's board of education in 1851 ordered that each school day be closed with a prayer and each Monday morning's work be started with exercises in Bible reading. However, the main curricular stress in the common schools was placed on literacy in the English language, on the 3 R's, geography, and singing. The grammar grades of San Francisco's elementary schools were expected to offer spelling, reading, writing, vocal music, arithmetic, geography, English and Spanish grammar, elocution, natural philosophy (general science), the use of globes, and U.S. history.

When in 1853 San Francisco's superintendent of schools, Colonel Thomas J. Nevins, first proposed a high school for boys and a female seminary, he had a board of education composed solely of former New Englanders. In this eastern tradition the high school was planned "to fit young men for practical duties and business of life or for the admission into any of the best colleges or universities in the United States." [1]

The course of study for the high school was to be "ancient and mod-

[1] William Warren Ferrier, *Ninety Years of Education in California—1846-1936* (Berkeley, Calif.: Sather Gate Book Shop, 1937), p. 80.

ern history, rhetoric, logic, composition, chemistry, geology, mineralogy, botany, intellectual philosophy, natural theology, political economy, Constitution of the United States, Constitution of California, algebra, astronomy, bookkeeping, the Latin, Greek, Spanish and French languages." [2] This was a pretentious curriculum for the time and for the available teachers, but a display of erudition was not unusual in the San Francisco of the 1850s.

John Swett was often amused by the vanity and conceit that school board members displayed in their suggestions for elaborate curricula. Swett rarely tired of telling school boards that their courses of study could be only as good as the teachers and textbooks they could find and were willing to pay for. Swett was fully aware that the free spirit of the West prompted pioneers to control their own educational programs locally, but as state superintendent he pushed through the legislature the 1866 Act to Provide for a System of Common Schools. This act authorized the state board of education to adopt rules and regulations for the conduct of schools, to establish a course of study for district schools, and to adopt a uniform state series of textbooks for such schools. It further required local districts to provide pupils with school supplies—ink, chalk, pens, and paper—at district expense and to establish a system of school libraries. The balancing of state and local control over the instructional programs in the public school began with the Swett administration.

This balancing was not achieved quickly in California because of the intermediate offices of the county board of education and the county schools' superintendent. As the district authority decreased, the county's position was enhanced. For many decades the state moved cautiously in its exercise of control over the curriculum.

State and County Interest in Curriculum and Textbooks

The foregoing observations show that most of what was happening educationally in early California schools was planned and executed by the pioneer teachers, principals, and local boards of education. Theoretically, curricular planning and the teaching of all courses were

[2] *Ibid.*

under the supervision of the state and county superintendents. Actually the state superintendent rarely was apprised of the courses of study in a given district until he received the annual October Reports through the county-school offices. This tradition of local control of the public schools with some state guidance and leadership, but with minimal state controls, was pushed further under the decentralization measures of the second constitution.

The first constitution's provisions for a state school system had been interpreted in terms of state aid for the common schools and state permission for locally supported high schools. The state issued teachers' certificates, but in questions of curriculum the legislature was satisfied with naming the subject areas that it hoped would be pursued and with the authorization of state textbooks. Indeed, textbook selection became the chief bone of contention.

In 1866, Swett succeeded in getting uniform textbooks adopted for the whole state, but his policy received a major setback as a result of an unfortunate textbook scandal that plagued the administrations of Superintendents Bolander and Carr in 1874 and 1875. On June 22, 1874, the state board of education called for bids on state textbook adoptions to be opened on January 5, 1875. On that day, the state board, with Superintendent Bolander as its secretary, adopted the Pacific Coast readers to replace McGuffey's, Cornell's geography to replace Monteith's, and Spencerian penmanship in place of Payson, Dunton, and Scribner's. Obviously, some publishers' representatives were going to lose business and some bookstores would have useless stocks. Also, many Californians had emotional attachments to books like McGuffey's readers. As a result, a sticky court case began in the sixth district court in Sacramento on February 3, 1875, and on April 19, 1875 the state supreme court declared the January 5 action of the state board null and void, although the state board had already ordered the new readers, geographies, and penmanship books. The supreme court decision was based on the fact that six months' notice of the proposed change had not been given.

In the meantime, the state board called for new bids on June 1, 1875, and proposed to reconsider bids of January 5, 1875, but they were enjoined from doing so by the county judge of Tehama County and the district judge of the fourteenth district. On December 13, 1875, a law was passed causing the old textbooks then in use to be the state-adopted textbooks. This ended the court's injunction, but it also temporarily ended the right of the state board to adopt textbooks. The legislature had taken over this job for the time being.

Ezra Carr, professor of agricultural chemistry and horticulture at the University of California, who had been elected to the state superintendency on the Republican ticket, was the innocent victim of this textbook scandal. In June, 1876, Carr was elected president of the California Teachers' Association, which hoped to save the principle of textbook adoption by the state board of education. But Carr's hands had been tied by the legislature just at the time when a revision of the constitution was in process. The constitution passed textbook adoption to the counties.

The whole affair became a political football, which temporarily returned all matters of textbooks and courses of studies to local districts and county boards of education and ultimately established the principle of free state textbooks, printed and furnished by the state of California. The first steps in this direction were taken by the constitutional convention of 1878–79. The Workingmen's party, organized by Dennis Kearney and C. C. O'Donnel, had 50 constitutional delegates who stood for free public schools, for emphasis on vocational education, and, above all, for free textbooks for all children of the state.

The educational committee of the convention proposed, among other things, that the state board of education be given power to fix a state course of study embracing reading, writing, spelling, arithmetic, geography, grammar, and history of the United States and in the higher classes some manual of government. But the committee did not want either the state board or the legislature to enforce uniformity of textbooks. This latter point was written into the constitution (Article IX), which assigned the adoption of textbooks to local boards of education and to the county superintendents, who were also to issue teaching certificates. The CTA had opposed all this decentralization in the new constitution.

After the new constitution was ratified on May 7, 1879 (by a vote of 77,952 to 67,134), the legislature required each county to have an appointed professional board of education that would certify teachers and adopt textbooks and courses of study.

When State Superintendent Fred M. Campbell was ending his term of office on December 28, 1882, he called a convention of all city and county superintendents in San Francisco. Many superintendents still preferred state adoption of textbooks, but they also wanted books printed by the state and issued free of charge to children.

The first step was achieved under Superintendent William T. Welcker, when a constitutional amendment was passed (Article IX, Section 7) to permit the state printing office to publish a state series of textbooks. This was the Perry Amendment, introduced by Senator George Perry of San Francisco, opposed by some public school teachers and administrators[3] but adopted by a majority of the electorate. Thereafter, the textbook situation in California was developed along the following lines.

1. In 1885, the legislators ordered the state board of education to adopt a state series of textbooks, although practically every county board had contracted for locally adopted textbooks for four years. On the request of Superintendent Welcker, State Attorney General Marshall ruled that county-adopted books should continue through the contractual period and that the state books were not the only ones that could be used legally. The state textbooks, incidentally, were being printed by the state printing office and sold to pupils at a price fixed by the state board, as the legislature had provided. Some details of this confused period are described by Cloud:[4]

> The man who put the new system of State-printed textbooks into operation was Colonel James J. Ayers, who was appointed in 1883 by Governor George Stoneman as Superintendent of State Printing. Colonel Ayers was a practical printer and a writer of considerable prominence. In his book *Gold and Sunshine, Reminiscence of Early California* he gives the arguments used by those who favored the Perry amendment. Their validity is hard to judge today, but they are given here simply to show the thinking in 1884 on the still vexing textbook problem. In part Colonel Ayers states:

> "The blighting effects of this combination [the schoolbook trust] were felt in every County in the State. Parents were not only obliged to pay extortionate prices for books, but the ring induced frequent and unnecessary changes in the series of textbooks used in the schools, and the parents would be compelled to buy a new set of books before the set their children already had were fairly worn—

> "I was called upon by the Legislature to make a report on the approximate cost the books could be furnished for by the state, and on the basis of this report a bill was drawn up and passed making the appropriations requisite for the State Board of Education to have a series of textbooks compiled."

[3] Roy Cloud, *Education in California* (Stanford, Calif.: Stanford Univ. Press, 1952), pp. 74 and 84.
[4] *Ibid.*, p. 85.

Colonel Ayers then describes his trip East, where he purchased a complete equipment of presses, type, bookbinding machinery, and an electro-typing outfit to duplicate the plates for the textbooks. He then states that with the delivery and installation of this material "the new departure in school books was inaugurated." He continues:

"It accomplished, almost from the beginning, the reform of the abuses that had so deeply entrenched themselves in the common school system, and purified it of the dangerous corruptions that were fastened upon it. Parents are now enabled to get the books at nearly cost price, and they are protected against the frequent and onerous charges which the greed of the school-book ring was in position to bring about."

Following the acquisition of the machinery for printing the State textbooks, the State Board of Education advertised for the submission of books which would be adopted. Local writers were favored, and, in a relatively short time, books in the various subjects were submitted. In their adoption, most series met the approval of the entire State Board.

The results of this controversy were that the state continued to adopt state series of textbooks, duplicating them from plates of the publishers. The confidence of local districts was restored when they were permitted to supply supplementary textbooks, although these were bought at local district expense.

2. In 1889, the CTA proposed legislation for free textbooks at local district expense, but the bill was vetoed.

3. California began to supply free basic textbooks for pupils in the elementary grade (1–8) in 1911. This practice still prevails, but supplementary textbooks can now be provided by the local district at district expense. The supplementary textbooks may not, however, be substituted for the state basic textbook.

4. Since 1917 the state has required secondary school districts to supply free textbooks to pupils at district expense. These books must be selected, however, from the approved list prepared by the state board of education.

From the foregoing discussion, it should be clear that textbooks adopted by the state and county boards of education were in effect the

California curriculum after 1880 and even from the superintendency of John Swett. Textbooks dominated the instructional programs not only in the public school classrooms but also in the normal schools, where the principal courses were concerned with the best use of existing books. In the struggle of county versus state control of texts and curriculum, the local district was the pawn and the state attained the dominating position. State control actually played into the hands of the Progressive Republicans elected in 1912.

Governor Hiram Johnson, with the support of a progressive legislature, promoted a series of education reforms, including the creation of the lay state board of education in its present form, the assignment of the state superintendent as executive secretary of the board, and the enlargement of the state department of education in elementary, secondary, and vocational education. These and other reforms opened a new era in curriculum development.

The Developmental Period (1910–1930)

After 1910, and particularly under Governor Johnson and State Superintendents Edward Hyatt and William C. Wood, the state school system experienced many new and modernizing improvements. First of all, the security of teachers was strengthened by a tenure law and a retirement system. The state department of education was enlarged to provide new statewide educational leadership, under which the state curriculum was developed, at first by the addition of new and experimental programs.

For example, the little-used junior college law was revived for junior college expansion, and junior high schools were legalized in 1915.[5] The new junior high school curriculum stressed instruction better fitted to the needs of adolescents and offered exploratory vocational courses in school shops and "domestic science" laboratories. The Smith-Hughes Act had given great encouragement to the state department in its endeavor to expand the vocational, agricultural, and home economics programs. Besides, kindergartens developed at local district expense, and the hiring of "home" teachers or tutors for handicapped pupils received legislative approval.

[5] Berkeley, California, and Columbus, Ohio, share the honor of experimenting with junior high school education as early as 1911.

Adult and continuation school programs developed rapidly after 1916 under the leadership of such men as Edward R. Snyder, a state department commissioner, and George Mann, chief of adult education. Rehabilitation of war veterans after 1920 and special schools and classes for the blind, deaf, and physically handicapped were begun under state and local district auspices.

The expansion of these and other scattered experimental programs with special curricula was given both unity and direction by the creation of California's first curriculum commission in October, 1927. The legislature sanctioned the creation of the commission by the state board of education, and the state board sought to use this appointed group of active teachers and school administrators to revise statewide curricula trends and to assist the board in the selection of state textbook series.

Another unifying influence over the massive but scattered curricular changes was the growing influence in California of John Dewey's experimentalism, or, as he preferred to call it, "instrumentalism." State department leaders, like Helen Heffernan (appointed commissioner of elementary education in 1926); city superintendents like John Sexson in Pasadena, Susan M. Dorsey in Los Angeles, Willard Givens in Oakland, Walter R. Hepner in San Diego; and county superintendents like Mark Keppel and Archie R. Clifton in Los Angeles led school districts and teaching staffs into the camp of progessive education. Schools of education, like that of Stanford University under the leadership of Ellwood Patterson Cubberley, were preparing teachers as supervisors in the experimental method of curriculum development geared to pupil needs. The California Congress of Parents and Teachers gradually threw its weight behind the new curriculum.

But the momentum of this unified program of experimentalism was suddenly though temporarily brought to a screeching halt by the stock market crash of 1929.

The Post-Depression Era (1935–1950)

As is usually the case when the economy is depressed, the financial needs of the state school systems took precedence over all other aspects of education from 1929 to 1935. There was much talk during these years about the cost of the diversified instructional program in California's counties and districts, as well as great interest in the elimination of "frills." Between 1930 and 1935, much of the legislature's interest and nearly all of the state board's interest in schools were concentrated on economies. The counties were in a still worse economic plight because of welfare programs. Though local school districts were occupied with budgets and salary schedules, as well as with federal emergency aid to education, it was the local district that made the greatest effort to save the instructional program. In fact, some of the new federal aid was turned into the creation of local district curriculum-improvement centers. So, if interest in the instructional program was kept alive in the 1930s, its most aggressive development was in local school districts and later in the county departments of education.

Some examples of these district and county school curriculum-revision programs are those of the Pasadena City Schools, of Santa Barbara County Schools, and of the San Diego Unified School District. In Pasadena, Superintendent Sexson ran an extensive experiment on a revised curriculum for a 6-4-4 school organization. The six-year elementary program was one of the standards in the state; but the four-year junior high school and the four-year senior high–junior college program called for new instructional programs. Santa Barbara County employed Paul R. Hanna of Stanford University in 1935 to reorganize the county courses of study. Dr. Hanna, formerly of Teachers College at Columbia University, had played an important role in the earlier statewide curriculum revision program in Virginia. Later, in 1938, he was employed as one of two chief consultants for the revision of the curriculum of the San Diego schools.

These local programs were supported, too, by consultancies, courses, and workshops in the schools of education of the University of California, University of Southern California, Claremont Graduate School, and other higher-education institutions of the state. The annual progressive education workshop at Claremont in and after 1939 provided specialists in curriculum improvement for teachers, school administrators, and coordinators of districts and counties involved in revisions of their instructional programs.

The state as a whole was then involved in the eight-year (1933–41) study of the Progressive Education Association through the participation of Berkeley's University High School and Los Angeles' Eagle Rock High School in this notable study. The study, it will be remembered, attempted to evaluate the comparative effectiveness of traditional and progressive high schools. Besides, the state was conducting its own thirty-school study (a little eight-year study) in California secondary schools.

The state legislature, although it was chiefly concerned in the 1930s with school finance, school organization, and the equalization of educational opportunities, did offer some general directives on school curricula. One important aspect of these directives was the development of legislation on required, prohibited, and permissive instruction for all the schools of the state.

Required, Permissive, and Prohibited Instruction

After 1880, county boards of education were required to prescribe annually a course of study for each elementary grade in the schools under their jurisdiction. Large city school districts have been specifically exempt from the curricular control of the county boards.

In the final analysis, however, the California governing body that has the freest hand with the public school curriculum and course of study is the state legislature. The legislature may require, permit, or forbid any course or type of instruction that it wishes, provided that it does not run contrary to the state or federal constitution.

Throughout most of our educational history, the legislature has used these extensive powers infrequently. It has chosen to sketch the major guideline and to leave specific details of curricular planning to the state board of education and to local boards, teachers, and school administrators. Yet the legislature since 1885 has been under pressure from the electorate and legislative lobbies to enact laws on what should or should not be taught in the schools of the state.

An early pressure on the legislature to require special instruction occurred in 1885, when the temperance movement was spreading in California. Not only were alcohol and tobacco banned from the school grounds, but eventually instruction in the evil effects of alcohol, narcotics, and tobacco was required (see the Education Code, Section 7852). The development of legislated curriculum in California can best be treated by a review of current required and prohibited instruction.

Immediately before and after World War I, lawmakers were induced to specify what must and what must not be taught in the public schools. Much of the legislation on courses of study was promoted and lobbied by special and vested interests and organized groups with a cause. Many if not most of these groups had laudable purposes.

Temperance groups, as already indicated, pressured the legislature for instruction on the effects of alcohol, tobacco, and narcotics on the human system. Physical education teachers through their organizations secured a legislative requirement of one hour of physical education a day from grade 7 through grade 12. Insurance companies promoted safety education and driver education. Veterans and patriotic organizations secured the legislation on the teaching of U.S. history, citizenship, and American institutions.

Scarcely anyone can quarrel with these courses, for they are worthy and desirable. A danger in this trend is that a full list of curricular requirements derived in this way may not add up to an integrated, unified, educational experience.

REQUIRED INSTRUCTION

The legislature has from time to time interested itself in the overall program of instruction, as we shall see in the next section. Our concern here, however, is with specifics as detailed in Part I, Division 7, Chapter 3, of the Education Code, which reads, "Specified required courses of study." These specified courses are best explained by the selected code sections now quoted:

1. *Training of Pupils in Morality and Citizenship*
   7851. Each teacher shall endeavor to impress upon the minds of the pupils the principles of morality, truth, justice, patriotism, and a true comprehension of the rights, duties, and dignity of American citizenship, including kindness toward domestic pets and the humane treatment of living creatures, to teach them to avoid idleness, profanity, and falsehood, and to instruct them in manners and morals and in the principles of a free government.

2. *Instruction in Manners and Morals; Effect of Alcohol and Narcotics*
   7852. Instruction upon the nature of alcohol and narcotics and their effects upon the human system as determined by science shall be included in the curriculum of all elementary and secondary schools. The governing board of the district shall adopt regulations specifying the grade or grades and the course or courses in which such instruction with respect to alcohol and narcotics shall be included. All persons responsible for the preparation or enforcement of courses of study shall provide for instruction on the subjects of alcohol and narcotics.

3. *Courses in History and Government*

7901. In all public and private schools located within the state, there shall be given regular courses of instruction in the Constitution of the United States, and in American history, including the study of American institutions and ideals. In all public and private schools located within the state, there shall be given instruction in the constitution of the State of California, and in California history and civics.

7902. Instruction in the courses required by Section 7901 shall begin not later than the opening of the eighth grade and shall continue in the high school course and in courses in state colleges, the universities, and educational departments of state, municipal, and private institutions, to an extent to be determined by the superintendent of public instruction.

7903. Basic instruction in geography, United States history, the Declaration of Independence, the Constitution of the United States, and in American institutions and ideals as prescribed by Sections 7901, 7902, and 7604 of this code shall be prerequisite to participation by pupils in advanced courses involving the study of problems in sociology, political science, economics, foreign trade, and foreign affairs.

4. *Instruction in Public Safety and Accident Prevention*

This instruction, with emphasis on "the avoidance of hazards upon streets and highways," is required in every elementary and secondary school of the state (Education Code 8001–8004).

5. *Fire Prevention*

A course of study in fire prevention dealing with the protection of lives and property is required in all elementary and secondary schools (Education Code 8051–8056).

6. *Driver Education and Driver Training*

There are two distinct types of this instruction. The first involves the rules, knowledge, habits, and attitudes of good automobile driving, while the second also includes behind-the-wheel driving and observation in dual control of automobiles. The first is required of all high school students; but the second has limited application, as follows.

8107. The governing board of the school district may prescribe regulations determining who can profit by and who shall receive instruction in automobile driver training, provided, however, that no pupil shall be permitted to enroll in automobile driver training unless such pupil is presently enrolled in a course of instruction in automobile driver education or has satisfactorily completed such course. The regulations shall be subject to such standards for driver education and driver training as may be prescribed by the state board of education.

No pupil under the age of 15 years and 6 months or who is not enrolled in either grades 10, 11, or 12 shall receive automobile driver training after July 1, 1960.

7. *Physical Education and Exercise*

8151.   Attention shall be given to such physical exercises for the pupils as may be conducive to health and to vigor of body, as well as mind, and to the ventilation and temperature of schoolrooms.

8155.   The aims and purposes of the courses of physical education established shall be as follows:

   a. To develop organic vigor.
   b. To provide neuromuscular training.
   c. To promote bodily and mental poise.
   d. To correct postural defects.
   e. To secure the more advanced forms of coordination, strength, and endurance.
   f. To promote such desirable moral and social qualities as appreciation of the value of cooperation, self-subordination, and obedience to authority, and higher ideals, courage, and wholesome interest in truly recreational activities.
   g. To promote a hygienic school and home life.
   h. To secure scientific supervision of the sanitation and safety of school buildings, playgrounds, and athletic fields, and the equipment thereof.

8159.   All pupils enrolled in the elementary schools, except pupils excused, shall be required to attend upon the courses of physical education for an instructional period in each school day, which shall be not less than 20 minutes exclusive of recesses and the lunch period.

8160.   All pupils enrolled in the junior or senior high schools, except pupils excused, shall be required to attend upon the courses of physical education for an instructional period in each school day, which shall be not less than the length of the regular academic periods of the school.

8161.   All pupils enrolled in the junior colleges, except pupils excused, shall be required to attend upon the courses of physical education for a minimum of 120 minutes per week. Where adequate facilities are available, a daily program is recommended.

8162.   The governing board of each district may grant temporary exemption to pupils who are ill or injured where a modified program to meet the needs of pupils cannot be provided and to pupils while enrolled for one-half, or less, of the work normally required of full-time students. Permanent exemption may be granted to a pupil who has reached his twenty-first birthday or a pupil who is enrolled as a postgraduate student. Exemptions are also made for students participating in R.O.T.C. and athletic programs.

PERMISSIVE INSTRUCTION

In California some courses are specifically required, as we saw above, and some types of instruction are prohibited in public schools, as we shall see below. Between the requirements and prohibitions lies a vast area of possible courses or programs that the state may merely permit. Some of these permitted programs of instruction can be given at local district expense only.

State control was never so loose that the local district could offer any course at any level, even though the district paid for it out of its own funds. As new areas of instruction developed or as new levels were opened, the state often showed its interest and gave its encouragement by making these areas or levels permissive.

So, in their day, evening school classes, adult education, kindergartens, agricultural education, junior high schools, and a number of innovations were not merely tolerated but specifically permitted by the legislature, particularly if these new areas were offered at local district expense. Obviously, some of what was at first permitted to local districts on an experimental basis has now become part of the regular statewide program and now receives state financial support. The following types of instruction, however, are still in the permissive category:

1. *Released Time for Religious and Moral Instruction.* This is not religious instruction in the schools, which was declared unconstitutional in the McCollum Case (Champaign, Illinois, 1940), but religious instruction given on school time but not on school property (Education Code 8201-1). This type of instruction is not widely used in California today (see page 160).

2. *Military Science and Tactics.* Specific permission is given for R.O.T.C. in California secondary schools (Code 8251).

3. *Instruction by Correspondence.* Correspondence courses, offered by the University of California or other colleges and universities accredited for teacher training, may be accepted by the state secondary schools for credit, provided the courses are a part of the students' program (Code 8301).

Besides the above, credit for work experience, aviation education, and field activities in outdoor science and conservation programs is permitted by code sections 8351-1, 8402, and 8425.

PROHIBITED INSTRUCTION

The state of California prohibits instruction that (1) reflects on pupils because of race, color, or creed; (2) has a sectarian, partisan, or denominational character; or (3) advocates communism. The code sections on these prohibitions are self-explanatory:

> *8451* No teacher in giving instruction, nor entertainment permitted in or about any school, shall reflect in any way upon citizens of the United States because of their race, color, creed, or national origin or ancestry.

> *8452* No textbook, chart, or other means of instruction adopted by the state, county, city, or city and county boards of education for its use in the public schools shall contain any matter reflecting upon citizens of the United States because of their race, color, creed, or national origin or ancestry.

> *8455* No teacher giving instruction in any school, or on any property belonging to any agencies included in the Public School System, shall advocate or teach communism with the intent to indoctrinate any pupil with, or inculcate a preference in the mind of any pupil for, communism.

> The Legislature in prohibiting the advocacy or teaching of communism with the intent to indoctrinate any pupil with, or inculcate a preference in the mind of any pupil for, such doctrine does not intend to prevent the teaching of the above subject but intends to prevent the advocacy of and inculcation and indoctrination into communism as is hereinafter defined, for the purpose of undermining the patriotism for, and the belief in, the government of the United States and of this State in the minds of the pupils in the Public School System.

> For the purposes of this section, communism is a political theory that the presently existing form of government of the United States or of this State should be changed, by force, violence, or other unconstitutional means, to a totalitarian dictatorship which is based on

the principles of communism as expounded by Marx, Lenin, and Stalin.

Finally, the Education Code includes among prohibited school experiences some activities that are cocurricular or even extracurricular. In this area, California's teachers and school administrators are prohibited from soliciting memberships or collecting funds for organizations not directly under the control of school authorities. This prohibition is obviously for the protection of pupils, parents, teachers, and school administrators. As a general rule, the boards of local school districts take annual or long-term action whereby they declare that such activities as school banking programs and the Junior Red Cross are an authorized part of the system's educational activities and that they are to be operated under the full control of school authorities. The state's prohibition against unauthorized membership campaigns and money-raising drives protects the boards and school authorities from many special groups that hope to use the organized efforts of the public schools to their own advantage. These endless drives, however worthy and socially valuable, dissipate the energies of teachers and pupils and often embarrass pupils from less affluent families. On their own local initiative, judicious school boards and administrators frequently limit the number of approved essay and art contests that a wide variety of clubs and organizations propose as cocurricular activities and make attractive by prizes and awards.

The Postwar Era (1946–1967)

From what has already been said about the instructional program in California, it should be patently clear that the state's curriculum has seldom been static for any long period of time. Almost every decade or score of years in our history has witnessed those instructional changes, at least, that were necessary to keep the curriculum abreast of the times. If this were true in the comparatively quiet and settled decades of the past, more rapid and revolutionary curricular changes could be expected during and after World War II, during the cold war era, and down to the present time. On the one hand, the moods of the California electorate and the legislature have evidenced changing attitudes on the instructional program; on the other hand, professional educators have made strenuous efforts toward the technical and sociological needs of our day. Selected examples of curricular change since 1946 will support this contention.

INSTRUCTIONS IN MORAL AND SPIRITUAL VALUES

During and immediately after World War II, a nationally felt need for improved instruction in morals, ethics, and human values occasioned some California experimentation and a renewed interest in this instructional area. Programs of released time for religious education were established, at least experimentally, after 1948.

In 1947, the U.S. Supreme Court had ruled that religious instruction of public school pupils in school buildings was unconstitutional.[6] Thereafter, some school districts in New York, California, and elsewhere tried the alternative of releasing children, on the request of their parents, for denominational instruction in the churches of their choice. The instruction was given during school hours but not on school premises and not by public school teachers.

This type of religious instruction was challenged in New York and this case, too (the Zorach Case of 1952), reached the U.S. Supreme Court. By a decision of six to three, the Supreme Court upheld the New York Court of Appeals in its judgment that release-time programs were not a violation of the U.S. Constitution's First Amendment and hence not unconstitutional.

Even before the Zorach decision, some California communities, the city of San Diego for one, established experimental or even extended programs of release time for religious education. There were, however, problems inherent in the program, such as administrative difficulties, a lack of parental enthusiasm, and positive opposition by some religious and denominational groups and by organizations devoted to the principle of church-state separation. So while the San Diego experiment was discontinued, other communities, mostly rural or with a fair amount of religious homogeneity, continued the programs for years.

It became apparent, however, that public schools would plow less controversial fields if they chose to cultivate a completely secular approach to offering instruction in morals, values, and human relation-

---

[6] See the case of the *People of Illinois ex rel. Vashti McCollum v. Board of Education of School District No. 71, Champaign County, Illinois, et al.* In 1940, the board offered optional religious instruction for pupils on the request of their parents. Mrs. McCollum sued the board and the case eventually reached the U.S. Supreme Court.

ships. John L. Childs of Teachers College at Columbia University had prepared an excellent guide for this type of instruction.[7] With this book and much other recent material, the instructional staffs of California's school districts and schools of education throughout the state have promoted value instruction by these among other means:

1. Instructional staffs of district and county offices have prepared teacher guides for instruction in values.[8]

2. In-service teacher-training programs in school districts and in college summer sessions have provided workshops and seminars on moral and spiritual values (at Occidental College), value instruction and human relationships (at San Diego State College), and other related topics.

3. There has been a noticeable increase in value considerations in a variety of preservice education courses—for example, in the philosophy and sociology of education (under axiology, ethics, and human relations), in psychology (personal adjustment), in health education (narcotics addiction and so on). These recent necessary stresses have been repeatedly encouraged by the Far Western Philosophy of Education Association.[9]

4. Owing to the recent availability of narcotics near and on school campuses, vulnerable school districts like Grossmont Union High School and Junior College Districts have mustered their full administration and instructional forces in the battles with narcotics addiction.

[7] *Education and Morals* (New York: Appleton-Century-Crofts, 1950).

[8] See *Spiritual Value*, San Diego City Schools 1948–54, and *The American Heritage Series* of the Department of Education, San Diego County. The five guides in the county series are: (1) How Every Teacher Can Emphasize Patriotic Occasions (1961), (2) Things to Think About, About America (1961), (3) Citizenship Education for Secondary Schools (1961), (4) Developing American Values in Our Schools (1961), and (5) Economic Education (1963).

[9] The association membership (professors of philosophy of education) has heard papers read and panel discussions on morals, values, and education in almost every annual meeting. Examples are: Fresno, California, 1962, "Morals, Morality, and Education"; Tempe, Arizona, 1963, "A Catholic Concept of Morality and Education," "Jewish Education and Its Moral Implication," and the philosophy of J. Bronowski as reflected in *Science and Human Values*; Hayward, California, 1964, "Man, Nature, and Religion"; San Fernando, California, 1965, "Buber and Education" and papers on the moral implication of extreme philosophies (logical positivism, existentialism, and the objectivism of Ayn Rand).

As a general rule, though, California's public schools have not created new courses on ethics and values, although there has been some experimentation with high school philosophy and ethics courses. More usually, value instruction is incorporated in social studies, health, and physical education courses. This is more in line with the state law that requires all California teachers at every grade level to give instruction in manners and morals.[10]

MATHEMATICS AND SCIENCE

An important educational side effect of the cold war is the increased interest in mathematics and science. This post-Sputnik effort "to keep up with the U.S.S.R." is not peculiar to California, but some shifts in emphasis in mathematics and recent developments in both mathematics and science seem characteristic of curricular development in this state. After 1938, the arithmetic program in the state's elementary schools went through this amazing series of changes:

1. The state curriculum commission and the bureau of elementary education had accepted the principle that children could learn arithmetic more rapidly and effectively when they had developed a readiness for it—that is, when they were more mature. Therefore, arithmetic in the first grade was kept entirely informal and the presentation of the fundamental processes was moved up in the grades.

2. Textbook plates purchased in the national market were revised to fit this principle, and the revision was not done particularly well. Obviously, the children in the primary grades and even in grades 4 and 5 could not be expected to attain the national testing norms, since instruction in some of the fundamental processes was delayed for them. This forced a heavy concentration of arithmetic skills in grades 6 through 8, for in these grades children were expected to measure up to national norms.

[10] Section 7851 of the Education Code reads: "Each teacher shall endeavor to impress upon the minds of pupils the principles of morality, truth and justice, patriotism and a true comprehension of the rights, duties and dignity of American citizenship, to teach them to avoid idleness and profanity, and falsehood, and to instruct them in manners and morals and in the principles of a free government." This is a law of long standing that was amended into the above form in the Statutes of 1963.

3. Since the slower learners and some average pupils could not master the heavy concentration of arithmetic in the sixth grade and junior high school, the whole program fell into disrepute. School districts created remedial courses in arithmetic and stressed "basic mathematics" in senior high schools. Some districts developed and administered basic arithmetic tests for pupils in the sixth, eighth, and eleventh grades. Pupils who failed in these tests were required to take remedial courses or "basic mathematics" in grades 7, 9, or 11.

4. By the end of World War II, a new state series with a more "normal" (that is, more commonly accepted) grade placement of arithmetic skills was adopted. The new series no longer confused elementary teachers with such techniques as the additive method of subtraction. However, in the 1950s, the security of older teachers was again threatened by the introduction of the concepts and techniques of "new mathematics." This necessitated a reorganization of preservice methods courses and a new emphasis on in-service teacher training.

5. The ultimate effects of the last shift were to reverse the 1930–40 trend of upgrading the introduction of arithmetic processes. Elementary and junior high school pupils are now introduced to these processes and even to algebraic and geometric concepts earlier than they were in the past.

In the related field of science, the upgrading and modernization of instruction were intended not only to improve the secondary and junior college program but to lay a firm foundation for scientific studies in the elementary grades and junior high schools. Perhaps the most heartening part of science instruction in California schools in recent years is the emphasis on science in the elementary grades and on the biological and physical sciences in the junior high schools.

The now-popular district and countywide science fairs have proved an incentive to science instruction at all grade levels and to a truly scientific approach to the problems of the biological and physical world. The fairs encourage and publicize the individual pupil's selection and solution of a problem of his own choice. Under the guidance of science teachers, elementary and secondary school pupils establish their method of attack on their chosen problems and have an opportunity, when the job is well done, to prove to the public what they have proven to their own satisfaction. The emphasis is of course on the scientific method as opposed to the memorization of textbook data.

LANGUAGE INSTRUCTION

The extensive use of the audiolingual method and language laboratories in foreign language programs and in the teaching of English as a second language (the ESL program) is by and large an outgrowth of World War II. Since the war took thousands of servicemen into many foreign countries, it suddenly became important that many Americans gain a rapid and effective use of languages as widely different as German, Italian, Russian, and Japanese. While California deserves no special credit for the development of these programs, it is fair to admit that alert educational officers of the U.S. Navy and the Marine Corps in California were experimenting in 1941 with the then-simple audio equipment in their training programs. Long before the Monterey language school gained prominence, the direct and conversational method was giving a new direction to language instruction.

In time these early crash programs enlisted the services of native speakers of foreign tongues, of a new breed of linguistics and of the growing electronics industry. This was a great boon for language teachers. They would no longer have to justify their existence on the basis that language instruction trained the mind (through the intricacies of grammar and syntax), that it was necessary particularly for college preparation, or that young people could be introduced to other cultures through the language of these cultures.

Foreign language instruction suddenly became a practical and very important business. Besides, the ESL program, which had proved itself effective abroad, was discovered (or perhaps rediscovered) by California teachers. Twice before (in 1916 and again during the FEEP days of the 1930s) serious attention was given to "English for the foreign-born" in adult education classes. But now it is recognized that we have a young "foreign-born" element at home—children whose first language is Spanish or Portuguese or Chinese. It had been known for a long time that these children did not always fare so well with normal English instruction, but now there was a readiness and an opportunity to do something about it.

After 1950, and particularly after 1955, California school districts, teacher-training institutions, and county and state education departments developed new enthusiasm for audiolingual methods in foreign language instruction, language laboratories, and the new ESL program. It was an expensive program for teachers who needed special training or retraining and for school districts that needed language laboratories or at least less expensive portable classroom equipment; but this did not keep the legislature from getting into the act. As will become evident, foreign language instruction became a state requirement in the elementary grades.

The development of the ESL program was long overdue. It has particular value today, however, for it can be used and in part supported by the compensatory education program and it serves well in English instruction in the inter-American "*Amigos*" exchanges, now popular in the secondary schools of California and in the instruction of exchange students at the college level. The foreign language requirement seems more important today, too, since the opportunities for travel abroad have increased and the uses for Spanish in California are many.

Californians today, including legislators, are in the mood to pit the academic against the practical, and the cockfights have become popular at all levels from the elementary grades to the graduate school. In elementary schools, foreign languages have gained respectability, whereas the social studies, when taken en masse, have lost it. Individual social studies like geography and history seem worthy enough at all levels. At the secondary and junior college level, no great head of steam has developed to move vocational and occupational courses forward on the instructional tracks, since these do not rank high academically. In their new enthusiasm for the academic, Californians in considerable numbers have welcomed the apparent decline of experimentalism.

On the national scene, experimentalism in education, particularly as it was expressed in the progressive education philosophy of John Dewey, had absorbed a series of attacks by the Navy's Vice Admiral Hyman George Rickover, Arthur Bestor of the University of Illinois, Robert Maynard Hutchins of Chicago University, Mortimer Adler, and the Council for Basic Education. In the 1950s, one of the chief California spokesmen for this conservative position was Max Rafferty, district superintendent and then state superintendent.

In California by the middle 1950s the controversy had centered around two major areas—namely, teacher education and "Deweyism," or "adjustment education." Teachers, it was said, were well instructed in methods (how to teach) but not so well instructed in their special subject areas (what to teach), and adjustment education neglected thoroughness in academic training. Under particular attack were "education courses" in schools. A further attack was launched on frills and on ineffective academic work.

In the late 1950s the chief educational concerns of the state legislature and of Governor Edmund J. Brown was financial. Secondary concerns for school district reorganization and equalized educational opportunities were in effect part of the financial problem. Furthermore, a school system that proposed to be economical would, in any man's book, be one that eliminated frills and ineffective schoolwork. There was, therefore, a revived interest at the state level in the general courses of study that specify "required and allowed" instruction in the elementary and secondary schools of the state (see the Education Code, Vol. I, Division 7, Chapter 2, Sections 7601–7760, pp. 349–56).[11]

The state's revived interest in the general courses was expressed in Assembly Bill No. 2564 of July, 1961. This bill was an amendment of the general courses of study. It was designed to specify academic areas of instruction, to break down the social studies into distinct subjects, and to separate English from the social studies. It further called for the teaching of the principles of grammar and a variety of literature in English classes, for foreign language instruction for all children, and for thoroughness in teaching. Since the 1961 law is an amendment of the code, only the pertinent changes of specific sections will now be quoted.

ASSEMBLY BILL NO. 2564
(*Approved by Governor July 20, 1961*)
Filed with Secretary of State
(*July 21, 1961*)

The People of the State of California Do Enact as Follows:

Section 1   Section 7604 of the Education Code is amended to read:

7604   The course of study in the elementary schools shall include instruction in the following prescribed branches in the several grades in which each is required pursuant to this article (commencing at Section 7601):

---

[11] Chapter 2 on the general courses of study precedes the chapters on specified, required, prohibited, and permissive instruction, which we have already discussed in this section.

a. Beginning in grade 1, and continuing through grade 6 or 8, as the case may be, instruction shall be given in all of the following: (1) reading; (2) writing; (3) spelling; (4) arithmetic, with emphasis on basic principles and techniques.

b. Beginning not later than grade 4 and continuing through grade 6 or 8, as the case may be, instruction shall be given in all of the following: (1) English as a separate subject with emphasis on thoroughness, and as a discipline separate from the subject of social studies; (2) geography; (3) history, including the early history of California and the history of the United States.

c. Beginning not later than grade 6, and continuing through grade 6 or 8, as the case may be, instruction shall be given in all of the following: (1) civics; (2) a foreign language or languages; (3) natural science; (4) health.

d. The course of study in the elementary schools shall include instruction, in the grade or grades prescribed by the county board of education of the city, county, or city and county, in all of the following: (1) art; (2) music; (3) such other studies, not to exceed three, as may be prescribed by the board of education of the city, county, or city and county.

Notwithstanding other provisions of this section to the contrary, a foreign language or languages may be but is not required to be included in the course of study in the elementary schools until June 30, 1965, and on and after July 1, 1965, such course of study shall include a foreign language beginning not later than grade 6 and continuing through grade 6 or 8, as the case may be.

The legislature declares that it is the policy of the state to foster and encourage foreign language programs in the elementary and secondary schools by which the children of California learn to speak and write foreign languages with the same facility with which children educated in schools of other countries speak and read foreign languages, in order that the children of California be adequately prepared to undertake their duties as American citizens in a world in which the ability to communicate with peoples of other countries in their own tongue is of ever increasing importance.

7700   The course of study for grades 7 and 8 of each elementary school, and for each junior high school, high school, or grades 11 and 12 of a four-year junior college shall be prepared under the direction of the governing board having control thereof and shall be subject to the approval of the State Board of Education. The course of study shall meet the requirements of this section. In addition to courses otherwise required by law, the course of study shall require of all pupils in grades 7 to 12, inclusive:

    a. Five years of instruction in the use of English, designed to teach the student to read rapidly and perceptively, to write clearly and correctly, and to present ideas orally. Such instruction shall include the principles of grammar and punctuation as instruments of reading and writing. Also a core of reading designed to familiarize the student with the variety of literary forms and to improve his reading ability shall be taught.

    b. Five years of history commencing with grade 7, to include all of the following: (1) twenty semester periods of American history emphasizing American institutions and ideals, and California history; (2) twenty semester periods of world history, the history of Western civilization, and world geography; (3) ten semester periods of American government emphasizing principles of the Constitution and the Declaration of Independence, and the principles of state and local government under the Constitution of this state.

For purposes of the history requirements prescribed by subdivision (b), in the case of schools which are not operated on the basis of semester periods, the time devoted to the respective courses shall be, as nearly as practicable, the equivalent of the required time as measured in terms of semester periods, and the State Board of Education shall, by regulation, prescribe the manner in which time during the school year shall be allocated for such purposes in those schools.

7701 The course of study for grade 7 and 8 of an elementary school and for junior high school shall be designed to fit the needs of pupils of the 7th and 8th, or of the 7th, 8th, and 9th, or of the 7th, 8th, 9th, and 10th grades and shall be designed to meet the requirements of Section 7700 so that upon completion of grade 12 any pupil will have completed the courses required by Section 7700.

7702 The course of study for grades 7 and 8 of an elementary school and for junior high school comprising the 7th and 8th grades only shall be designed to fit the needs of pupils of the 7th and 8th grades but shall be designed to meet the requirements of Section 7700, so that upon completion of grade 12 any pupil will have completed the courses required by Section 7700.

7751   The course of study for grades 11 and 12 of a four-year junior college shall be designed to meet the needs of pupils of the 11th and 12th grades of the public schools and shall be designed to meet the requirements of Section 7700, so that upon completion of grade 12 any pupil will have completed the courses required by Section 7700.

7752   The course of study for four-year high schools shall be designed to fit the needs of pupils of the 9th, 10th, 11th, and 12th grades of the public schools and shall be designed to meet the requirements of Section 7700 so that upon completion of grade 12 any pupil will have completed the courses required by Section 7700.

7754   The course of study for senior high schools shall be designed to fit the needs of pupils of the 10th, 11th, and 12th, or of the 11th and 12th grades, and shall be designed to meet the requirements of Section 7700 so that upon completion of grade 12 any pupil will have completed the courses required by Sections 7604 and 7700.

It is interesting to note that the chief criticism of the above law by school board members and school administrators concerned the requirement of foreign language teaching in all elementary schools for almost all elementary pupils. The main reason for this criticism lay in the lack of elementary teachers prepared to do the job.

A major effect of the 1961 law was, however, the tightening of state controls over the instructional program. The next and somewhat indirect state control over the curriculum was the Fisher Act revising requirements for state teachers' credentials. This bill will be discussed in Chapter 5.

THE CALIFORNIA TEACHER—

HIS TRAINING, CREDENTIALS,

AND PROFESSIONAL ORGANIZATION

During the three days after Christmas in 1854, State Superintendent Paul K. Hubbs conducted the first California state teachers' meeting in San Francisco. Approximately 100 teachers from many California settlements attended. Not more than 20 percent of these teachers were normal-school trained (that is, had attended normal schools for a year or two after graduating from elementary schools). Of the remaining 80 percent, some would have had only an eighth-grade diploma.

In contrast to this motley mass of poorly trained teachers, Superintendent Hubbs was a liberally educated lawyer. A native of New Jersey, Hubbs was then 54 years old. He had secured legislative sanction for this state meeting that he intended to use to share the problems of school finance with his teachers. It was also an occasion to discuss textbook needs, courses of study, and teaching methods. However, never having taught school himself, Hubbs approached the meeting as a politician bent on creating public enthusiasm for the new school system. As a businessman, he was furious at the meager state apportionments ($38,187 for 1854) and at the teachers' salaries, which dropped from an average of $955 per year to as little as $58.32 (probably for the minimum term).

The pioneer teachers attending the meeting in San Francisco were therefore not an affluent lot. For many of them teaching was not the only source of income. What they lacked in financial return, however, they made up for in hopes and in their zeal to improve the lot of the California educator. The chief result of the San Francisco conference was a sense of unity that held the teachers of California together in a state system. Before 1854, most pioneer teachers worked in small groups or even alone in isolated communities. The earliest of these pioneers began teaching before, during, or immediately after the Mexican War.

Pioneer Teachers—
Their Training and Certification

The historical records of early California communities often feature the first schoolmaster or schoolmarm. There are available, therefore, many choice bits of information about early California teachers and some striking examples of great courage and of extraordinary enthusiasm for the development of schools in this one-time Wild West.[1] A few examples of some of these pioneers and of their work follow.

Monterey will not let us forget the place of the Hartnell family in its educational history. William Hartnell, a Britisher, came to Monterey in 1834, married into a Mexican family, and fathered 21 sons and daughters. Hartnell, in many ways an unusual man, opened a school near Monterey, which he variously dubbed El Colegio de San José and El Seminario Patricinio. Something of a rover in his early days, he had both a good education and a fairly adequate command of at least six languages. So, with little aid from his hired help, he offered a curriculum of the 3 R's, English and Spanish grammar, German and Latin studies, philosophy, bookkeeping, and Christian doctrine. Adherence to the faith of the *padres* was required of teachers by Mexican law.

An early teacher of a quite different character was Reverend S. V.

---

[1] See the records of local historical societies; William Warren Ferrier, *Ninety Years of Education in California* (Berkeley, Calif.: Sather Gate Book Shop, 1937); and Roy Cloud, *Education in California* (Stanford, Calif.: Stanford Univ. Press, 1952).

Blakelee, a graduate of Western Reserve College who came overland in 1849 and opened a school in San Jose. His classes met in a massive tent of blue drilling used in the mining regions. In an early letter about Blakelee's school, San Jose's Reverend J. W. Douglass noted: "By the way, Mr. Blakelee is taking among the Mestizos as a teacher. He makes them sing the multiplication tables and 'Morning Bells,' etc., and gets along with their tempers, etc.; and I believe is a good teacher." [2]

Many pioneer teachers were men of the cloth, women of the veil, or persons of missionary propensities. They sprang from every conceivable denominational stock—Baptist, Catholic, Congregationalist, Episcopal, Methodist (including the African M.E. branch), Mormon, Presbyterian (both "old school" and "new school"), United Brethren, and associates of the American Bible, Home Missionary, and Tract Societies and of the Dutch Reformed Church.

In May, 1854, J. J. Moore, a Negro, opened a school for colored children in the basement of St. Cyprian's A.M.E. Church in San Francisco. The original enrollment of 23 pupils soon increased to 44. Many of these pioneer teachers found themselves in the classroom by sheer accident. Some had the scantiest preparation for their new venture; others were well trained by the standards of the time—graduates of high schools, academies, normal schools, or even of eastern colleges and universities.

Among the best trained were the clergymen and missionaries who chose to use their spare time and supplement their meager salaries by teaching school. At the opposite extreme were men like William Marston, a devout Mormon elder with scarcely rudimentary preparation for teaching. In his own writing, his carefully dotted capital "I's" were only one peculiarity in a most unusual system of capitalization. As a speller he was, to say the least, unconventional. But this was insignificant in the San Francisco of 1848, for the chief course in the curriculum was manners and morals, because the chief purpose of the school was to make decent young people out of potential rowdies. As a result, the first qualification of a teacher was his own decency and uprightness. And all of this was itself in the true New England tradition, where clergymen had long qualified teachers on the basis of their moral character.

No account of pioneer teachers of character could omit reference

[2] The letter is quoted from Ferrier, *op. cit.*, p. 47. We have no idea what the "etc." signify.

to Olive Isbell Mann, who is reputed to have opened "the first American school in California." Olive Isbell, born in Ashtabula County, Ohio, in 1824, married Dr. Isaac Mann, who traveled with his bride in 1846 in a wagon train from Mt. Pleasant, Iowa, to Sutter's Fort and then to Santa Clara. John C. Frémont gave members of the Mann party temporary lodgings in the dilapidated Santa Clara mission buildings, one of which, a stable, was used by Mrs. Mann for a school. Boxes were used for desks and a stone floor in the center of the room was the hearth, from which smoke ascended through a leaky roof. Her hand was the only available slate and a lead pencil the only school supply. She taught 25 children for two months, after which Isaac Mann built Monterey's first hotel and she opened a school in a room of the old adobe custom house of Monterey. The enrollment there grew from 25 to 56 before the Manns moved to French Camp to raise cattle. Olive Isbell Mann died in Santa Paula on March 25, 1899. She had long been counted the dean of California public school teachers.

Her masculine counterpart in this deanship was undoubtedly John Swett, the son of a New England schoolmaster, who served successively and successfully as an elementary schoolteacher, principal, state superintendent of public instruction, and then as a high school teacher in San Francisco. He also served in various capacities in the California Teachers' Association. At the 1913 commencement of the University of California, President Wheeler conferred the L.L.D. degree on John Swett, remarking that "it will show this venerable educator that from the lowest to the highest of our educational institutions acknowledgment is freely made of his service to the state and the nation." Scarcely two months later, on July 31, he enjoyed his eighty-third birthday at his home in Contra Costa County, amid his family, friends, and old associates. On August 22 he died, leaving a life whose motto had been, "Be ashamed to sleep without having accomplished some worthy deed." In November, 1921, John F. Swett, Jr., deposited the books and papers of his father in the library of the University of California. These papers are a treasure of early California's educational history.

Swett had come to California originally to mine for gold, but he was appointed a teacher in Rincon School in San Francisco in 1853 and became its principal in 1854. He was both an idealist and a happy warrior in the cause of education. In the spirit of Horace Mann, Swett carried his curriculum and achievements to the people. At Rincon School, parents and other San Francisco citizens were able to witness the outcome of the curriculum. To prove that his courses of study were bringing results, Swett held spelling bees and other public exercises, including the examination of pupils before their parents, recitations, and songs, some of which he composed himself. Swett brought a mixture of idealism, pedantry, and New England background to this hymn, which he wrote and had his pupils sing for their parents:

> Great God protect the common school,
>   That glorious birthright of the free,
> The guerdon of the people's rule,
>   Palladium of liberty.
>
> Here may free children come and learn
>   To emulate their patriot sires,
> And Freedom's altars ever burn
>   With Liberty's unsullied fires.
>
> Eternal source of truth and light,
>   Our joyful thanks to thee we raise,
> And consecrate with new delight
>   The schoolhouse by our songs of praise.
>
> Our hymns and prayers ascend to thee
>   That we are made no tyrant's tool,
> Free sons and daughters of the free,
>   Free children of the common school.

But this display of erudition and idealism gives only one side of Swett's character. He had a very human and Yankee business side, too. He was able to talk to his pupils, his school boards, and the public in terms of the rough realities of his day. When he was earning $2,000 a year as principal of Rincon School, he was being paid in city scrip, which was always discounted—usually 5 to 10 percent, but up to 40 percent at times. This prompted his anonymous poem, "Random Rhymes for School Teachers by a Poor Ped," in a local paper:

> As well suppose that a game of euchre
> Will fill your pockets with filthy lucre,
> As think that teaching the city's scholars
> Will line your pocket with silver dollars.
> Mum is the word, and nothing to say;
> Live "on faith" and expect no pay.

Swett rarely tired of telling school boards that their courses of study and their instructional programs could be only as good as the teachers and textbooks they could find and were willing to pay for. Swett did not have the opportunity to create the first normal school in California, but he did create the original state board of examiners and a substantial system of diplomas and certificates for teachers.

The Evolution of Teacher Training in California

It should be remembered that the first state normal school in the United States was established in Lexington, Massachusetts, in 1839 and that there were but seven state normal schools in the whole country by the end of 1854. When teacher-training classes for elementary teachers were set up in San Francisco in 1862, this state normal was the thirteenth in the United States—only Massachusetts, New York, Connecticut, Michigan, New Jersey, Illinois, Pennsylvania, and Minnesota (that is, only nine of the existing 31 states) had state normals before California.

California's desperate problem of getting qualified teachers in the 1850s and 1860s caused Superintendents Andrew J. Moulder and Swett to propose these measures to the state legislature: (1) the creation of a state board of examiners for teachers in 1859; (2) the establishment of a state normal school in 1859; (3) the establishment and financing of state teachers' conventions and state and county institutes for teachers in the 1850s, 1863, and 1866; (4) the formation of a state board of normal-school trustees in 1863; and (5) the creation of teaching diplomas (credentials) in 1863 and life diplomas after 10 years of service in 1866.

The development of state normal schools in California followed this sequential pattern:

1862 Normal-school classes were opened in San Francisco.

1872 The first normal school was moved from San Francisco to San Jose. (It eventually became San Jose State College.)

1882 Los Angeles State Normal was created. This school was later developed into a four-year state teachers' college and eventually, in 1919, became UCLA (the Westwood campus was developed later).

1889 The Northern California State Normal was established
Chico.

1897 San Diego State Normal was established at Fifth and
Streets in San Diego. (Dr. Samuel Black left the state superintendenc
to become the first principal [president] of San Diego State.)

1899 San Francisco State Teachers' College was created (the pre
ent San Francisco State College).

Until 1900 normal schools in California offered two-year teacher
training courses after graduation from the eighth grade. As in othe
states, the normal-school courses were lengthened to three years, an
admission was then granted only to high school graduates. When th
four-year program began in 1925, the normal schools were classified a
state teachers' colleges. They remained training schools for teacher
only, until they became state colleges with departments other tha
the education department. Here is the sequence:

1908 Santa Barbara State Teachers' College was created. Thi
school became the University of California's Santa Barbara campus i
1948 and moved its location to Goleta, California.

1911 Fresno State College was created.

1913 Humboldt State College was established at Arcata in Hum
boldt County.

1947 Los Angeles, Long Beach, and Sacramento State college
were created.

1957 San Fernando State College was created out of an extensio
program of Los Angeles State in San Fernando Valley.

1959 San Diego State College began teacher training in Imperia
Valley. The State College of Alameda County at Hayward was create

1967 The nineteenth college in the state college system was ap
proved for opening in 1970. The location is to be in Kern County
near Bakersfield. A president was appointed to set up plans in th
summer of 1967.

Thus, there are now 19 campuses in the state college system, to be
examined in detail in Chapter 6.

In the 1890s, when most teacher training in California was pro-
vided in the normal schools, the University of California and Stanford
University established schools of education. As early as 1880, the an-
nual convention of the California Teachers' Association passed a reso-

lution urgently requesting that a department of education be established at the state university. This was done in the 1890s, and in 1905
the CTA annual convention urged the establishment of a practice or
laboratory school on the Berkeley campus. It is interesting to note that
Ellwood Patterson Cubberley left the superintendency of the San Diego
city schools to begin another new department of education at Stanford
University in 1898.

THE LICENSING OF TEACHERS

A summary of the development of teacher certificates, credentials, and licenses in California can be sketched as follows:

1852 Examination for teachers was first required by the state.

1859–60 County superintendents were authorized to appoint
county boards of examiners with the right to grant one-year county
certificates to teachers.

1863 Legislation provided for (1) state educational diplomas
(valid for six years), (2) first-grade certificates (valid for four years),
(3) second-grade certificates (valid for four years), (4) third-grade
certificates (valid for two years). An oath of allegiance was required
of all persons receiving certificates.

1866 *Life diplomas* were provided for teachers with 10 years of
experience.

1874 Equal salary was to be paid to both men and women if they
held the same certificates.

1879 County board of education was granted the right to certify
teachers.

1887 A Grammar School Course Certificate permitted the holder
to teach in any California high school.

In 1893, the legislature offered grammar-grade certificates to normal-
school graduates, and a system of life diplomas was created for credentialed or certificated teachers after a number of years' experience.
An 1897 supreme court ruling (*Mitchell v. Winnek,* 117 Cal. 520)
confirmed the legislature's right to prescribe the qualifications needed
for teaching credentials, even though Article IX of the constitution
gave county superintendents and county boards the control over
teachers' examinations and teaching certificates.

On April 12, 1900, a special California Educational Commission made these recommendations regarding the certification of teachers:

1. No changes should be made that impair the validity of existing certificates, and such certificates should be renewable as heretofore.
2. Statistics show that the formal examination as a basis for certification is becoming obsolete and that the credential basis is rapidly increasing in favor. Also, that our professional training schools are supplying as many teachers as the schools require.
3. The large excess of certificated teachers in the State makes it practicable to raise the requirements for teachers' certificates.
4. (a) High school certificates should be issued on credentials only; (b) elementary, kindergarten, and special certificates should be based on credentials or on examinations in accordance with higher standards than now prevail; such examinations should be held not oftener than once a year; (c) the issuance of primary certificates and of educational diplomas should be discontinued.[3]

The educational commission likewise recommended that the completion of a high school course or its equivalent be required for admission to state normal schools. This recommendation was enacted into the state law in April, 1902, but the effective date of the law was set as July, 1906. By this time, the minimum educational requirements for all candidates for teaching were established, but the licensing of teachers was still confused.

The counties had constitutional authority to "certificate" elementary school teachers, and this authority was extended in 1879 to "grammar-grade" certificates. However, the supreme court in 1897 recognized the right of the legislature to establish qualifications for state teaching "credentials." Thereafter, a teacher could be licensed by either a county certificate or a state credential. Today, California teachers need both state credentials and a certificate from the county in which they are employed, but county certification is achieved by the mere filing of state credentials in the county office. The changes from older forms of licensing to current practice came gradually in this order.

The state developed "general elementary" and "general secondary" teaching credentials before 1920, which permitted the teacher to teach any subject at the level indicated, elementary or secondary. In addition, because of teacher shortages during and after World War I, "special teaching credentials" were developed in adult education, art,

[3] Cloud, p. 102.

some economics, industrial arts, and physical education. The requirements for "special credentials" in these special fields were less stringent
than those for general credentials.

In and after the 1920s, therefore, California-certificated employees
fell into one or another of these categories: (1) Teachers with general
elementary credentials were permitted to teach any subject in any elementary grade (1–8). (2) Teachers with general secondary credentials
were permitted to teach any subject (regardless of their majors and
minors) in any secondary school in grades 9–14. (3) Teachers with
the more recent "general junior high" credential were permitted to
teach any subject in grades 7–9 of either elementary or secondary
schools. (4) "Special credential" teachers were permitted to teach in
their areas of specialization in junior or senior high school or in an
adult class if they held adult education credentials.

Besides the above, a "general administrative" credential was devised
to cover all school administration from the superintendency to princi-
palships and vice-principalships, and "a general kindergarten-primary
credential" was available for teachers who wished to teach classes from
the kindergarten through grade 3. Thereafter, particularly in the
1920s, the variety of state credentials began to multiply as did the detailed specification of educational requirements for each credential.
Many subdivisions of special credentials and credentials for school
administration and supervision began to appear.

With the multiplication of special credentials and the creation of
limited administration credentials—for example, for elementary or
secondary principals and for supervision and the direction of instruction—the whole credential system became very complicated. The com-
plication was intensified by the addition of credentials for school
nurses, librarians, and special types of teachers. Finally, the bookkeeping on credential requirements in the state department of education,
in colleges of education, and even in county offices and local district
offices became very complex, arduous, and confusing. By 1950, therefore, the state board and state department of education, school administrators, and the California Teachers' Association were searching for
a drastic simplification of the credentialing of teachers, which had
earlier been complicated still more by county teaching certificates issued for use within a given county.

Much consultation followed in many association committees and in
governmental agencies. A number of widely varying plans for new
credentials were proposed. Some proposals called for the original basic

three credentials (elementary, secondary, and administration); others proposed five, six, or more basic credentials. Differences of professional opinion developed just when the legislature, in a conservative mood, had become very critical of teacher-education courses and enthusiastic for a highly structured academic training for all teachers, including elementary and kindergarten-primary teachers. The result was the highly controversial Senate Bill No. 57, which produced the Fisher Act that Governor Brown signed and filed with the secretary of state in 1961.

Under the Fisher Act the old system of general and special credentials was discontinued in favor of this set of standard credentials:

1. The standard teaching credential with specialization in elementary, secondary, and junior college teaching. Five years of college preparation are required, although the fifth year can be completed by an elementary teacher during the first five years of his teaching experience. The prospective teacher is required to have an academic major and minor other than the education major heretofore accepted for elementary teachers. Secondary teachers and junior college instructors are permitted to teach in their major and minor fields only, though they may teach their specialties in the elementary or junior high school grades.

2. The standard designated-subject credential, which qualifies the teacher for work in that subject area only, also requires five years of college preparation. Here again the teacher credentialed in a special area may teach his subject in elementary, junior high, and high schools and in junior colleges.

3. The standard designated-services credential may be given after five years of college work to prospective workers in pupil-personnel (guidance, counseling, and so on) and health services. School nurses were already required to hold an R.N. and a public health nursing diploma.

4. The standard supervision credential, requiring six years of college preparation, is required for principals, vice principals, and supervisors.

5. The standard administration credential is reserved for central office administrators—superintendents (state, county, and district) and school business executives who have completed seven years of college preparation for their work.

In addition, the Fisher Act set a ceiling on the number of education courses (social and psychological foundations, methods, testing, evaluation, curriculum courses, and the like) that a candidate for teaching may be required to take. Considerable stress is placed on general education and academic majors and minors for all credential programs from the standard elementary to the standard administration credentials.

Precise definitions of what constitutes an academic (nonpractical) course have been attempted, though they have been subject to criticism and varied interpretation. In general, courses in natural and social sciences, humanities, mathematics, and fine arts have been specified as academic, which is not the case with practical courses in agriculture, business, health, home economics, industrial arts, and physical education.

The number of professional education courses permitted in a credential program have been scaled down from 12 units for elementary teachers to two for junior college applicants. Though these state guidelines may be varied by individual colleges certified for recommending credential candidates, the general education and academic requirements are such that little room is left for normal teacher preparation as it was understood in California up to 1960.

What professional educators considered to be the normal teacher-education program was precisely the bone of contention between those who favored and those who opposed the Fisher Act. The proponents of the bill contended that the chief aspect of teacher education was to prepare candidates academically in their major and minor subject areas. So the chief purpose of the bill was to limit so-called methods courses or education courses. The contention of professional educators, on the other hand, was that the academic preparations of teachers, while essential, does not assure success in teaching and that the successful teacher must also have an understanding of children and youth (educational psychology, child growth, and development), must serve as a guide and counselor to young people (guidance and counseling) and as a competent instructor (methods), and must be a fair evaluator of pupil achievements (tests and measurement).

In this controversy between the academically minded and the professional educator, the proponents of the Fisher bill aligned themselves with the academic or conservative viewpoint; and they did effect a radical change in teacher education in California. The full details of this change in the preparation of teachers for California schools are specified in 16 pages of legislation—Sections 13187–13199 and 13292 of the California Education Code of 1965—and represent the original and much-amended Fisher Act, including the 1965 Senate Bill No. 908, which again amends the above sections.

Although there is as yet no simple and sure interpretation of the Fisher Act, Bass and Wolpert[4] detail the situation as it was understood in 1963.

Professional Organization and the Status of Teachers

Since 1851, California's state superintendents of public instruction have called upon the pooled resources of the assembled body of California teachers to aid in the development of the state's educational system. Although there was no plan in the 1850s to create a state association of public school teachers, the steps taken by the state superintendents and the legislature inevitably led to the formation of such an association.

With the benefit of hindsight and ample documentation, we will trace the progress toward the formation and development of the California Teachers' Association.

STATE TEACHERS' MEETINGS

1. In 1851 the state legislature permitted annual meetings of teachers.

2. Superintendent Paul K. Hubbs called the first annual meeting in San Francisco on December 26–28, 1853. Because of travel conditions and scarce lodgings in San Francisco, only 100 teachers attended. In a Benecia meeting on August 12, 1856, 60 teachers discussed (a) a uniform system of schools in California communities, (b) the place and value of women teachers in public schools, (c) Bible reading in public schools (recommended by the teachers).

3. Although the state meetings could not be held every year, when they were held California teachers had the opportunity to discuss these topics, among others and to make their suggestions to the state super-

---

[4] Theodore Bass and Arnold Wolpert, *Teaching in California* (San Francisco: Chandler Publishing Company, 1963), Ch. 2.

intendent: (a) teaching methods and uniform educational practices, (b) available textbooks and a proposed state series to guide the instructional program, (c) the strengthening of the local district organization and the need for strong state support of education, (d) legislation that would be advantageous to a growing school system.

STATE TEACHERS' INSTITUTES

1. The legislature in 1859 provided funds for state teachers' institutes and required the state superintendent to address county institutes.

2. The first state institute was held in San Francisco on May 27–31, 1861. Some items discussed were: (a) gymnastics, or physical education, (b) discipline and corporal punishment of pupils, (c) when to introduce formal grammar, (d) the need for a state teachers' journal.

3. The second state institute was held in Sacramento on September 23–25, 1862. Some important matters of business at this meeting included: (a) the effective use of memory in the classroom, (b) accommodation for state adoption of uniform textbooks, (c) the appointment of a committee to plan and publish a teachers' journal for California.

4. The third institute was held in San Francisco in May, 1863. Actions taken were: (a) a resolution adopted and a petition planned for voters to ask for higher state school revenues, (b) agreement to publish *The California Teacher* (first issued in July, 1863), the first teachers' journal in California.

THE CALIFORNIA TEACHER

This publication was considered the official journal of the state department of instruction—a "must" for county superintendents and trustees as well as for teachers and anyone interested in better California schools. Its objective in the words of Theodore Bradley, principal of Denman School, San Francisco, and chairman of the editorial committee, was: "To elevate the office of teacher to the rank of a professional . . . not only desired by every friend of Education, but believed absolutely essential to obtain the full advantage of our school system." It aimed to: aid teachers in their influence for good; promote free state or public schools; perfect the system of public instruction from primary schools to the university; develop sound, professional education; encourage professors in academies and colleges to suggest what is most needed for sound learning; provide professional encouragement and aids to teachers.

The journal continued for 13 years, from 1863 to 1876. Its chief result was to give rise to the California Educational Society, which was planned on May 9, 1863, and which took over the publication of *The California Teacher* on June 18, 1864.

THE CALIFORNIA EDUCATIONAL SOCIETY (1863–1873)

This first organization of California teachers was open to male graduates of normal schools who held state credentials or diplomas. It proposed to distinguish worthy from unworthy members of the teaching profession, making expulsion from the society equivalent to the loss of the right to teach.

The society admitted women members in 1867 and reduced dues from $10 to $5 for women. The society worked hard for free and better schools in California, but it died mainly because its small, select membership had little statewide influence. The depression of 1873 helped its demise. Two years later, the teachers of California were organizing their forces to influence the second state constitution. This new organization has operated since as the California Teachers' Association.

Teachers and the general public alike sought a new type of state school organization and hence a new state constitution. So if the CTA got off to a good start on June 10 and 11, 1875, it was in no small measure due to the vital needs for educational reform at the time. Under the leadership of Superintendent John Swett, it put pressure on the legislature and worked valiantly on plans for revision of Article IX of the constitution.

The association asked for a public school system that would include "primary and grammar schools and such high schools, normal schools and technical schools as may be established by the legislature or by municipal or district authority." A four-year term of office for county school superintendents was written into the new constitution on the recommendation of the CTA, which also recommended a $1,500-a-year salary for county superintendents.

THE CTA OLD-STYLE ORGANIZATION (1875–1909)

From its founding in 1875 the CTA was the only teacher organization in California until 1893, when the teachers of southern counties (Santa Barbara, Ventura, Los Angeles, Orange, San Bernardino, Riverside, and San Diego) organized a Teachers' Association of Southern California with headquarters in Los Angeles.

These two associations functioned separately but cooperatively until 1909, when the southern organization became the present California Teachers' Association, Southern Section. There were, in effect, four independent teachers' associations in the state: the CTA in San Francisco, the Northern California Teachers' Association, the Southern California Teachers' Association in Los Angeles, and the San Joaquin Valley Teachers' Association in Fresno and Bakersfield.

THE MODERN CTA (1910–1960)

As early as 1902, there was a proposal to bring all four teachers' associations under a single organization to be known as the California Teachers' Federation, but the proposal failed. So, in 1906, the CTA incorporated and called for a Greater California Teachers' Association. But only in 1909 did all four associations finally unite under the CTA, the three lesser groups becoming the CTA, Northern Section; the CTA, Southern Section; and the CTA, San Joaquin Valley Section. The united association immediately employed a full-time executive secretary.

Thereafter, the CTA became a great power and it eventually grew to its 1967 membership strength of 160,042 teachers. In the years from 1910 to 1967 it has stood for and secured legislation for a better system of education in California as well as for legal rights and benefits for teachers. To enumerate all the improvements in California education for which the CTA is responsible (wholly or in part) is to relate much of the development of education in California after 1875, but a list of examples should suffice.

EDUCATIONAL DEVELOPMENTS PROPOSED
AND SUPPORTED BY THE CTA

1. Inclusion of kindergartens and junior colleges in the state system on a regular basis.

2. Establishment of the ADA basis of state support of education.

3. Improvement of teacher-training facilities (from normal schools to state teachers' colleges and then to state colleges).

4. Improvement of professional requirements for teachers' credentials.

5. Enactment of California's teacher-tenure law.

6. Establishment of minimum salary laws for teachers (constitutional and legislative).

7. Development and improvement of the state teachers' retirement system.

8. Equalization of educational opportunities for all California children and youth.

9. Development of professional services in the state department of education and the county schools departments.

10. Implementation of better educational services for handicapped children.

Along with these and many other improvements, the CTA has developed its own services to teachers in the following areas:

1. Teacher-placement services in the state CTA office and the section offices.

2. Legal assistance to teachers in professional matters.

3. Establishment and encouragement of credit unions, insurance plans, and purchasing services for teachers.

4. Provision of facilities for association and special group meetings in the state headquarters and section offices.

5. Publication of the CTA Journal, research studies, and the like.

6. Improvement of professional standards.

7. Cooperation with the NEA, other state teachers' associations, and the World Confederation of the Organizations of the Teaching Profession (WCOTP).

The CTA has helped improve salaries, job security, satisfactory working conditions, and the general welfare of the profession. Indeed, its chief aim has been to develop and improve the professional status of teachers.

THE CTA'S INTERNAL ORGANIZATION

The central headquarters of the CTA, long located in San Francisco, now occupy a building in Burlingame. The move from San Francisco to the more adequate headquarters of Burlingame was necessitated by the large and still growing membership of the association. In the fall of 1967, the membership was in excess of 160,000. This vast professional body is headed by a state president and state board of directors of nine members. The ruling of the association is determined by the state council on education composed of 365 delegates from all sections of California.

As may be expected, the size of the CTA paid staff has grown with the organization and because of the increased services to teachers. Bass and Wolpert summarize these services briefly as follows:

> In addition to policy determination and legislative activity, CTA maintains a Reserch Department, a Field Service Department for program and problem consultant service, a Public Information Department (publications and public relations), a Professional and Legal Services Department, and a Commission for Higher Education. CTA carries on programs in ethics and personnel standards, in teacher education and certification, in determining educational policy for the profession, in improving the financing of public education, in aggressive promotion of teacher welfare in such areas as salaries, retirement, tenure, leaves, teachers rights, and the like, and in special services such as insurance, purchasing, placement, and credit unions.
>
> Affiliated with the CTA are more than 700 local teacher associations serving virtually all California teachers.[5]

The association has been particularly blessed by the character, ability, and long tenure of its state executive secretary. On August 13, 1927, Roy Cloud, then superintendent of schools in Redwood City, was chosen as the CTA executive secretary, and he held this position for 20 year, until August 31, 1947. Arthur F. Corey succeeded Cloud and served for another 20 years, until July 1, 1967, when he was succeeded by Jack D. Rees.

An organization so extensively spread over all California has had

[5] *Ibid.*, p. 84.

to establish sectional headquarters. Currently there are six sections with elected presidents and appointed executive secretaries and staffs: (1) the Bay Section in Burlingame, (2) the Central Section in Bakersfield, (3) the Central Coast Section in Salinas, (4) the North Coast Section in Arcato, (5) the Northern Section in Chico, and (6) the Southern Section in Los Angeles. This last section, the largest of all, extends from Santa Monica south to the Mexican border and across the whole state from east to west.

The CTA maintains a government relations executive and staff in Sacramento. Its major placement services are in the headquarters in Burlingame and Los Angeles.

CTA AFFILIATES AND NEA RELATIONS

The CTA Affiliated Associations include 18 California Associations: (1) Childhood Education, (2) Health, Physical Education, and Recreation, (3) School Administrators (CASSA), (4) Secondary School Administrators (CASSA), (5) Supervision and Curriculum Development, (6) Business Education, (7) Adult Education (The California Council for Adult Education), (8) Elementary School Administrators (CESAA), (9) Home Economics, (10) Industrial Education, (11) Junior Colleges (CJCA), (12) Scholarship (California's Scholarship Federation), (13) Retired Teachers, (14) School Nurses, (15) Libraries (School Library Association of California), (16) Agricultural Teachers, (17) Adult Education Administrators (CAAEA), and (18) Supervision of Child Welfare and Attendance (CASCWA).

The California Teachers' Association has always worked closely with the National Education Association. Both organizations are almost 100 years old and both have a similar organizational structure. Not only have administrators and supervisors been included in each group; they have given much leadership to both groups. The California Association of School Administrators is the state counterpart of the American Association of School Administrators of the NEA. There are the American Association of Secondary School Administrators and the California Association of Secondary School Administrators for high school principals and the AAESA and CAESA for elementary school principals. Likewise, the supervisors and directors of curriculum have their organizations. But the Classroom Teachers compose the largest groups, though subject-matter groups (in industrial arts, mathematics, physical education, and social studies) within the association are many.

The California Teachers' Association Journal and the National Education Association Journal, the house organs of each of the associations, publish the organizational structure of the association under their boards of directors and their executive secretaries.

During most of their long years of service, the CTA and NEA had no competitive organizations. On April 15, 1916, however, the American Federation of Teachers met in Chicago, drew up a constitution, and applied for a charter with the American Federation of Labor, but even before 1916 a few teachers' locals had already affiliated with the AFL. John Dewey himself was influential in the organization of teachers' unions.

The California Federation of Teachers was organized in 1919. It grew slowly until World War II, though there was some noticeable increase of locals in and after 1934. The federation now has some 50 locals in California's school districts as well as in colleges and universities. Because of the massive membership of the NEA (over one million in 1967) and the CTA (over 160,000), the AFT and CFT have been reluctant to publish their comparatively small but growing membership, which in 1962 was estimated at 70,000 for the AFL and 5,000 for the CFT.[6]

The policies of the federation include:

1. Membership for classroom teachers only. School administrators may not join the AFT and CFT.

2. Strenuous effort to improve teachers' salaries and welfare benefits.

3. A no-strike policy (written into the AFT constitution), liberally interpreted since 1946 as to when and where strikes seemed necessary to overcome intolerable working conditions.

In California, there has been a recent tendency of the CFT locals to secure the sole rights of collective bargaining with a district or with a college system, as these rights are defined in the labor code.

[6] See *ibid.*, and T. M. Stinnett and Albert J. Huggett, *Professional Problems of Teachers,* 2nd ed. (New York: Macmillan, 1963), pp. 421–27.

HIGHER EDUCATION

IN CALIFORNIA

In 1966, the American Council on Education listed 176 California college campuses accredited to offer some higher-education courses from the freshman and junior college level through the highest levels of postgraduate studies.[1] These campuses, including eight campuses of the University of California and the 19 of the California state college system, served a gross registered enrollment of 813,852 Californians in 1967, including part-time extension students. The public junior colleges, the largest group (76 colleges in 66 school districts), had a total enrollment of 487,458 in the fall of 1966.[2]

The next largest enrollment is in the state college system's 19 campuses, where 177,324 undergraduate and graduate students were enrolled in October, 1966. Eight campuses of the University of California (not including the California Medical College in San Francisco) en-

[1] American Council on Education, *Accredited Institutions of Higher Education*, (Washingon, D.C., 1966), pp. 6–15.
[2] California State Dept. of Education, *The Junior College Story* (Sacramento: Bureau of Junior College General Education, August, 1966).

rolled 87,036 undergraduate and graduate students in October, 1966.

Finally, California has many private colleges, some of which have very high quality programs and substantial enrollments, as this list shows:

	Location	Men	Women	Total
California Institute of Technology	Pasadena	1,400	30	1,430
Claremont Colleges	Claremont	2,287	1,608	3,895
Immaculate Heart College	Los Angeles	93	1,211	1,304
Loyola University	Los Angeles	2,759	314	3,073
Occidental College	Los Angeles	957	646	1,603
St. Mary's College	Moraga	995		995
Stanford University	Palo Alto	8,601	2,565	11,166
University of San Francisco	San Francisco	3,973	1,591	5,564
University of Santa Clara	Santa Clara	3,375	959	4,334
University of Southern California	Los Angeles	14,186	4,437	18,623
Total		38,626	13,361	51,987

In enrollment and many other respects, California now ranks first among the states in the field of higher education. It provides, for instance, more post-high school education opportunities than any other state. This is remarkable, because when California gained its statehood in 1850 some other parts of the country had been in the business of higher education for more than 100 years. Harvard College was founded in 1637, 231 years before the founding of the University of California. Moreover, as was the case in many other states, when higher education came to California it came by way of private and denominational schools.

Initially, it was not always easy to say whether these private academies, seminaries, and institutes were colleges in the true sense of the word or merely high-grade secondary schools. An older private college might set the date of its founding at a time when it was not a true college. For example, San Jose's Notre Dame Academy developed into Notre Dame College. On the other hand, the first San Francisco Academy of 1850 realistically changed its name to the English Classical High School in 1854. Indeed, a family boarding school for boys that opened in June, 1853, became California College in 1854, which by 1868 was to be the inceptive base of the University of California.

The University of California

The glorious history of this great university can be sketched here only in brief. Though the university was founded on March 21, 1864, the founding was preceded by a long planning period between 1849 and 1867. The history of the university falls into four main periods.

PLANNING

The University of California was a mere idea in the constitutional convention of 1849. The delegates seemed to want to use funds from federal land grants for common schools to build a university. Early legislatures did little more than talk about the idea; however, the legislature in 1851 made the governor and the state superintendent of public instruction *ex officio* members of a future university board that was permitted to begin operation after it had acquired $20,000.

In 1853, a group of Congregational and Presbyterian ministers, seeing the need for a college, planned one and opened it in a building in Oakland on property bounded by 12th, 14th, Franklin, and Harrison Streets. Three students were enrolled in this "Academy of Mr. Durant," which was briefly known as Contra Costa Academy after Durant acquired the first 140 acres of the present Berkeley site of the University of California. Though the new site was available in 1858, on June 11, 1860, the College of California, a continuation of the old academy, opened in Oakland. The first class of this college was graduated with B.A. degrees on June 1, 1864, in the Oakland Presbyterian Church.

Now that there was indeed a College of California, the idea of a university for California was resurrected, particularly as there was evidence that federal land grants for agricultural, mining, and mechanical arts would be available through the first Morrill Act when it was signed by Abraham Lincoln. The California College Board of Trustees, alert to the situation, proposed a speeding-up of the process. On October 9, 1867, the board met with the state superintendent of public instruction and offered their Berkeley site to the state for a state university. The California college board stood willing to disincorporate if this land were accepted by the state and donate all its assets to the new university, which would become a land-grant college.

The state legislature accepted the gift on March 21, 1868, and a week later made the first appropriation of funds for the University of California. The business affairs of the university were vested in a board of regents of 23 members—seven *ex officio* (the governor and lieutenant governor, the speaker of the assembly, the superintendent of public instruction, the presidents of the Agricultural Society, the Mechanics Institute, and the university) and 16 regents appointed by the governor for 16-year terms. Professor La Conte of the College of California was selected by the board as acting president during the construction period; but, on August 16, 1870, Durant of the old California College became the first UC president. To date, 13 educators have held this very important office.

DEVELOPMENT

The university opened its classes in the old college building in Oakland, but accessible funds made possible the erection of buildings on the Berkeley site. The state had created a university fund, which grew from the resources of the Morrill Act and private donors. In 1873, Herbert H. Toland had opened a medical school, Toland Hall, on Stockton Street in San Francisco. When he turned it over to the university, it became Toland College, to which California's first dental college was added. In 1878, S. Clinton Hastings endowed Hastings College of Law with a sum of $100,000 donated to the university. Besides the buildings in Berkeley, the university acquired Hastings law school and Toland Hall medical college in San Francisco.

The presidents of this period were: Henry Durant (1870–72), Daniel Coit Gilman of Yale (1872–75), who resigned to become the first president of Johns Hopkins University in 1878; John La Conte (1876–81), who began his service as acting president of UC; William T. Reid (1881–85); and Edward S. Holden (1885–88).

EXPANSION

Shortly before the opening of Leland Stanford, Jr., University in Palo Alto in 1885, the real expansion of the University of California began under presidents Horace Davis (1888–90), Martin Kellogg of

Lick Observatory (1893–99), and Benjamin Wheeler (1899–1919), who made UC a prominent cultural center by bringing such eminent professors as Josiah Royce to Berkeley.[3] President Wheeler also brought William James to the Berkeley campus to discuss the then-budding philosophy of pragmatism with the professors of UC.

Under Wheeler and under General David Prescott Barrows (1919–23) and William Wallace Campbell (1923–30), the university farm and college of agriculture at Davis was opened in 1909 and UCLA was developed out of the original normal school (1919–27). Lick Observatory at Mt. Hamilton and the Scripps Institute of Oceanography at La Jolla were attached to the university.

THE RECENT PERIOD

Within the past two decades, Santa Barbara State College has become UCSB, and new campuses have been built in Riverside (UCR), La Jolla (San Diego's UCSD), and Irvine (UCI). By 1966, there were nine campuses of the university spread across the state.[4]

During Robert Gordon Sproul's presidency (1930–58), the University of California became the world's largest university. And by the time Clark Kerr (1958–67) resumed his full professorship in 1967, the university was well into the stormiest period of its recent history. Harry B. Wollman, acting president in the spring of 1967, was succeeded by Charles J. Hitch.

While all the presidents assisted the regents in building this great institution and in securing funds and husbanding the resources of the university, the provosts and chancellors on each campus guided the deans, professors, and the academic senate in the development of its extensive educational and research programs.

[3] To speak of bringing Josiah Royce to California from Harvard is a strange anomaly, for this eminent philosopher and professor was born in Grass Valley, California, in 1855 and was himself an 1875 graduate of the University of California. His hobby was California history, much of which he knew from personal experience in Sacramento Valley and San Francisco. Though he went to Germany to study Hegel, he had already gained much of his own idealism and his conception of "the majesty of the community" from his pioneer mother, whose basic lessons were that "we are saved through the community and by loyalty."

[4] The present campuses are located at Berkeley (the oldest and largest), Davis ("The Farm"), Irvine (the newest and smallest), Los Angeles (UCLA), Riverside, San Diego (originally the Scripps Institute of Oceanography but now a vastly expanded campus with a school of medicine), San Francisco (the California Medical College and an affiliated art institute), Santa Barbara, and Santa Cruz. Each campus is directed by a chancellor under the president.

By state law, the university is directed to provide instruction in the liberal arts and sciences and the professions; it has gained the exclusive jurisdiction in higher education over instruction in law and over graduate instruction in medicine, dentistry, veterinary medicine, and architecture (see the Education Code 22551).

The board of regents, whose legal authority was written into the state constitution by constitutional amendment (see the Constitution, Article IX, Section 9, as amended on November 5, 1918), has become a very powerful body of men with long terms of office (16 years for each of the 16 appointed members).

The constitution makes the university a "public trust" to be administered by a corporation known as The Board of Regents of the University of California with full powers of organization and government, "subject only to such legislative control as may be necessary to insure compliance with the terms of the endowments of the university and the security of its funds."

A board with such extensive constitutional powers and long term of office sees legislatures come and go and looks to the legislature for large appropriations with no strings attached. It is only natural that the board of regents has often been a thorn in the side of the legislature, and the legislature has become wary of the creation of any other state board over which lawmakers could exercise so little effective control. The legislature exercised such caution recently when the Board of Trustees of California State Colleges was created.

Nevertheless, the political history of California since 1964 has, in the minds of many educators, underlined the wisdom of the constitutional provisions for the University of California. These provisions have tended to keep the university and its academic atmosphere insulated from the contradictory political pressures, which could result from changing political complexions of the legislature and the top administrative echelons of state government. The University of California, like Oxford and Cambridge, has worked in an atmosphere of freedom and indifference to the political changes of parties and dynasties.

Even those *ex officio* officers on the board of regents who were elected on partisan tickets—the governor, lieutenant governor, and speaker of the assembly—were a distinct minority on the board, and the appointed regents had so long a tenure (16 years) that any allegiance to the politics of the governor who appointed them had time to fade. Moreover, operating as a constitutionally organized corporation, the board of regents has been free to manage its own debits and credits for educational progress, for the students, and for the benefit of the state and the nation.

The resources of the university are many, including its vast properties and equipment spread across the state, its distinguished faculties, and its extensive endowments. Its annual income is derived not from the state budget alone but from research grants and other assistance from the federal government and many foundations. The board of regents has jealously guarded its constitutional freedom of operation, including the offering of tuitionless education to tens of thousands of students. It seemed unreasonable to them to cut back California's best educational opportunities at a time when personal income in the state set a record high of $66,127,000,000. However, in the 1966 gubernatorial campaign, the state was seen to be in dire financial straits. The expensive and independent university organization became a campaign issue.

In the January 1967 meeting of the board of regents, Governor Ronald Reagan's first meeting as a regent, President Clark Kerr was removed from his office. In less symbolic actions, the governor proposed these economy measures affecting the university:

1. A 10 percent cut across the board in the university and state college budgets and in welfare budgets.

2. Proposed tuition of $200 to $400 in addition to current fees of students in higher education.

3. A freeze on filling new professional positions and on replacements, despite increasing enrollments.

4. A delay, at the very least, in the improvement of professors' salaries.

Almost simultaneously, the constitutional independence of the board of regents was threatened by Assemblyman Carl Britschi's Bill No. 57. This proposed constitutional amendment (Assembly Constitutional Amendment No. 7), to be submitted to the people in 1968, is designed to limit the financial independence of the board.

These changes, proposed or threatened, predict a new kind of higher education for California. However, unless one is a prophet or the son of a prophet, he had better not specify the outcome, for no business is as fraught with danger as that of a seer.

The private colleges and universities of California must look at the 1967 debate with mixed emotions. After all, they were the pioneers of higher education in California, and down the years they have had difficulty in competing with a massive and comparatively inexpensive public education system of colleges and universities. That private colleges here had a hard time in California's "professor market" was reflected in a late 1966 meeting of the California Council for Higher Education, whose president is Arthur G. Coons, president emeritus of Occidental College. Coons, with Milton Kloetzel of USC and Father Charles S. Casassa of Loyola University, supported Easton Rothwell's (Mills College) position against increases (of 5 percent) in the salaries of university and state college professors. Rothwell noted that the increase "will put the private institutions in a different position with regard to both faculty recruitment and student tuition." The vote for a salary increase lost by a nine-to-nine tie in the CCHE.[5]

That the private colleges in California and other states have had an increasingly difficult problem of competing with state colleges and the university goes without saying. It would be ungrateful for Californians to forget or to overlook the contributions they have made and now make to higher education.

Private Colleges and Universities in California

The precedent of Durant's Contra Costa Academy (the parent institution of the University of California) and the older American tradition of church-inspired and privately endowed colleges encouraged many—literally hundreds—of private colleges to spring up in California. Some 30 of these older institutions remain today as accredited colleges and universities. The dates of their origin as colleges may be disputed in some cases, but we list their appearance in historical order, by the dates they claim for their founding—whether as "academies" or colleges.

1851	University of the Pacific, Stockton (Methodist)
	University of Santa Clara, Santa Clara (Jesuit)
1852	Mills College, Oakland (Private, girls)
1855	University of San Francisco (Jesuit)

[5] See *The California Professor*, Vol. 1, No. 3 (January, 1967), p. 1.

1861 Chapman College, Orange (Disciples of Christ)
1863 St. Mary's College, Moraga (Christian Brothers)
1868 Notre Dame, Belmont (Catholic, girls)
      College of the Holy Names, Oakland, Los Gatos (Catholic, girls)
1880 University of Southern California (Methodist, now private)
1882 Pacific Union College, Angwin (Seventh Day Adventist)
1885 Stanford University, Palo Alto (Private)
1886 Pomona College, Claremont (Congregational)
1887 Occidental College, Los Angeles (Presbyterian)
1890 Dominican Convent, San Rafael (Catholic, girls)
1891 La Verne College, La Verne (Brethren)
      California Institute of Technology, Pasadena (Private)
1898 St. Patrick's Seminary, Menlo Park (Catholic, Sulpician)
1901 Whittier College, Whittier (Quaker)
1902 Pasadena College, Pasadena (Nazarene)
1907 Redlands University, Redlands (Baptist)
1911 Loyola University, Los Angeles (Jesuit)
1916 Immaculate Heart College, Los Angeles (Catholic, girls)
1924 California-Western, San Diego (Methodist, private)
1925 Claremont Colleges, Claremont (Private)
      Mt. St. Mary's, Los Angeles (Catholic, girls)
1926 Scripps College, Claremont (Private)
      St. John's, Camarillo (Catholic)
1937 George Pepperdine College, Los Angeles (Church of Christ)
      Claremont Men's College, Claremont (Private)
      Harvey Mudd College, Claremont (Private)

It will be noted from the list that there were several high points of activity in the development of private colleges. The first occurred in the 1850s and 1860s, when all colleges in California were private. Then in the 1880s a new series of denominational and private colleges was begun, giving USC, Stanford, Occidental, Pomona, La Verne, Whittier, Redlands, and so on. Finally, immediately before and after the depression there was another high point. Some of the older institutions were established for denominational purposes, often for the training of the clergy and church workers. Others have partly or entirely disassociated themselves from the denomination that founded them. All depended heavily on endowments. As a general rule, each has special objectives that state colleges do not propose to meet.

The California State College System

The century-old and still growing state college system has made an important place for itself under the California sun. Beginning with the first California State Normal School in San Francisco in 1862, the system has many years of varied experience behind it. Its normal school experience and its short years as state teachers' colleges have been traced in detail in Chapter 5.

After World War I, teachers' colleges were involved in a three-year curriculum for the sole purpose of training teachers. However, by 1923 the colleges in Chico, Fresno, San Diego, San Francisco, and San Jose were permitted to offer B.A. programs in elementary education, art and music education, junior high school education, and home economics. Even as late as 1935, the legislature indicated that

> the primary function of the state colleges is to train teachers, and there shall be no extension of the curriculum of any state college which will carry it into any other field of higher education; provided that as a secondary function courses in liberal arts may be given, but such courses shall only be such as appropriate as courses of instruction for students intending to enter the teaching profession.

However, when the legislature specified that a declaration of intention to become a teacher was not to be a prerequisite for admission to state colleges, it opened the door to a second higher education system in the state. This system has been developing for the past 30 years, making higher education easily accessible to many California areas. That this accomplishment was achieved against some odds and opposition should be clear from this sequence of events:

1. After 1935, the state college baccalaureate program was extended to B.A. and B.S. programs in the liberal arts, sciences, agriculture, business administration, economics, engineering, foreign languages, journalism, nursing, premedical, psychology, sociology, social welfare, and a variety of other fields.

2. Probably as a precaution, the university once seemed disposed to expand its services by the statewide absorption of normal school and state colleges into the university system, as was done in Los Angeles and Santa Barbara.

3. The state colleges were authorized to confer the master of arts degree as early as 1949. Later, masters of science, business administration, and social work were authorized as the various campuses in this 19-campus system were able to develop programs. The first Ph.D. authorized in a California state college was conferred in chemistry at San Diego State College in June, 1967, after a joint program of training supervised by SDSC and UCSD.

4. With the expansion of local junior colleges, much of the lower division work of the state colleges has been eliminated. Many students now enter the state colleges in their junior or at least sophomore years.

5. In the 1960s, the control of the colleges passed from the state board of education and the state superintendent of public instruction to the board of trustees of the California state colleges and to a chancellor of the state college system. These legally constituted offices now have as their single interest the development of this vast higher-education program.

There are still some understandable residual problems in the developing system. In its bid for professional staff, for example, the state college system is caught between the considerable differentials in salaries, privileges, and working conditions available in the university and the increasing salary schedules of the junior colleges. Other battles of the state college system are being fought in the California Coordinating Council for Higher Education, as we shall see on page 212. It should be noted here, however, that the state colleges have been helped rather than hindered by the growing junior college system, because the slackening of lower-division work in the state colleges enables them to put a heavier concentration of effort on upper division and graduate work.

The Junior Colleges of California

Junior colleges have multiplied and progressed in California as in no other state or nation. In 1907, the California junior college law made post-high school education in the public school systems legal.

The initial spurt in junior college development after 1911 did not continue in the 1920s, but the development of California junior colleges resumed in the 1940s, and academic courses were added to provide lower-division college training. As general junior college programs and city colleges began to appear, the inevitable accreditation of junior colleges and increased enrollment followed. By 1958–59, 96,027 students were enrolled in the public junior colleges of 27 junior college districts of California. By 1960, enrollment reached 145,000. In 1961, the state projection for junior college enrollment indicated that there would be 300,000 junior students in California by 1966, whereas there were in fact 459,400 students enrolled in junior colleges that year.

A brief summary of the history and purpose of California junior colleges is outlined in the following excerpts from *The Junior College Story*.

> California was the first state to enact legislation creating public junior colleges. A 1907 law, proposed by Senator Anthony Caminetti of Amador County, allowed the board of trustees of a high school district to provide post-high school courses in the high school. These courses were to approximate the courses in the first two years of four-year colleges and universities.

> Although the 1907 law was permissive, no school district made any move in this direction until 1910, when the Fresno High School offered post-high school classes. Santa Barbara High School followed this move in 1911. There were 16 high schools in 1917 offering postgraduate courses, with total enrollments of 1,259.

> During this period, the attorney general of the state ruled that high schools could not collect state aid for such post-high school courses. The decision resulted in a law being introduced by Senator John Ballard of Los Angeles. This legislation used the term "junior college courses" rather than "post-high school courses" and allowed the districts offering junior college courses to collect state aid for attendance.

> In 1921, legislation was enacted which allowed the formation of separate junior college districts. Modesto junior college district was the first to be formed under this law.

> The great expansion of the public junior college system came after World War II. The increase in technological advancement, the status symbol of attending a college, and the development of automation caused a tremendous upsurge in college attendance.

> By July, 1966, there were 66 districts maintaining 76 public junior

colleges. The 66 districts maintaining junior colleges are composed of one high school district, six unified school districts, and 59 separate junior college districts.

As of the fall of 1965, the total enrollment in California public junior colleges was 459,400. The five largest were Los Angeles City College, with 16,798; College of San Mateo, with 15,893; Orange Coast College, with 15,238; Long Beach City College, with 15,132; and Los Angeles Valley College, with 14,865.

The five smallest colleges were Palo Verde College, with 448; Mt. San Jacinto College, with 671; Lassen Junior College, with 687; College of the Siskiyous, with 718; and Taft College, with 731.

As might be expected, the smaller colleges are generally located in sparsely settled mountain or desert areas, while the largest colleges are in metropolitan or densely populated areas. The six junior colleges of the Los Angeles City Junior College District enroll 16 percent of the total junior college population of the state.

In 1959, legislation was enacted which authorized the development of a master plan for higher education. A *Master Plan for Higher Education in California, 1960–1975,* was published in 1960.

This document—over 300 pages in length—is now the "basic text" that outlines the role, purpose, and function of each of the three segments of higher education—the junior colleges, the state colleges, and the University of California. Specifically, the role of the junior college is indicated as follows:

1. To provide the first two years of college education for those students wishing to transfer to a four-year institution.
2. To grant the Associate in Arts degree to those students who complete successfully a prescribed two-year program of studies.
3. To offer vocational-technical training, general education, and other appropriate programs to prepare youth for occupations which require no more than two years of training.
4. To provide satisfactory counseling services.
5. To offer remedial courses for those students who may profit by such instruction.[6]

[6] Bureau of Junior College General Education, *The Junior College Story* (Sacramento: California State Dept. of Education, August, 1966). See also the Bureau's *Directory of California Junior Colleges—1966–1967* (October, 1966) and the 1966 Junior College Directory of the American Association of Junior Colleges, pp. 10–15.

Although there has been some agitation for a new state board of junior colleges, their administration is likely to remain as it is for some time. Briefly, various responsibilities rest with three groups. Again, from *The Junior College Story*:

> Junior colleges are locally administered by boards of trustees elected by the voters of the district. Under Education Code provisions, boards of trustees may adopt such rules and regulations as may be necessary to enable the board to exercise the powers and to perform the duties conferred or imposed upon the board of statute.
>
> The state board of education is composed of 10 members appointed by the governor, with the advice and consent of two-thirds of the senate. The term of office is four years. "The board shall adopt rules and regulations not inconsistent with the laws of this State . . . for the government of the . . . secondary schools . . ." (Education Code Section 152).
>
> The Department of Education shall be administered through: (a) The State Board of Education, which shall be the governing and policy determining body of the department. (b) The State Director of Education in whom all executive and administrative functions of the department are vested and who is the executive officer of the State Board of Education.
>
> "The State Superintendent of Public Instruction is *ex officio* Director of Education" (Education Code Section 354).[7]

Besides these responsibilities, the report also mentions the advising responsibility of the CCHE, which we shall now discuss.

The Master Plan for Higher Education

The increasing California population, the gradually expanding opportunities for higher education in the state, and the growing competition between institutions, both private and public, offering education at the tertiary level have forced the state government to examine higher educational opportunities and services and institutional relationships and to seek a master plan for higher education.

The master plan was initiated on February 1, 1960 (see Senate

[7] *Ibid.*, pp. 7–8.

Journal—1960 regular session—page 42, paragraphs 4 and 6). As the advisory Coordinating Council for Higher Education (CCHE) develops suggestions for the state government and as these suggestions are enacted into law, they are included in the Education Code (Part 4, Division 16.5, Sections 22500 and following). The sections include provisions for the appointment of CCHE members and for a professional staff and director.

The council is composed of representatives of the state boards for higher education and junior colleges and private colleges, as well as professional educators and laymen representing the general public. The balance of representation can be seen in the following outline.

1. University of California: the president and two regents, with three other regents serving as alternates.

2. California state colleges: two trustees, with two alternates (also trustees).

3. Independent colleges: one representative educator each from Stanford University, Occidental College, and the University of San Francisco (formerly Loyola).

4. Junior college representatives: the state superintendent of public instruction, one trustee, and one president of a public junior college, with one alternate.

5. The general public: three laymen from various sections of the state.

In 1966 and again in 1967, Arthur G Coons, former president of Occidental College, served as president of the council. The functions of the council, which serves in an advisory capacity to the governor and the legislature, were written into this section of the law.

> *22703* The co-ordinating council shall have the following functions, advisory to the governing boards of the institutions of public higher education and to appropriate state officials: (1) review of the annual budget and capital outlay requests of the university and the California State Colleges, and presentation of comments on the general level of support sought; (2) advice as to the application of the provisions of this division delineating the different functions of public higher education and counsel as to the programs appropriate

to each segment thereof, and in connection therewith shall submit to the Governor and to the Legislature within five days of the beginning of each general session a report which contains recommendations as to necessary or desirable changes, if any, in the functions and programs of the several segments of public higher education; and (3) development of plans for the orderly growth of public higher education and the making of recommendations on the need for and location of new facilities and programs.

In addition, the legislated Master Plan for Higher Education in California of 1960 gave these guidelines to the council:

22550 The Legislature hereby finds and declares that the University of California is the primary state-supported academic agency for research.

22551 The university may provide instruction in the liberal arts and sciences and in the professions, including the teaching profession. The university has exclusive jurisdiction in public higher education over instruction in the profession of law, and over graduate instruction in the professions of medicine, dentistry, veterinary medicine and architecture.

22551 The university has the sole authority in the public higher education to award the doctoral degree in all fields of learning, except that it may agree with the state colleges to award joint doctoral degrees in selected fields.

22606 The primary function of the state colleges is the provision of instruction for undergraduate students and graduate students, through the master's degree, in the liberal arts and sciences, in applied fields and in the professions, including the teaching profession. Presently established two-year programs in agriculture are authorized, but other two-year programs shall be authorized only when mutually agreed upon by the Trustees of the California State Colleges and the State Board of Education. The doctoral degree may be awarded jointly with the University of California, as provided in Section 22552. Faculty research is authorized to the extent that it is consistent with the primary function of the state colleges and the facilities provided for that function.

22651 Public junior colleges shall offer instruction through but not beyond the 14th grade level, which instruction may include, but shall not be limited to, programs in one or more of the following categories: (1) standard collegiate courses for transfer to higher institutions; (2) vocational and technical fields leading to employment; and (3) general or liberal arts courses. Studies in these fields may lead to the Associate in Arts or Associate in Science degree.

From the foregoing sections of the code, it is understandable that the CCHE needs to consider many of its problems in the light of conflicting interests in California's massive, expensive, and sometimes conflicting systems of higher education. The university and state, junior, and private colleges all have their legal rights and vested interests in this massive program. The rights, interests, and ambitions of each of these groups, as considered by the coordinating council, have posed a variety of problems and areas of discussion.

Some of the major problems or suggestions that have come before the Council include the following:

1. The functions of the state colleges in serving "regional needs" for higher education and as being "teaching institutions" as opposed to those dedicated to research. The California state colleges have evidenced interest in becoming a second university system with all the rights and privileges of a university system. This ambition to date has been frustrated.

2. The differentials in professorial salaries and the current competition in the "professorial market" have produced recommendations for comparative salary schedules, in which both the state colleges and private colleges have had an interest.

3. Consideration of various types of research expected of the various colleges and universities of the state—for example, the research that is merely good scholarship (keeping up with the developments and literature in a given field) versus creative or original research (leading to the development of a new drug, a new technology, or an improved exploration of anthropological, geological, or oceanographic phenomena). It will be noted that the university has been designated as the primary agency for research, especially of the latter type.

4. The creation of a state system of junior colleges under a special state board apart from the state board of education, under which the junior colleges now function.

5. The development of new degrees, as the "teaching doctorate" as opposed to doctorates conferred on research technicians.

6. The overall problem of who does what in higher education in California so as to provide ample tertiary education facilities in the most economical manner.

Finally, few would deny that the master plan for higher education and the CCHE were not long overdue in a state that has seen the development of massive and competitive systems of higher education. Moreover, only the naive fail to see the struggle to maintain or improve their status by the vested interests on or outside of the CCHE. If there were easy answers and a simple division of labor in the areas of higher education in California, we would have them now. Those who are sincerely interested in the development and organization of education in California cannot but wait in anxious expectation for the final outcomes of the master plan in 1975.

RESIDUAL PROBLEMS

AND CURRENT TRENDS

Any serious reader in the history of California education is forced to pronounce the traditional "Well done!" with enthusiastic overtones. He cannot fail to notice the leadership of great educators in the past, and, if he is perceptive, he will suspect that a considerable share of the glory has been earned by the nameless thousands of devoted teachers, administrators, legislators, and publicly minded citizens. Through the combined efforts of leaders and workers in the public and private schools, California compares most favorably with the rest of the nation and the rest of the world in educational achievements. Indeed, California's practice has often set the pace in the educational vanguard. In many areas, it is still blazing the trail.

To imply, however, that the developmental task is done would be to close one's eyes to the educational problem that the state government, the people, and the school boards have yet to solve. However, lest we belabor this point, which has been apparent in the whole book, it should be sufficient to conclude this study with pointed reference to remaining problems and, where present educational efforts justify it, to mark the direction in which California is going. It should be clear at the outset that the chief school problem of California has not changed much with the passing of the years. It is the problem of repeated and continuing population explosions.

The state set itself up in business in 1850 with a mere 100,000 citizens. The population soon doubled, trebled, and quadrupled, until 1880 when the U.S. Bureau of the Census provided these population figures:

1880	864,694
1890	1,213,398
1900	1,485,549
1920	3,426,861
1930	5,677,251
1940	6,907,387
1950	10,586,223
1960	15,717,204

As was noted in Chapter 1, the state's 1930 population of 5,677,251 was nearly doubled by 1950 (10,586,223) and nearly trebled by 1960 (15,717,204). In 1964, when the state's estimated population reached 18,084,000, California passed New York as the most populous state. Indeed, in July, 1964, the California department of finance estimated 18,234,000 Californians and the July 1, 1967, estimates reached 19,505,050. The department's projections are for 21 million in 1970 and for 28 million for 1990.

Reduced to school enrollment, these population explosions alert educators to the basic problem of the system. The 1966 public school enrollment in all grades, including enrollment in special classes, was 5,290,719, which represented a 3.4 percent gain, or an actual increase of 174,939 over the fall of 1965. The 1960 total enrollment was only 65.2 percent of 1966, which showed 3,791,000 more than in 1950.

Against this background of continuing growth of California's population and school enrollment, it will be easier, though not entirely simple, to indicate in outline form the residual problems of the state school system.

School Facilities for Growing Enrollments. The increase of 3,791,000 public school pupils from 1950 to 1966 requires a minimum of 12,500 additional classrooms in existing school buildings or in the new schools. Though there have been some double sessions and the provision of temporary classrooms, local bonds supported by state funds from school building bonds have kept the problem fairly well in hand.

However, as preparedness is the key to the solution, the state, counties, and local districts (particularly the larger ones) have prepared and will need to continue population and enrollment projections. Only when the state knows what to expect in a school district in the way of enrollment can it be prepared to meet it with adequate school facilities.

One study by the state department of finance, as a single example, gives promise of surprising corrections. As an instance of the projections we can review the enrollment trends in all California state colleges. These are the 1960 actual and estimated full-time enrollments:[1]

	Full-time	Part-time	Total
1958	44,528	35,563	80,091
1960	58,600	50,200	108,800
1965	98,950	97,150	196,100
1970	145,200	143,950	289,150
1975	180,650	177,900	358,550

The total enrollment in California state colleges for the fall of 1966 was 169,520, of which 110,274 were full-time enrollees. Obviously, the finance department gave more accurate projections for full-time enrollment than for part-time, which includes extension courses. Extended services, however, do not involve the college building program.

State college building programs are planned in the light of enrollment projections, available land, and the policies of the trustees. Buildings on the San Diego campus, for example, are being constructed for a maximum enrollment of 28,000. In 1967–68 this campus enrolled just short of 20,000, but the finance department has predicted 32,300 enrollees by 1975. At that time, the building program will need to be increased or the enrollment curtailed. Many additions to the staff will also be needed.

An Adequate Teaching Staff for California's Schools and Colleges. Adequate staffing is a corollary to growing enrollments. For years Californians have ben handicapped with a shortage of adequately

[1] California Department of Finance, *Projection of Enrollment for California's Institutions of Higher Education, 1960–1975* (Sacramento, 1960), p. 35.

trained teachers and professors.[2] Up to the present or recent past, at least, the teacher-training institutions of the state have not been able to supply the need for trained teachers, so school districts and California colleges have sought to meet the residual need by recruiting well-trained teachers and professors from other states. The whole problem, as may be expected, is related to providing attractive salaries. Even in the 1962–63 school year, when the average salaries for California teachers were $8,601 in junior colleges, $7,570 in secondary schools, and $6,800 in elementary schools, the California Teachers' Association was anticipating typical maximum salaries at $11,000.[3] The 1966–67 state median salaries are $7,813 (elementary), $8,922 (secondary), and $10,900 (junior college). This brings state maximums of public schools and junior colleges to $15,000. Already in the 1965–66 academic year, the salary range of junior college instructors and professors was $5,400 to $12,931 without the doctorate and $14,009 with it.[4]

The 1966–67 salary schedules of California state colleges had a range of $6,168 for teaching assistants to $16,212 for full professors with five years of teaching credit in that rank. The range of pay at the several campuses of the University of California in 1967 was $7,800 to $20,800. These figures do not take into consideration the additional recompense for extension and summer-session work or that which comes from research grants.

In this area of higher education, the junior college schedules are in an advantageous position, since they are made by competing junior college districts whereas state college salaries are set by the board of trustees of the California state colleges and the chancellor's office and fitted by the legislature into the state budget. University salaries are, of course, set by the board of regents, which has enjoyed considerable independence from state budgetary and legislature controls.

The Financial Support of Public Education. In the 1967–68 school year, the state plans to spend 1,754 million dollars, or 54 percent of the general fund of the state. In an inflationary period, when all costs and

[2] See, for example, Theodore Bass and Arnold W. Wolpert, *Teaching in California,* rev. ed. (San Francisco: Chandler Publishing Company, 1963), ch. 1.
[3] *Ibid.,* p. 46.
[4] State Department of Education, *Salary Schedules for Teaching Personnel in California Public Junior Colleges, 1965–1966* (Sacramento: Bureau of Junior College Education, 1966).

salaries are on the rise, there cannot be a noticeable reduction in educational costs. Neither will there be an easing of demands on more state and federal funds by property owners who are annually reminded of increased assessments for local school districts. Time alone will tell whether the old percentage formula of 55-40-5 or 55-42-3 (local, state, and federal) will be allowed to stand. Federal aid has of course been increasing, but the percentage of state aid has not increased.

It should not be concluded, however, that all residual problems are financial. There are other problems that will challenge California educators and legislatures in the years ahead. These can easily be detected in a summary of current educational trends in California.

School District Reorganization. The trend toward consolidation in school district reorganization will undoubtedly continue, though there remain many citizens who will oppose it. Much unification and consolidation has been achieved since the Strayer Report, and, given the state's good intentions and adequate machinery for unification, most of the battles with little independent districts should be won within the next decade.

Junior College Reorganization. In the fall of 1967, the legislature authorized the state superintendent to nominate members for the new board of managers for the California junior colleges. State superintendent Max Rafferty made these nominations in April 1968. By the action, the state board of education is being relieved of its responsibility for the supervision of the junior colleges, which as yet are being operated by city and junior college districts. The tendency is to separate the junior colleges of California from the districts that created them.

Coordination of Higher Education Services. The establishment of the California Council for Higher Education was an indication of the state's interest in clarifying the responsibilities of the various agencies currently involved in higher education. It has been advantageous to bring together representatives of the University of California, the California state colleges, private colleges, and universities and private and public junior colleges for the purpose of analyzing who does what in higher education. The recommendations of the Council that have been accepted are now written into the law. There is, however, still much work for the council to do.

Curriculum Development and Control. The direct interest of the state legislature in public school curricula during the last decade stands in marked contrast to the district and county curricular reorganization activities so prevalent from 1935 to 1950. It has been noted already that the legislature has defined specific curricular requirements, like foreign language instruction in the elementary grades, and has turned the direction of the instructional program to stress the traditional academic subjects as opposed to the more general area approach to the social studies, for example.

In the junior colleges, moreover, the recent stress on lower-division college work seems to have overshadowed junior college programs of terminal and vocational education and an earlier interest in apprenticeships in vocational junior colleges. In effect, the trend is to stress *college* in the junior college program.

As is usual in California education, the specialists in every area of the curriculum seem to be blazing new trails; but, since many of these directions are not yet clearly marked, it would be folly to list them as trends.

Teacher Training and Credentials. One of the most marked changes of direction in California education in recent years is the state's expressed intent to make subject-matter specialists of all public school teachers, including those in the kindergarten and elementary grades. The stress on the academic and the ceilings placed on the much-maligned education courses are at the center of this trend.

Finally, there are trends that can at the moment be classified as mere hopes or needs. We need mention but two. One is toward a second university system in California, or a third if you will. A state that will have from 20 to 30 million people could make good use of a state university system alongside the existing university campuses and private colleges and universities. The other hope is for another statewide study of the entire public school system—its organization, financial structure, curricula, and services. After all, a quarter of a century has passed since the Strayer Report.

A FRAMEWORK OF DATES

IN CALIFORNIA HISTORY

Since the topical arrangement of this book is not conducive to a sequential overview of the story of California and its public school system, this chronological outline is appended. It should be of particular value to those who wish to study the important events of California's history in the order in which they occurred. The chronology falls naturally under such headings as Indian origins, Spanish ambitions in California, Mexican California, and the present state of California, so the sequence of events is arranged in strict historical order.

Indian Origins

California Indians were a modest portion of the descendants of Asian immigrants who brought a neolithic culture to America. Before their arrival in California, the immigrant Indians had developed the finest flints, seagoing boats, some pottery, and the ability to spin, weave, and make nets. However, the avant-garde of Indian culture in Central and South America had already discarded the primitive neolithic culture of the California Indian by the first century of our era. The advanced Incas of Peru and Mayans in Guatemala and the

Yucatán peninsula had developed an agricultural economy based on Indian corn that resembled somewhat earlier cultures of the Old World. These early Indian cultures produced rich textiles, fine pottery, and ornaments of gold, silver, and copper. Later they built cities with canals, gardens, great temples, and pyramids. Standing armies, schools, and systematic religions were developed, along with an adequate mathematical system, accurate calendars, and hieroglyphic recordkeeping.

In and after the seventh century, Toltec invaders of south and central Mexico adopted and improved the Mayan culture of Yucatán. A few key dates will outline the achievements of the Aztecs and contrast them with the California Indians.

1196   The Aztecs began to make capital of the previous Mayan and Toltec cultures. With a superior military and political sense, the Aztecs gradually extended their control over Mexico and some colonies in Central America.

1325   Mextili became the capital of the Aztec empire, which harbored an advanced agricultural economy, commerce, and simple industries. An educational system preserved and developed mathematical knowledge, astronomy, architecture, engineering, and a variety of arts.

1500   The interest of Spain and Portugal in the conquest of the Caribbean—namely, Cuba, Puerto Rico, Florida, and Honduras—and South America—Brazil and Peru—precluded any serious interest in Mexico and California until Balboa's discovery of the Pacific Ocean.

1513   Vasco Núñez de Balboa crossed the isthmus of Panama and discovered the Pacific.

1519   Hernando Cortés invaded Mexico from Vera Cruz to Mexico City, the domain of Montezuma II (1480–1520), the last Aztec Emperor of Mexico.

Cortés, determined to reach the Orient from the west, sent ships to find the "northern straits." This expedition discovered Lower California, thought to be an island. The Indians there were reported to be stubbornly pagan and cruel opponents of Christianity and Spanish civilization.

1542   The Spanish viceroy Mendoza commissioned Juan Rodríguez Cabrillo to explore the coasts of California. Cabrillo discovered San Diego Bay on September 28, 1542, and named it San Miguel because of the feast of San Miguel (Michaelmas) on September 29 in the Spanish ecclesiastical calendar.

Despite Spanish claims to California and the occasional appearance of Spanish galleons on the coast from 1542 to 1769, the Indians of southern and central California continued unconcerned in their neolithic way of life. Their primitive culture was markedly inferior to the Aztecs and the well-organized northern tribes, the Klamaths, Modocs, and Shastas.

The Yuma tribes of southern California, like the Diegüeños, were food gatherers. Because of the climate they found little use for clothing. They had little interest in fighting and only the crudest of weapons. Green leaves and roots were their vegetables, while their meat courses included fish, bear, snails, caterpillars, crickets, frogs, horned toads, and even skunk.

As fighters, California Indians were no match for the Aztecs, nor did they offer much serious resistance to the Spanish conquistadors. Fortunately for them, they had little need for resistance until the Spanish occupation of California in 1769. Up to that time, the California Indian was challenged merely to survive and to pass along his primitive culture from one generation to the next.

Spanish Ambitions in California

From 1542 to 1769, California was scarcely more than a name in Spanish imperial history. Spain had repeatedly staked out claims in California and was determined to protect the claims from any intrusions by the British and Russian imperialists. The Spanish crown and the viceroys in New Spain were beset with problems more pressing than the colonization of California.

1492 Ferdinand's conquest of Granada put an end to Moorish power in Spain. This crusade and the future military involvements of Spain provided a rich source of eager conquistadors committed to the Christian and Catholic cause and very loyal to the Spanish crown.

1512 Ferdinand Magellan, sailing to the Orient from Spain, went through the southern tip of South America by the Straits of Magellan and discovered the Ladrones Islands (later called the Philippines). Thereafter, New Spain (in Mexico and California) became a contact with the Far East.

1516 The Hapsburg Charles of Ghent, as Spain's Charles I, brought the Netherlands into the Spanish political and religious arena. In 1519 Charles became Charles V of the Holy Roman Empire, and there were revolts at home.

1519–56 Spain was not only building an empire in the New World but was getting into an endless series of conflicts with neighbors in Europe and competitors on the high seas. Spain became deeply involved in the problems of the Holy Roman Empire and in religious conflicts that came out of the Protestant Reformation, especially during the Thirty Years War. The financing of fleets and the maintenance of armies in Europe repeatedly emptied the treasury, which had to be refilled with gold from America and by favorable trade with colonies.

1556–98 Franco-Spanish wars had flared up repeatedly in 1521–29, 1535–38, 1556–59, and 1589–98. Philip II of Spain (1556–98), as successor of Charles I, added fuel to the flames. He was very Spanish, very Catholic, very efficient, and very anti-British, especially anti-Elizabethan. He often fought for the Hapsburg cause outside Spain.

This man, for whom the Philippines were named, fought the French (1556–59), won a naval battle against the Turks (Lepanto, 1571), lost Tunis for Spain (1574), conquered the Portuguese throne (1580), lost a fleet to Francis Drake at Cádiz (1587), and built the Invincible Armada (130 vessels with some 34,000 sailors and soldiers) and lost it to the English (Drake, Howard, and Hawkins, July 21–29, 1588).

1577–79 Francis Drake, with Elizabeth's secret commission "to annoy the King of Spain in his Indies," sailed his ship the *Golden Hind* through the Straits of Magellan and up the west coast of the Americas to Drake's bay, north of San Francisco. He named the land New Albion, for the English, but despite the brief English threat in northern California, the Spanish crown and the viceroys of New Spain showed little interest in the colonization of California.

1595 The Portuguese navigator Sebastián Rodríguez Cermenho was appointed by the Spanish viceroy to explore and mark the entire course of his return voyage from the Philippines to Mexico. Cermenho, sailing the well-loaded *San Augustín*, entered San Francisco Bay and had his chaplain, Fray Francisco de la Concepción, christen the site San Francisco. On November 30, 1595, the *San Augustín* was driven ashore and broken up in a squall. The Indians picked up the silks and porcelain from the ship, while the Spanish crew escaped in a launch to Monterey Bay and finally reached Navidad in sad condition on January 7, 1596.

It is clear that Francis Drake never noticed San Francisco Bay and that Cermenho and his tattered crew discovered Monterey Bay seven years before Sebastián Vizcaíno took possession of Monterey for Spain in 1602. This staking out of claims for Spain and England had little noticeable effect on the California Indian, who was still very much in possession of his land.

1602 Five years before the settlement of Jamestown in Virginia, Luis Velasco of New Spain ordered Sebastián Vizcaíno to explore and claim the coast of California for Spain. Sailing from Acapulco, Mexico, on May 5, 1602, Vizcaíno rediscovered San Miguel and rechristened it San Diego de Alcalá, after a newly sainted Franciscan friar. Sailing to the north, Vizcaíno also named Santa Catalina, Santa Barbara, and Point Concepción before he landed in Monterey Bay and named it for Viceroy Gaspar de Zúniga, Count of Monterey. Vizcaíno sailed into Monterey Bay on December 16, 1602.

1769–1823 The Franciscans established twenty-one missions, taught Indians adobe building skills, agriculture, animal husbandry, and Christian doctrine. Girls were taught cooking and sewing. The missions (approximately thirty miles, or one day's travel, apart) and their dates of establishment are:

San Diego, July, 1769
San Carlos, June 3, 1770 (Carmel)
San Antonio de Padua, July 14, 1771
San Gabriel, September 8, 1771 (Los Angeles was an Asistencia to San Gabriel)
San Luis Obispo, September 1, 1772
San Francisco, October 9, 1776 (Mission Dolores)
San Juan Capistrano, November, 1776
Santa Clara, January 12, 1777
San Buenaventura, March 31, 1782
Santa Barbara, December 4, 1786
Purísima Concepción, December 8, 1789
Santa Cruz, September 25, 1791
Soledad, October 9, 1791
San José, June 11, 1797
San Juan Bautista, June 24, 1797
San Miguel, July 25, 1797
San Fernando, September 8, 1797
San Luis Rey, June, 1798
Santa Inez, September 17, 1804

San Rafael, December 14, 1817
San Francisco Solano, July 4, 1823

The earliest Spanish towns grew up in the shadows of the missions or near the *presidios*. The government organization, though based on the Spanish colonial pattern, seems to have "just growed" like Topsy. The viceroy resided in Mexico City with his *reiño*. The principal mission town of Monterey, because of its historical and geographic importance, soon became the seat of the territorial governor, in charge of the militia and the *presidios*. Town affairs were run by the *alcaldes* and their councils. This left the missions and the holders of larger land grants quite independent.

Legally the Indians were the king's wards, so the mission lands were considered to be a royal domain held for the Indians. Hence, the *padres*, going about the king's business of civilizing the natives, were deeply loyal to the throne, which spoke for both church and state. But, since the mission lands had to be managed and run, the *padres* were actually the government on them.

In more settled dioceses and archdioceses of New Spain, the bishops and archbishops controlled church properties. They had the right to use the regular clergy, but the priests and monks felt responsible only to their own superiors in Mexico and to the king. So the process of secularization of the missions had different meanings at different moments in history.

The diocese of California was created in 1783 and Bishop Reyes was sent to California to manage church affairs in his newly acquired ecclesiastical domain. The Franciscan *padres*, who by then had established six missions, had been taking orders from their mother house, the College of San Fernando in Mexico, and they were caught by surprise at this early secularization attempt. Indeed, Bishop Reyes had no surplus of secular or diocesan clergy available to take over the work of the missions. So the *padres*, or regular clergy, gained another thirty years of peace before the matter of secularization was again seriously considered by the Spanish *cortes*.

Later attempts to secularize the missions (in 1813, 1826, 1830, and 1846) were destined to remove mission property from all ecclesiastical control.

1784 Fray Junípero Serra died on August 28 at the age of seventy-one.

1786 Pedro Fages, as military governor of California, was empowered to make private land grants outside existing towns, missions, and Indian villages. These private grants became *ranchos* when devoted to cattle and stock raising and *haciendas* when their chief purpose was agricultural.

1790–92 Don Diego de Borica became governor of California and instituted reforms in the government and in education. Borica was succeeded by José Joaquín Arrillaga, who was in turn succeeded by Pablo Vincente Solá, the last Spanish governor of California.

1808 After Madrid capitulated to the forces of Napoleon and accepted Napoleon's brother Joseph as king, the creoles of Mexico used Viceroy José de Iturrigaray to get a greater share in government.

1810 Miguel Hildago y Costilla (1753–1811), a Mexican priest steeped in French revolutionary philosophy, initiated a revolt among the creoles in Guanajuato, seized Guadalajara, and marched on Mexico City. He was executed on July 31, but José María Morelos y Pavón (1765–1815), a mestizo priest and lieutenant of Hildago, continued the revolution. Declaring independence from Spain in 1813, he became head of an independent government, but he too was captured and shot in 1815.

1811–23 Californians were little affected by progress and setbacks of early Mexican revolts. The governors and the *padres* remained loyal to the Spanish viceroys and the crown. Many of the *padres* seemed confused by the royalist claims of the self-proclaimed creole Emperor Agustín I of Mexico. In November, 1823, Governor Arguello received official notice of the birth of the new Republic of Mexico and notified the Mexican minister of state of his allegiance.

The net results of the revolutionary period of California can be summed up as follows:

1. Supplies and reinforcements did not reach California from Mexico, and soldiers were not paid.

2. Most schools, apart from the mission schools, were closed chiefly because of the lack of teachers and funds and a shortage of books and supplies.

3. The continuing loyalty of the *padres* to the Spanish crown made them suspect to the new government and opened the door to a new wave of secularization of the missions.

4. The fidelity of the Spanish governors and other California royal-

ists to the crown of Spain caused the new Mexican governments to be suspicious of the loyalty of all Californians. This suspicion caused Mexican authorities to turn California into a penal colony, which in turn discouraged Monterey and local governments and ultimately turned many Californians against the government in Mexico.

5. Although the Mexican government inherited Spain's suspicion of foreign invasion and foreign trade, Californians were more friendly to foreign trade, to the settlement and intermarriage of incoming traders with Californians, and to the introduction of Yankee schools in California.

6. A rash of Indian revolts in and after 1824 threatened the missions, the *ranchos,* and the *haciendas.*

Mexican California

1824–34   The Republic of Mexico, born November 19, 1823, framed its constitution after that of the United States. The Province of the Californias (Upper and Lower) began to function as a Mexican state in January, 1824. The troublesome years that followed the birth of Mexican California witnessed a show of loyalty to the Republic and untoward events in this order:

1. In January, 1824, a *junta* of prominent citizens (military, civil, and ecclesiastical) was called to establish the government of the province of California. The *padres* were conspicuous by their absence, and they soon protested new taxes on mission products.

2. José María Echeandía, the first constitutional governor of California, was appointed *jefe político* and *comandante militar* of both Californias. His intent to move his capital from Monterey to the south created north-south strife of jealousy.

3. The soldiers revolted in Monterey in 1828 and again in 1829.

4. A peaceful Yankee invasion of California began in 1826, and by 1830 the Mexican government directed the governor of California to distribute public lands to settlers who would become Roman Catholics and could prove two years of residence in California. Other foreigners —Swiss, French, British, and Russian—were soon attracted to California.

5. Because Mexico used California as a penal colony, riots occurred between native Californians and Mexicans.

6. In 1828, the news of the expulsion of Spanish friars from Mexico reached California, but California expulsion was temporarily postponed.

1834–44 In 1834, the Mexican government secularized the California missions, depriving the Franciscans of control. While a few friars continued to serve in the mission areas until 1845, the effective years of the missions and mission schools ended in 1834. During their sixty-five years in California, the Franciscans assisted some 90,000 Indian baptisms and 28,000 marriages. Many Indians died under the restrictions of civilized life and from the white man's diseases, so only 30,000 mission Indians were returned to their old way of life in 1834. In California today, there are hardly more than 20,000 full-blooded Indians.

The secularization of the missions by Governor Figueroa, completed by Governor Pío Pico, was a gradual process begun on September 13, 1813, by the Spanish *cortes*. To the Mexican government it meant the organization of mission communities into towns and the distribution of surplus lands to the neophytes under secular rather than ecclesiastical administration. The missions were allowed to keep a separate *rancho* for the support of a place of public worship and for the support of a curate to hold church services.

As early as 1826 unmarried Indians who had been Christians from childhood and married Indians who had been Christians for fifteen years were permitted by law to leave the missions, but few did.

In 1833, secularization of the missions began in earnest, and in 1834 a widespread destruction of mission cattle and properties was effected. This discouraged some of the *padres*, who gave up their care of the remaining properties. From 1836 to 1842, the systematic spoliation of mission properties began. The appointed secular *mayordomos* of the missions used mission grain and cattle as government supplies and paid government debts by orders on various mission products.

Some Indians received portions of mission lands as a basis for creating Indian *pueblos*, but many of them neglected their lands and turned to drinking and stealing. At this point not a few Indians returned to their former neolithic way of living. Ultimately the Indian *pueblos* that had been substituted for mission control were complete failures.

After the death of Figueroa on September 9, 1835, governors Alvarado and Micheltoreno made efforts to restore the missions to their former glory, but they were ineffective. Finally, Governor Pío Pico authorized the sale and rental of mission estates to raise money for defense against war with the United States.

During the years of the demise of the educational endeavors of the missions, the governors and *alcaldes* of California explored other educational possibilities. The Mexican Californian was still the frontiersman, remote from the national capital. As a Mexican citizen, the average Californian had little more interest in education than Spanish colonials had. However, the governors improved the schools of Monterey, Santa Barbara, and Los Angeles. Figueroa opened new schools at Sonoma, Santa Clara, San Jose, San Gabriel, San Luis Rey, and San Diego. He permitted William Hartnell to open a college at San Jose—El Seminario de San Jose—as a normal school and college. In 1830, the tenth governor, Juan Bautista Alvarado, encouraged the establishment of schools and established typesetting and printing classes in San Jose; he even employed teachers from the United States when funds were available. In 1840, Governor Pío Pico planned special taxes for education. Teachers were to be paid from the public treasury and compulsory education was recommended.

1844–46 The last two years of Mexican California witnessed an acceleration of the turmoil that followed Figueroa's death in 1835. Revolution, civil war, the short-lived secession of California from Mexico—these were only manifestations of a great general movement toward independence for California. The Mexican governors were often considered as foreign rulers by Californians. Britain, France, Russia, and the United States watched closely the deterioration of Mexican control over California. Mexico ordered foreigners out of California, and it came as no surprise when the flag of the United States was raised at Monterey on July 7, 1846.

1846–48 The Mexican War continued for twenty months and five days after July 7, 1846. It was not an extraordinarily difficult time for Californians, but most California schools were closed during the war. By the terms of the Guadalupe Hidalgo Treaty, signed on February 2, 1848, California, New Mexico, and the northern portions of Sonora, Coahuila, and Tamaulipas were ceded to the United States. The United States paid Mexico fifteen million dollars and assumed the obligations of Mexico on the land it ceded.

1848–50   California remained under United States military government from the day the treaty was signed to December 17, 1849, when the first state government took office in San Jose, the first state capital. On September 9, 1850, the state of California was admitted to the Union. The 1848 population of 15,000 Californians grew to 90,000 in 1849 because of the gold rush. Although the 1849 constitution established a state school system on paper, the first schools that opened after the war were private schools. San Francisco alone experimented with an elected school board in 1848.

The Educational History of California (1849–1967)

Chapters One, Two, and Six offered some details of the early history of California schools. Our purpose here is to list the highlights of this history as they fall into six discrete periods.

THE ARCHITECTURAL ERA OF THE STATE SCHOOL SYSTEM, 1850–1880

Although the 1849 constitution called for a state school system, its development was left to the legislators. That the system did not grow rapidly is evidenced below.

1851   The first laws on public education were enacted by the legislature. In the hope of getting schools into operation rapidly, the legislature permitted the use of state school funds by private schools.

1853   Of California's 17,821 children, 3,314 were enrolled in school. Judge Marvin, the state superintendent of public instruction, reported that 232,000 acres of public land had been sold to create a state school fund.

1856   California had 367 public schools, 486 teachers, and 35,722 enrolled pupils. It had nearly 250,000 inhabitants, as against its 1850 population of 92,595.

1857–60   Before 1856, the state legislature had already authorized the following administrative structure and financial procedures:

1. State board of education composed of the governor, the surveyor general, and the superintendent of public instruction

2. The office of the county superintendent of schools
3. County boards of examiners for teachers
4. A public (nonsectarian) system of elementary schools
5. A state school fund derived from the sale of public land
6. A state school tax and maximum county and district tax rate.

The legislature was importuned to put more public land up for sale and to provide more money for schools through increased taxes. By 1860 an extensive system of elementary schools with some grammar-grade classes was functioning, but secondary schools and higher education were offered only by private academies and colleges.

1861 San Francisco graduates its first public high school class. The high school began as Union Grammar School in 1856 and became San Francisco High School in 1858.

1862 The legislature authorized the first state normal school, established in San Francisco and later moved to San Jose.

1863 Wartime economies due to the Civil War curtailed the development of the state school system. John Swett was elected state superintendent of public instruction.

1868 The legislature created the University of California on March 21.

1875 A highly centralized system of public elementary schools, grammar-grade instruction, and a state university had been achieved. Although state school apportionments had reached $498,509 in 1874 and $1,215,247 in 1875, state aid to education was not adequate. The financing of public education was a major cause of the revision of the state constitution.

1879 On May 5, Californians ratified the new constitution, which effected these educational changes:

1. Decentralized the state system by increasing the authority of the county superintendent over curriculum, textbooks, and teacher certification.

2. Increased the minimum school term to six months.

3. Increased the term of office of state and county superintendents to four years.

4. Made the University of California and its board of regents a public corporation, which was to manage university business without legislative interference.

THE MODERNIZATION OF THE STATE SCHOOL SYSTEM, 1880–1925

1883   The Perry Constitutional Amendment, adopted by a majority of the electors, approved the printing of state school textbooks to be sold at cost to pupils.

1886   A series of laws, legal opinions, and court cases for state aid for public high schools was begun. On March 20, 1891, a law approving union high school districts was passed and contested in the courts. The matter of state aid for high schools was ultimately settled in a 1902 constitutional amendment.

1887   On May 7, the cornerstone of Stanford University was laid by the former governor Leland Stanford and his wife. The university began its work on October 1, 1890, under President David Starr Jordan.

1907   The first California junior college law was passed, permitting city and district high schools to offer work in grades 13 and 14.

1908   State support was approved for evening elementary and high schools.

1909   The employment of children during school hours was prohibited by state law.

1910   The direct-primary law removed state, county, and district school offices from partisan politics.

1911–17   The election of Governor Hiram W. Johnson on the Progressive Republican ticket was a signal for much progressive school legislation, examples of which are:

1. County school boards were permitted to provide transportation for pupils (1911).

2. The first California teacher-tenure law was passed (1912).

3. The California Teachers' Retirement System was begun, modestly at first (1913).

4. Poll tax as a source of revenue for schools was repealed (1915).

5. School districts were permitted to levy taxes for kindergartens, which were to be operated at district expense (1915).

6. Physical education was required at all school levels (1916).

7. Smith-Hughes classes in agriculture, vocational training, and home economics were approved in California (1916).

8. High schools were required to furnish pupils with free textbooks purchased at local district expense (1916).

1920 State aid for all public education (kindergartens, elementary and secondary schools, and junior colleges) was approved as was the apportionment of state school funds on the average-daily-attendance basis.

1923–24 The two-year normal school was abandoned in favor of four-year state teachers' colleges, which were permitted to grant the B.A. degree. The use of radio in public schools was approved.

THE PREDEPRESSION AND DEPRESSION YEARS, 1925–1937

1925–26 These years were marked by a war between a progressive state superintendent (Will C. Wood) and an economy-minded governor (Friend William Richardson).

1927 State Superintendent William John Cooper improved state school financing, encouraged progressive practices in public school, and in 1929 became the U.S. Commissioner of Education.

1928 Mark Keppel, former Riverside city superintendent and Los Angeles county superintendent of schools, died on June 16 at the age of sixty-one. Keppel had long served as a distinguished leader, an effective superintendent, and a member and officer of the CTA. He had worked hard for the codification of California School Law.

1929 California's first school code was published. On September 10, Los Angeles Junior College was opened in buildings vacated by UCLA when UCLA moved to Westwood. The stock market crash did not have an immediate effect on California education, but its ultimate effects were nearly catastrophic. They included these setbacks for public education in California:

1. County welfare cases were so numerous that most counties could not carry their share of school support.

2. The one-hundred-million-dollar perpetual school fund was taken from the public schools by Governor Rolph to balance an ailing state budget.

3. Teachers' salaries and expenditures for school supplies were reduced drastically.

4. The educational programs were cut to bare essentials with the elimination of all so-called frills.

5. Most districts failed to provide adequate funds for building maintenance and replacements and new buildings needed for an increasing population.

1933 The Riley-Stewart constitutional amendment transferred to the state the support that counties had previously raised for schools, since most available county funds were needed for welfare cases. This involved a complete reorganization of school finance and a drastic revision of the 1929 school code.

1933–34 Federal aid to education came to California by the way of WPA projects, the NYA, and CCC camps. The adult education program in California was revived to give constructive occupations to the jobless. It was heavily supported by Federal Emergency Education funds.

1935–36 A minimum state teachers' salary of $1,320 per year was adopted by the state, which permitted the establishment of district teacher-retirement systems as supplements to the small state retirement benefits of $600 per year.

1937–38 The experience gained by educators in providing practical or rehabilitation education for the jobless provided the incentive for vocational education courses and for apprenticeship training in revived junior colleges. As the junior college program was revived, it offered terminal courses, vocational education, and academic or lower-division college courses, in that order. Vocational courses in high schools and junior colleges made a solid foundation for the training of workers in new industries and in national defense programs after 1939.

NATIONAL DEFENSE EDUCATION, WAR TRAINING,
AND POSTWAR SCHOOL ISSUES, 1939–1952

1939–40 Job training of adults for the new war industries had the effect of making regular secondary eductaion more practical and of greater use for graduates entering the business world, national defense industries, and the armed services. If the depression had brought a great influx of jobless people to California, national defense efforts and World War II were to bring still more service-connected defense-industry families to California. Many of these people were housed in military or defense projects, which provided no taxes for school districts until the federal government began to subsidize these school districts by in-lieu-of-tax payments.

1940–45 The financial strain on local school districts forced repeated constitutional amendments to increase state aid and apportionments to local districts. The financial crisis during Governor Earl Warren's administration forced the state to study the possibility of reorganization of school districts and to adopt state apportionments that would equalize educational opportunities and costs.

1945 The Fair Equalization Law expanded and adjusted state aid to local districts on an equalizing basis.

1946 The commission on the reorganization of school districts began to function.

POSTWAR TRENDS AND CURRENT ISSUES IN PUBLIC EDUCATION, 1947–1967

The legislature has repeatedly revised the Fair Equalization Law and improved the size and methods of state apportionments. Curriculum-revision programs have attempted to improve instruction in science, mathematics, and foreign languages.

A revision of the state's complex method of teacher certification produced the new standard teaching credentials, which stressed the academic training of teachers and put ceilings on the number of education courses required.

1957 Early signs of an impending conservative revolution in California education became apparent.

1962 Max Rafferty was elected to the state superintendency on a conservative program for California education.

1966 Rafferty was reelected, and Ronald Reagan was elected as state governor on a platform of greater economy, especially in welfare and education programs.

1967 Economical management of public education was recommended to the legislature and school authorities.

THE GOVERNORS OF CALIFORNIA

JULY 1, 1769, TO JULY 1, 1969

Although California was claimed as a part of the Spanish empire on September 28, 1542, Spanish governors of California (as opposed to governors of Las Californias, that is, Lower and Upper California) date from the colonization of California in 1769.

Ten Spanish governors were followed by sixteen Mexican governors, including Pío Pico, who served twice. The Mexican governors were followed by seven U.S. military governors from July 7, 1846, to December 20, 1849, and thirty-three elected governors of the state of California. A complete list of these governors follows.

Spanish Governors, July 1, 1769, to November, 1822

1. Gaspar de Portolá, 1768–70
2. Felipe de Barrí, 1770–75
3. Felipe de Neve, 1775–82
4. Pedro Fages, 1782–91
5. José Antonio Roméu, 1791–92
6. José Joaquín de Arrillaga, 1792–94
7. Diego de Borica, 1794–1800
8. José Joaquín de Arrillaga, 1800–14
9. José Argüello, 1814–15
10. Pablo Vicente de Solá, 1815–22

Mexican Governors, November, 1822, to July 7, 1846

1. Pablo Vicente de Solá, November, 1822
2. Luis Argüello, 1822–25 (acting)
3. José María de Echeandía, 1825–31
4. Manuel Victoria, 1831–32
5. Pío Pico, 1832 (20 days)
6. José María Echeandía, 1832–33 (in the south only)
7. Agustín Vicente Zamorano, 1832–33 (in the north only)
8. José Figueroa, 1833–35
9. José Castro, 1835–36 (acting)
10. Nicolás Gutiérrez, 1836 (acting, 4 months)
11. Mariano Chico, 1836 (3 months)
12. Nicolás Gutiérrez, 1836 (acting, 3 months)
13. Juan Bautista Alvarado, 1836–42
14. Manuel Micheltorena, 1842–46
15. Pío Pico, 1845–46
16. José María Flores, 1846–47

United States Military Governors, July 7, 1846, to December 20, 1849

1. Commodore John D. Sloat, July 7, 1846
2. Commodore Robert F. Stockton, July 29, 1846
3. Captain John C. Frémont, January 19, 1847
4. General Stephen W. Kearney, March 1, 1847
5. Colonel Richard B. Mason, May 31, 1847
6. General Persifor F. Smith, February 28, 1849
7. General Bennett Riley, April 12, 1849

Governors of California, December 20, 1849, to January 3, 1967

1.	Peter H. Burnett	Ind. Dem.	December 20, 1849
2.	John McDougal	Ind. Dem.	January 9, 1851
3.	John Bigler	Dem.	January 8, 1852
4.	John Neely Johnson	Amer.	January 9, 1856
5.	John B. Weller	Dem.	January 8, 1858
6.	Milton S. Latham	Lecomp. D.	January 9, 1860
7.	John G. Downey	Lecomp. D.	January 14, 1860
8.	Leland Stanford	Rep.	January 10, 1862
9.	Frederick F. Low	Union	December 10, 1863
10.	Henry H. Haight	Dem.	December 5, 1867

11.	Newton Booth	Rep.	December 8, 1871
12.	Romauldo Pacheco	Rep.	February 27, 1875
13.	William Irwin	Dem.	December 9, 1875
14.	George C. Perkins	Rep.	January 8, 1880
15.	George Stoneman	Dem.	January 10, 1883
16.	Washington Bartlett	Dem.	January 8, 1887
17.	Robert W. Waterman	Rep.	September 13, 1887
18.	Henry H. Markham	Rep.	January 8, 1891
19.	James H. Budd	Dem.	January 11, 1895
20.	Henry T. Gage	Rep.	January 4, 1899
21.	George C. Pardee	Rep.	January 7, 1903
22.	James N. Gillett	Rep.	January 9, 1907
23.	Hiram W. Johnson	Prog. Rep.	January 3, 1911
24.	William D. Stephens	Rep.	March 15, 1917
25.	Friend W. Richardson	Rep.	January 8, 1923
26.	Clement C. Young	Rep.	January 4, 1927
27.	James Rolph	Rep.	January 6, 1931
28.	Frank Merriam	Rep.	June 2, 1934
29.	Culbert Olson	Dem.	January 2, 1939
30.	Earl Warren	Rep.	January 4, 1943
31.	Goodwin Knight	Rep.	October 5, 1953
32.	Edwin G. Brown	Dem.	January 5, 1959
33.	Ronald Reagan	Rep.	January 3, 1967

THE ORGANIZATION

OF THE CALIFORNIA EDUCATION CODE

The education code of the 1960s was recodified at the 1959 regular session of the California legislature. It was the third and last attempt to bring all state laws on public education together into one document. The current code, which supercedes the 1929 school code and the 1945 education code, is a massive document of 2,368 pages, including frontmatter, tables of contents, appendixes, and indexes. The code is available for sale in two volumes published by the Documents Section of the state of California.

The codification and indexing of this extensive legal publication represent improvements over the earlier codes. It is now easier to find specific laws on public education. Although no teacher or school administrator could be expected to have a comprehensive knowledge of the whole code, it does seem desirable that public school employees have an overview of the state law as it is organized in the code.

Apart from the tables of contents, the table of cross references (of current code sections and of those of the previous code), and extensive indexes, the code offers in its frontmatter a list of the members of the state board of education and of the board of trustees of the California state colleges as well as directories of the state department of education and the county superintendents of schools.

The legal material proper (1,728 pages) is organized into two major parts: statutory law (specific laws on schools and education, which compose the code proper) and an appendix of constitutional and general laws from twelve other California codes as these apply to the organization and management of public schools. The following outline of the code and its appendix gives an overview of all California laws on education. (The numbers in parentheses are sections.)

The Education Code (1959–1967)

Part 1   *General Provisions and the Organizational Structure of the Public School System (1–5000)*

    Division   1   *General provisions (1–100)*
        Chapter 1   Establishment and construction of the code, including rights of persons now holding office or holding certificates and credentials, and definition of code terms
        Chapter 2   Administration and certification of oaths
        Chapter 3   Language of instruction (the English language)

    Division   2   *State educational agencies (101–600)*
        Chapter 1   State board of education—powers and duties
        Chapter 2   State superintendent of public instruction—powers and duties
        Chapter 3   State department of education
        Chapter 4   State Council of Educational Planning and Coordination
        Chapter 5   National defense education

    Division   3   *County organization (601–900)*

    Division   4   *Local educational agencies (local boards, districts, and superintendents) (901–1600)*

    Division   5   *Organization and reorganization of districts (1601–5000)*

Part 2   *Educational Program and Personnel (5001–15000)*

    Division   6   *System of public instruction (types of schools, classes, facilities, and libraries) (5001–7500)*

    Division   7   *Educational program (types of courses and instruction) (7501–9200)*

    Division   8   *Instructional materials (books and teaching aids) (9201–10500)*

Division 9 Pupils (admission, attendance, expulsion) (*10501–12900*)

Division 10 Employees (employment conditions, certification, classified employees, and retirement) (*12901–15000*)

Part 3 Property, Transportation, and Finance (*15001–22499*)

Division 11 School sites and construction (*15001–15800*)

Division 12 Management and control of property and equipment (*15801–16800*)

Division 13 Supplementary services (*16801–17150*)

Division 14 State financial support and management (budget, ADA, etc.) (*17151–20100*)

Division 15 County financial support and management (*20101–20500*)

Division 16 Local school district financial support and management (*20501–22499*)

Before continuing with the education code, it will be of value to give a more detailed breakdown of Division 14, since it gives the particulars of the methods of state apportionments to local school districts. This detailed breakdown should throw some light on our treatment of state apportionments in Chapter Three.

The complex financial partnership between the state and the local school district is spelled out in 290 pages of law arranged in the first four chapters of Division 14:

Chapter 1 State financial management and control

Chapter 2 Sources of maintenance and disbursement of the state school fund

Chapter 3 Computation of allowances and apportionment from the state school fund

Chapter 4 Federal aid for education

The local school district should be especially interested in the seventy-four pages of Chapter 3. For those who need an overview of it or need to refer to the code, we offer this outline from the code's index.

Chapter 3 Computation of allowances and apportionments from state school fund (17601–18461)

home economics extension work, insurance for athletic teams, and notices of election) (*31001–31999*)

Appendix to the Education Code

The 345-page appendix to the code quotes extracts from the state constitution and from seventeen other California codes of law that apply to the organization, management, and control of public and private education in the state.

THE STATE CONSTITUTION

Besides quoting all of Article IX (on education), the code lists extracts from Article IV (on legislation), Article XI (on cities, counties, and towns), Article XII (on corporations), Article XIII (on revenue and taxation), and Article XX (on the eight-hour work day and subversive persons and groups) as these apply to education in the state.

EXTRACTS FROM CALIFORNIA CODES

Seventeen codes besides the education code have laws that schools must observe. These are:

1. Agricultural code (on market milk and milk containers)

2. Business and professions code (on cosmetology classes, educational uses of horse-racing license fees, and retail liquor stores—not to be licensed for properties in the vicinity of schools, public playgrounds, churches, and hospitals)

3. Civil code (on safe water for drinking and fire protection and the liability for accidents on public property)

4. Code of civil procedure (on Sundays and holidays, mechanics liens, eminent domain, and public records)

5. Elections code (as it applies to the election of school boards and elected school officials)

6. Government code (on legal residences; on the state seal, flag, and emblems; on the liability of public employees and public entities and indemnification of public employees; on dangerous conditions in

public properties; on liabilities, claims, and defenses). Extensive extracts from this code deal further with public officers and employees, wage and salary deductions (including withholding taxes), appointments, nominations, commissions and oaths of office, official bonds, resignations and vacancies, air travel insurance, and public works and public purchases and contracts.

Finally, after defining the relationships between the departments and agencies of the state, the specific laws applicable to schools and school employees are listed: the state civil service, the state retirement system, federal old age, survivors insurance, and so on.

7. Health and safety code (on control of communicable diseases, sanitation, fire, and earthquake protection and on the care of physically handicapped children and mental health problems)

8. Insurance code (as it applies to insurance for schools, camps, common carriers, and workmen's liability)

9. Labor code (on employment of minors, working conditions of persons employed by public agencies or for public works, and safety for workmen in schools and public works)

10. Military and veterans code (on state militia and California Cadet Corps; on emblems and veterans memorials)

11. Penal code (on molestation and annoyance of minors, on loiterers on school grounds, etc.)

12. Public resources code (on acquisition, administration, protection, and reforestration of forest lands by counties and tax adjustment for such lands)

13. Public utilities code (on charter party carriers of passengers and the basis of charges for these services). This code does not apply to school bus contractors, who are compensated by parents of children attending public, private, and parochial schools.

14. Revenue and taxation code (on equalization of property taxes by the state board of equalization and technical guidance on the distribution of tax money from properties on the secured roll and the unsecured roll, on redemptions, and on intangibles). Also outlined here are exemptions from the sales-and-use taxes for school cafeteria meals and exemptions from vehicle license fees by educational institutions.

15. Street and highways code (gives school districts the right to collect taxes for access roads to school buildings even if by so doing the district exceeds its maximum tax rate)

16. Vehicle code (gives regulations for school buses and requirements for drivers and regulates student licenses in driver training courses). This code also details the liability of public agencies that own and operate buses and the requirements for traffic signs, signals, and markings for street crossings at schools and for school bus signals. It further regulates the speed of school buses and the special stops they must make and lists special lighting equipment, safety belts, and the size of school bus lettering. Finally, it defines violations of the code, penalties, and the disposition of fees, fines, and forfeitures collected.

17. Welfare and institutions code (details the law governing juvenile courts, juvenile halls, ranches, and camps, California Industries for the Blind, and coordination of programs for handicapped children). This code also regulates the use of federal funds for the welfare and education of Indians, including medical attention for sick and injured Indians.

Finally, the code includes three validating acts from the general laws of California of 1962 and 1963. These acts validate the organization, boundaries, acts, proceedings, and bonds of public bodies (for example, boards of education), and they provide limitations of time within which legal actions may be commenced in connection with the new validated acts, which might have previously appeared to be invalid.

THE ADMINISTRATIVE ORGANIZATION

OF THE STATE SCHOOL SYSTEM

California's system of public education has become so extensive that a practical means of identifying its organization and its state, county, and district administrative personnel had to be prepared by the state department of public instruction. Therefore, since 1950, the department's bureau of research has published annually a *Directory of Administrative and Supervising Personnel of California's Public Schools,* which includes the school organization of the state department, the 58 counties, and the 1,413 school districts in the state. The school district data includes the grade levels served by a given district and its current school enrollment.

The stated purposes of the 1966 directory are to give the following information:

1. Names and addresses of the members of the state board of education and the professional staff of the state department of education

2. Names and addresses of the members of the various commissions and committees that are advisory to the state board of education

3. Names of the fifty-eight county superintendents of schools and their administrative and supervisory staff members, addresses, and telephone numbers

4. Names of superintendents of schools and their administrative and supervisory staff members in the 1,413 school districts in the state, addresses, and telephone numbers

5. Addresses, telephone numbers, enrollments, and grade spans of all the schools in the state

6. Alphabetical indexes of personal names in the directory, the names of school districts (including nonoperating districts), and the names of all schools

The directory is based on a complete coding system that covers state and county operations and the coded identification of all districts and schools in the state. This codification is of particular importance for the data-processing equipment now used in the state department, county offices, and large school districts. It is the intent of the department to use the coding system for all official state documents.

The system identifies state offices with an initial S and department divisions as S-001, S-002, and so on. The bureau in the division appears as S-002-0010, S-002-0031, and so on. The fifty-eight counties are identified 01 through 58 and districts within counties are, for example, 58-010. Finally, schools in the districts are listed as 58-010-002 and so on.

The following outline of the coded directory with some explanatory notes gives an overview of California's educational agencies and their identification.

The State Offices

S-000   State Board of Education

The ten appointed members, with the state superintendent as the secretary and executive officer of the board.

S-001   State Superintendent of Public Instruction

This elected officer also serves as director of education inasmuch as he heads the state department. His office includes the chief deputy superintendent, the assistant superintendent in charge of the Los Angeles office, secretaries, and a special assistant to the superintendent.

S-002 *Division of Departmental Administration*

The division and its bureaus are headed by the chief deputy superintendent, who is responsible for these functions:

Bureau of Educational Research (S-002-0010)
Fiscal Office (S-002-0020)
Legal Office (S-002-0030)
Investigative Office (S-002-0031)
Personnel Office (S-002-0040)
Bureau of Publications (S-002-0050)
Bureau of Systems and Data Processing (S-002-0060)
Educational Data Processing Project (S-002-0061)

S-003 *Division of Instruction*

This massive division, under the direction of an associate superintendent, seems to reflect the superintendent's involvement with and interest in instruction. The bureaus and agencies under this division include:

Bureaus of Elementary and Secondary Education (S-003-0010)
Bureaus of Audio-visual and Library Education (S-003-0020)
Bureau of Pupil Personnel Services (S-003-0030)
Bureau of Health Education, Physical Education, and Recreation (S-003-0040)
Bureau of National Defense Education Act Administration (S-003-0050)
Foreign Language Placement Project (S-003-0060)
Vocational Education (S-003-0070)
   Manpower Development and Training Program (S-003-0071)
   Bureau of Agricultural Education (S-003-0072)
   Bureau of Business Education (S-003-0073)
   Bureau of Homemaking Education (S-003-0074)
   Bureau of Industrial Education (S-003-0075)

S-004 *Division of Libraries (State Library)*

The state librarian heads this division.

S-005 *Division of Public School Administration*

The division chief is an associate superintendent responsible for these bureaus and services:

Bureau of Administrative Services (S-005-0010)
Food Services Office (S-005-0020)
Bureau of School Apportionments and Reports (S-005-0030)
Bureau of School District Organization (S-005-0040)
Bureau of School Planning (S-005-0050)

Agency for Surplus Property (S-005-0060). State warehouses in Sacramento, San Leandro, and Los Angeles operate under this agency.

Bureau of Textbooks and Publications Distribution (S-005-0070)

S-006   Division of Special Schools and Services

A deputy superintendent is chief of this division, responsible for these bureaus and schools:

Bureau for Physically Exceptional Children (S-006-0010)

Bureau for Handicapped and Mentally Exceptional Children (S-006-0020)

State Special Schools (for the blind, deaf, and cerebral-palsied) (S-006-0030). These schools include: California School for the Blind, 3001 Derby Street, Berkeley 94705; California School for the Deaf, 2601 Waring Street, Berkeley 94705; School for Cerebral-Palsied Children (Northern California), Lake Merced Boulevard and Winston Drive, San Francisco 90000; School for Cerebral-Palsied Children (Southern California), 4339 East State College Drive, Los Angeles 90032.

S-007   Division of Higher Education[1]

The chief of this division is an associate superintendent responsible for these bureaus and services:

Bureau of Adult Education (S-007-0010)

Civil Defense Education (S-007-0011)

Bureau of Junior College Administration and Finances (S-007-0020)

Bureau of Junior College General Education (S-007-0030)

Bureau of Junior College Vocational-Technical Education (S-007-0040)

Bureau of Readjustment Education (S-007-0050)

Bureau of Teacher Education and Certification (S-007-0060)

S-008   Office of Compensatory Education

This division, newly created in 1967,[2] is headed by an associate superintendent, who is responsible for these bureaus:

[1] It should be remembered that the state department of education does not now have any responsibility for the University of California or the California state colleges. For purposes of coordination, however, the state superintendent is an *ex officio* member of the board of regents of the University of California and of the board of trustees of the California state colleges.

[2] The compensatory education office in the state department is the latest of many expansions necessary to cooperate with massive federal aid programs. The office of this division, which began as a bureau, is currently headed by California's first Negro associate superintendent, Wilson C. Riles.

Bureau of Compensatory Education—Administration and Finance (S-008-0010)

Bureau of Community Services (S-008-0020)

Bureau of Program Development (S-008-0030)

Bureau of Program Evaluation (S-008-0040)

Compensatory Education School Educational Bureau (S-008-0050)

Bureau of Teacher Education for Disadvantaged Children (S-008-0060)

Bureau of Intergroup Relations (S-008-0070)

S-009   California Maritime Academy

The academy, which trains officers for the merchant marine, has long enjoyed special status apart from the California state colleges and special schools. It has its own board of governors, whose membership includes the chief deputy state superintendent, acting for the superintendent. The executive officer of the academy is a retired U.S. Navy rear admiral.

S-010   Committee on Credentials

This state committee now has the important duty of implementing the revised teaching-credential program provided for in the Fisher Act, which took effect on January 1, 1964 (see Chapter Five). The superintendent recognizes the importance of this committee by the fact that he himself serves as its chairman.

S-011   Advisory Compensatory Education Commission

The commission of fourteen members is chaired by Associate Superintendent Riles, who is the commission's executive secretary. The membership represents social welfare organizations, the California School Board Association, California's university, the state colleges, Catholic schools, the American Jewish Committee, Mexican-Americans, and the state senate.

S-012   The State Curriculum Commission

This commission was originally created by the state board of education to secure professional guidance on the curriculum for the whole state and on the study of state textbooks for adoption by the board. The state superintendent is chairman of the commission, whose membership includes professors, elementary and secondary school administrators and teachers, and directors of education in large city districts.

S-013   Commission on Equal Opportunities in Education

The fifteen-member commission includes civic-minded citizens from all parts of the state.

S-014   State Teacher-Retirement System

This extensive organization is quite naturally put under the direction of the state department of education.

S-015   State Committee on Public Education

The latest of the state department's committees and commissions was created, like those that preceded it, by the state board of education. Title V of the California administrative code lists the rules and the organization of this and other state educational committees.

County Schools, Offices, and School Districts

The fifty-eight California counties are coded in alphabetical order in this manner: Alameda (01-000), Alpine (02-000), Imperial (13-000), Los Angeles (19-000), San Diego (37-000), San Francisco (38-000), Sierra (46-000), Yuba (58-000). These eight counties are selected because they are widely different in size and organization, and they together serve therefore as representative examples of county and district structures throughout the state. Enrollment data used is drawn from the 1966 directory.

ALAMEDA COUNTY

Alameda County is a large and thickly populated East-Bay county.

01-000-000   Office of the County Superintendent (in Hayward)
  01-010-000   Alameda City Unified District (enrollment 11,407)
    01-010-0010   Donald Lum Elementary School, first of thirteen elementary schools in the district
    01-010-6005   Alameda Adult School
    01-010-6010   Alameda High School
    01-010-6015   Encinal High School

01-020-0000 Albany City Unified District (enrollment 2,494). The district has four elementary schools, a high school, and an adult school.

01-030-0000 Amador Valley Joint Union High School District (enrollment 1,267)

01-040-0000 Berkeley City Unified District (enrollment 16,809)

    01-040-0010 Columbus Elementary School, the first of seventeen elementary schools

    01-040-6005 Berkeley Evening High School

    01-040-6010 Berkeley Senior High School

    01-040-6015 Berkeley Senior High School (West Campus)

    01-040-6020 Garfield Junior High School

    01-040-6025 McKinley Continuation High School

    01-040-6030 Willard Junior High School

    01-050-0000 Castro Valley Unified District (enrollment 9,808)

    01-060-0000 Emery Unified District (enrollment 623)

01-080-0000 Green Joint Elementary District (enrollment 161)

01-090-0000 Hayward Unified District (enrollment 30,113). This district has forty-three elementary schools and five high schools.

01-100-0000 Irman Elementary District (enrollment 27)

01-110-0000 Livermore Elementary District (enrollment 6,222)

01-120-6000 Livermore Joint Union High School District (enrollment 2,073)

01-170-0000 Oakland City Unified District (enrollment 66,223). This district includes sixty-six elementary schools and twenty-seven high schools, including adult and technical high schools. The junior colleges in Oakland are operated by their separate junior college district.

01-180-0000 Peralta Junior College District

    01-180-7000 Peralta Junior College (enrollment 8,231)

    01-180-7005 Laney Junior College (enrollment 3,043)

    01-180-7010 Merritt College (enrollment 5,188)

Other Alameda County districts include San Leandro, San Lorenzo, and Sunol Glen elementary.

ALPINE COUNTY

Alpine County is a sparsely populated, mountainous county south of Lake Tahoe.

02-000-0000   Office of the County Superintendent (at Markleeville)
    02-010-0000   Alpine County Unified School District (enrollment 116)
       02-010-0010   Clay Elementary School (enrollment 45)
       02-010-0020   Lincoln Elementary School (enrollment 37)

The Alpine county and district superintendents are one and the same person. The only other administrators are the elementary school teaching principals. There are less than two hundred pupils in school in the entire county.

IMPERIAL COUNTY

Imperial County, at the southeastern end of the state, is a flat, agricultural, and semidesert area. A concentration of urban population includes the cities of Brawley, Calexico, El Centro, and Holtville.

13-000-0000   Office of the County Superintendent (at El Centro). The county office operates these two special schools:

   13-990-0010   Juvenile Hall School, grades 1–7 (enrollment 9)

   13-990-0020   Kepley School for Physically Handicapped Children
      13-010-0000   Brawley Elementary District (enrollment 3,487)
         13-010-0010   Barbara Worth School, the first of seven elementary schools in the district
      13-010-6000   Brawley High School District (enrollment 1,294)
         13-020-6005   Brawley High School. The district superintendent is also principal of the high school, which offers courses in grades 9 through 12.
      13-030-0000   Calexico Elementary District (enrollment 2,616)
         13-030-0010   De Anza Intermediate School (a junior high school with grades 7 and 8)
         13-030-0020   Dool Elementary School, the first of four elementary schools in the district
      13-040-6000   Calexico Union High School District (enrollment 907)
         13-040-6005   Calexico High School
      13-050-0000   Calipatria Unified School District (enrollment 1,279). The district has three elementary schools and a high school that enrolls 324 students.

The other districts in the county are El Centro Elementary District, Central Union High School District; Holtville Union Elementary School

District, Holtville Union High School District; Imperial Junior College District, Imperial Unified District; San Pasqual Unified; and seven very small elementary districts.

LOS ANGELES COUNTY

In striking contrast to Imperial County, Los Angeles County has a concentration of seven million people, three million of whom are served by the Los Angeles City Unified School District (enrollment 662,565). There are districts in Los Angeles County as small as the Wilsona Elementary School District (enrollment: 79) in Lancaster.

19-000-0000   Office of the County Superintendent
   19-520-0000   Los Angeles Unified and Los Angeles College District
   19-920-0000   Wilson Elementary District with one elementary school

SAN FRANCISCO CITY AND COUNTY

San Francisco offers a unique situation in that it has a combined city-county government and a combined city-county school district, with a single city-county head of education and a city-county central administration. It is currently the third largest school district in California, ranking after Los Angeles City Unified District and San Diego City Unified District. The San Francisco district operates all the elementary and secondary schools in the city-county and the City College of San Francisco (grades 13 and 14).

SIERRA COUNTY

The county superintendent of this northeastern mountainous county is also the district superintendent of the Sierra-Plumas Joint Unified School District, which laps over into Plumas County to the north. The unified district enrolls about 800 pupils in four elementary schools, two junior-senior high schools (at Alleghany and Loyalton), and one high school at Donnieville, the county seat. The elementary schools serve grades 1 to 6 only.

YUBA COUNTY

This small, mountainous county adjoins Sierra and Plumas counties. It has 24 elementary schools in 6 elementary districts, two high schools (one at Wheatland and one at Marysville) and a junior college at Marysville. The junior college enrolls almost 2,500 students from a wide mountainous area.

SELECTED BIBLIOGRAPHIES

Books and resource materials on California and its school system are extensive and are not always easily available. These bibliographies, therefore, are organized on the basis of the availability of resource materials.

Books in print in 1966, government documents, and recent periodicals

Albrecht, Gustav. "A Survey of Teacher Opinion in California," *Phi Delta Kappan.* Vol. 42, no. 3 (December, 1960).

American Council on Education. *Accredited Institutions of Higher Education.* Washington, D.C., 1966. The council prepares booklets semiannually for the Federation of Regional Accrediting Commissions for Higher Education. This book lists all accredited colleges in California as of September, 1966.

Bancroft, Hubert Howe. *California Pioneer Register and Index, 1769–1800.* Baltimore: Regional Publishing Co., 1964.

Bass, Theodore, and Arnold Wolpert. *Teaching in California.* San Francisco: Chandler Publishing Co., 1963.

Bolton, Herbert Eugene. *Guide to Materials for the History of the United States* (in the Principal Archives of Mexico). New York: Kraus Reprint Corporation, 1965.

Brown, Kenneth. "The Conservative Revolution (in California) in Historical Perspective," *Phi Delta Kappan.* Vol. 42, no. 3 (December, 1960).

California Education Code. Sacramento: California Department of General Services, 1966.

California State Department of Education. *Directory of Administrators and Supervisory Personnel of California Public Schools*. Sacramento, 1966.

California Teachers' Association. *Teachers' Legal Guide*. Los Angeles: CTA Southern Section, n.d.

————. *CTA Journal, Centennial Edition 1863–1963* (May, 1962).

————. *Financing California Public Schools* (December, 1967).

Chapman, Charles Edward. *Colonial Hispanic America: A History*. New York: Macmillan, 1938.

Crouch, Winston W., *et al. California Government and Politics*. Englewood Cliffs, N.J.: Prentice-Hall, 1957.

Dana, Richard Henry. *Two Years Before the Mast*. New York: New American Library, 1964.

Hunt, Maurice P., Max Rafferty, and Harry A. Fosdick. "Education: California's Disaster Area," *Phi Delta Kappan*. Vol. 47, no. 3 (November, 1965).

Hyink, Bernard L. *Politics and Government in California*. New York: Thomas Y. Crowell Co., 1959.

Langer, William L. (ed.). *An Encyclopedia of World History*. Boston: Houghton Mifflin, 1948.

Lummis, Charles F. *The Spanish Pioneers*. Glorieta, N.M.: Rio Grande Press, 1963.

Moehlman, Arthur B. *School Administration*. Boston: Houghton Mifflin, 1951.

Rafferty, Max. "Children of Uranus," *Phi Delta Kappan*. Vol. 42, no. 1 (October, 1960).

Robinson, Don. "The Conservative Revolution in California Education," *Phi Delta Kappan*. Vol. 42, no. 3 (December, 1960).

Stone, James C. *California's Commitment to Public Education*. New York: Thomas Y. Crowell Co., 1961.

U.S. Office of Education, *Federal Aids for College Students*. Washington, D.C.: Government Printing Office, 1966.

Basic books and resources no longer being printed but generally available in adequate libraries

Atherton, Gertrude F. *Golden Gate Country*. New York: Duell, Sloane and Pearce, 1945.

Bancroft, Hubert Howe. *Chronicles of the Builders of the Commonwealth: Historical Character Study*. San Francisco: The History Company, 1890.

————. *History of California*. Santa Barbara: W. Hebberd, 1963. Vols. 18–24, 34, and 35.

————. *The New Pacific*. New York: The Bancroft Company, 1914.

Bolton, Herbert Eugene. *Cross, Sword, and Gold Pan.* Los Angeles: The Primavera Press, 1936.

———. and Ephraim D. Adams. *California's Story.* New York: Allyn and Bacon, 1922.

Chapman, Charles Edward. *The Founding of Spanish California: The Northwestward Expansion of New Spain, 1687–1783.* New York: Macmillan, 1916.

———. *A History of California: The Spanish Period.* New York: Macmillan, 1921.

Cloud, Roy W. *Education in California.* Stanford: Stanford University Press, 1952.

Engelhardt, Charles Anthony (Father Zephyrin). *The Missions and Missionaries of California.* Santa Barbara: Mission Santa Barbara, 1929.

———. *Mission San Luis Obispo in the Valley of the Bears.* Santa Barbara: Santa Barbara Mission, 1933.

———. *Mission San Carlos Borromeo.* Santa Barbara: Santa Barbara Mission, 1934.

———. *The San Diego Mission.* San Francisco: James H. Barry, 1920.

———. *The San Luis Rey Mission.* San Francisco: James H. Barry, 1921.

Ferrier, William Warren, *Ninety Years of Education in California, 1846–1936.* Berkeley: Sather Gate Book Shop, 1937.

Hunt, Rockwell D. *A Short History of California.* New York: Thomas Y. Crowell Co., 1929.

Norton, Henry K. *The Story of California.* Chicago: A. C. McClurg & Co., 1923.

Old and rare books and papers, including books published privately and by unknown publishers

Carr, William G. *John Swett, the Biography of an Educational Pioneer.* Santa Ana, California, 1933.

Colton, Walter. *Three Years in California.* 1850.

Hittell, J. S. *History of California.* San Francisco: Pacific Press Publishing House, 1885.

Royce, Josiah. *California.*

———. *California from the Conquest in 1846 to the Second Vigilance Committee in San Francisco—A Study of American Character.* New York: Alfred Knopf, 1948.

———. "The Squatter Riot of '50 in Sacramento," *Overland Monthly.* Vol. 6.

Swett, John. *A History of the Public School System in California.* Printed privately in 1876.

———. *Public Education in California.* 1911.

Swett, John. *American Public Schools.* New York: American Book Company, 1900.

Tuthill, Franklin. *The History of California.* 1866.

Among the old and rare materials, resources needing special mention

1. Early California newspapers and journals, such as *The Californian* (the first newspaper in California, once edited by Reverend Walter Colton), *The California Star* (from 1847), *Pacific News* (from 1856), *Pacific* (1851–81), the San Francisco *Daily Herald* and *Evening Picayune,* the San Diego *Herald* (*Union*), and *Overland Monthly* (an official state department publication, 1886–1904).

2. Records of official documents, such as *Annals of San Francisco,* and the collected resources of the California Historical Society and the dozens of local historical societies, such as those in Sacramento, San Diego County, and La Jolla.

3. The minutes of early boards of education.

4. Publications of the California Teachers' Association: *The California Teacher* (1864–76), *The Pacific School and Home Journal* (1877–83), *The California Teacher and Journal of Home Education* (1883–87), *Sierra Educational News* (1904–50), and *CTA Journal* (1950–).

5. Masters theses and doctoral dissertations in California colleges and universities.

INDEX

A
B
C
D
E
F
G
H
I
J